The Augustów Roundup
of July 1945

ALSO BY TERESA KACZOROWSKA
AND FROM MCFARLAND

*Children of the Katyn Massacre: Accounts of Life After
the 1940 Soviet Murder of Polish POWs* (2006)

The Augustów Roundup of July 1945

Accounts of the Brutal Soviet Repression of Polish Resistance

TERESA KACZOROWSKA

Translated by HALINA KORALEWSKI
Edited by BOŻENA U. ZAREMBA

Afterwords by Danuta Kaszlej,
Zbigniew Kaszlej *and* Nikita Pietrov

McFarland & Company, Inc., Publishers
Jefferson, North Carolina

Published by special arrangement with Bellona Publishing House.
All photographs are from the author's collection.

Library of Congress Cataloguing-in-Publication Data

Names: Kaczorowska, Teresa, author. | Koralewski, Halina, 1946– translator. | Zaremba, Bożena U., 1960– editor.
Title: The Augustów roundup of July 1945 : accounts of the brutal Soviet repression of Polish resistance / Teresa Kaczorowska ; translated by Halina Koralewski ; edited by Bożena U. Zaremba.
Other titles: Obława Augustowska. English | Accounts of the brutal Soviet repression of Polish resistance
Description: Jefferson, North Carolina : McFarland & Company, Inc., Publishers, 2023 | Includes bibliographical references and index.
Identifiers: LCCN 2022023290 | ISBN 9781476689043 (paperback : acid free paper) ♾ ISBN 9781476646848 (ebook)
Subjects: LCSH: Augustów Roundup, 1945—Personal narratives. | Anti-communist movements—Poland—Augustów (Województwo Podlaskie)—History. | Counterinsurgency—Poland—History—20th century. | Augustów Forest Region—History, Military—20th century. | Political persecution—Augustów Forest Region—History—20th century. | Atrocities—Augustów Forest Region. | Poland—History—Occupation, 1939–1945. | BISAC: HISTORY / Wars & Conflicts / World War II / General | HISTORY / Europe / Poland
Classification: LCC DK4600.A9 K3313 2022 | DDC 943.8/32—dc23/eng/20220517
LC record available at https://lccn.loc.gov/2022023290

British Library cataloguing data are available

ISBN (print) 978-1-4766-8904-3
ISBN (ebook) 978-1-4766-4684-8

© 2023 Teresa Kaczorowska. All rights reserved

No part of this book may be reproduced or transmitted in any form or by any means, electronic or mechanical, including photocopying or recording, or by any information storage and retrieval system, without permission in writing from the publisher.

Front cover images, *clockwise from top*: Michał Wołąsewicz in 1941; Zyta Kucharzewska; Stanisław Wysocki's father, Ludwik Wysocki; Father Wysocki's sister, Aniela; Klemens Świerzbiński; Father Wysocki's sister, Kazimiera; Władysław Stefanowski, alias "Grom." *Background*: the Lebiedzianka River in the Augustów Primeval Forest, where the resurgence unit under Władysław Stefanowski, alias "Grom," was stationed (all photographs are from the author collection)

Printed in the United States of America

McFarland & Company, Inc., Publishers
Box 611, Jefferson, North Carolina 28640
www.mcfarlandpub.com

Table of Contents

From the Author	vii
From the Translator: Historical Backdrop to the Augustów Roundup	xi
Marian Tananis (Sejny): "Traitors are the worst"	1
Krystyna Świerzbińska (Augustów): "When we came back from Siberia, my father was gone"	31
Fr. Stanisław Wysocki (Suwałki): "Our farm was an oasis for the insurgency"	47
Tadeusz Jagłowski (Augustów): "Our parents waited for their son's return until their death"	70
Józef Kucharzewski (Giby): "I heard the moans of my tortured sister"	85
Marian Bućko (Augustów): "Our family is waiting for the explanation of this crime"	100
Teresa Staśkiewicz (Augustów): "The Augustów Roundup is still alive"	117
Afterword—Why Is This Book Needed?	129
Afterword—The Augustów Roundup: Crime with No Statute of Limitations	147
Notes	151
Selected Sources	163
Index	165

From the Author

The goal of *The Augustów Roundup of July 1945: Accounts of the Brutal Soviet Repression of Polish Resistance* is to shed light on the Augustów Roundup—a barely known, still unsolved, yet most ruthless Stalinist crime in post–World War II Poland, which sometimes is also referred to as the "July Roundup," "Little Katyń" or "Another Katyń." It was carried out by regular troops of the Red Army and Internal Troops of the 62nd Division of the NKVD (People's Commissariat for Internal Affairs), aided by members of the UB (Polish secret police), MO (Citizens' Militia), and 160 Polish soldiers of the First Infantry Regiment of the Praga District of Warsaw. These forces, numbering approximately 45,000 men, raided the Augustów Primeval Forest (located in the northeast region of Poland) and its surroundings to carry out an extensive pacification. Over 7,000 people suspected of involvement in the Polish Anti-Communist Resistance—the underground movement favoring independence from the Soviet Union—were imprisoned in dozens of places in Augustów, Suwałki, Sejny, and Sokółka counties. In barns, pigsties, warehouses, and sheds that belonged to local farmers, the Soviets created the so-called "filtration camps," where the detainees were subjected to interrogation, beating, and torture—methods of cruelty and terror developed by the Stalinist apparatus. Sometimes, the captors restrained prisoners with barbed wire or kept them under the open sky in flooded pits.

Only some of those arrested during the Roundup returned to their homes. To this day, no one knows what happened to a large number of Poles who went missing without a trace—how and where they were murdered or where their bodies were buried. Until now, it has been assumed that the number of Augustów Roundup victims was 592. That figure agrees with the evaluation of the Białystok branch of the IPN (National Remembrance Institute), which is conducting an investigation. However, in light of recent research, especially the release of some decoded cryptograms by Nikita Petrov of the Association "Memorial" in Moscow, the number of victims is now estimated at 2,000.

I have made an effort to examine this only recently uncovered crime through the testimony of seven residents of Augustów, Suwałki, and Sejny counties. I met with each of them in person, sometimes several times. They include a soldier of the Augustów Primeval Forest division of the Polish Underground and an Augustów Roundup survivor, Marian Tananis from Sejny (b. 1929), who is a former insurgent sentenced after World War II to 15 years in communist prisons. The rest of the protagonists of this story are family members of the Roundup victims—sons, daughters, and siblings of those murdered. Some of them had been deported deep into Russia. For example, Krystyna Świerzbińska—a daughter of a Home Army soldier from Jaziewo killed in the Roundup—survived deportation to Siberia. Another one, Marian Bućko from Krasnybór, was imprisoned in Soviet camps for political prisoners along with his father, platoon leader Konstanty Bućko. Others witnessed this drama as children. (Particularly unsettling is the chapter about Monsignor Stanisław Wysocki from Suwałki, who was only seven years old when, in July 1945, he lost his father and two sisters.)

These seven testimonies—illustrated by period photographs and accompanied by archival documents as well as contemporary photos—are based on facts and authentic experiences of real people and verified by historical sources and local archives as well as family documents and collectibles, which make them especially impactful. Not only do they make the Augustów Roundup and tragic postwar Polish history more familiar, but they also serve as a valuable educational tool. They show the real trauma that many families suffered after the mysterious disappearance of their fathers, husbands, and siblings, who were often their sole providers. They reveal the suffering of people who were deprived of a chance to visit the graves of their loved ones and who lived amidst lies, uncertainty, and fear. Families of those lost in the Augustów Roundup were spared from death yet lived for decades with the stigma of the "families of bandits" attached to them by the communist regime. They, too, are the victims of this Soviet murder.

At the same time, this book reminds us that the people from the region affected by this crime still remember, suffer, and wait for its explanation; they also wait for the uncovering of their loved ones' burial place. Many of them energetically work towards revealing the truth, most often through the Association for the Memory of the 1945 Augustów Roundup Victims (Związek Pamięci Ofiar Obławy Augustowskiej 1945). They participate in frequent events remembering the victims of the Augustów Roundup, such as the unveiling of an epitaph in their honor at the Jasna Góra Monastery in Częstochowa (May 3, 2014) or the dedication of the cross (June 14, 2014) commemorating the insurgents killed in a major battle with the Soviet forces in charge of the Augustów Roundup, on Lake Brożane. Families of those murdered also work with the IPN. They participate in DNA testing to help prosecutors identify those killed in the Augustów Roundup. They do hope that the exhumation to be conducted by IPN will uncover the body remains of their relatives, buried in secret in 1945, so that they will be able to light a candle in memory of the victims.

Working on *The Augustów Roundup* was not an easy task. I had to struggle with similar problems that I faced while writing the books about the tragedy of the Katyń massacre.[1] I am glad, however, that I managed to finish the book on the Augustów Roundup, which is shown from the perspective of actual victims and witnesses. The fact that the book was published on the 70th anniversary of the crime that is so little known in Poland and around the world is especially significant.

I am thankful to the heroes of this publication for opening their hearts to me, which sometimes posed a challenge to them. I also offer words of thanks to Nikita Petrov of the Association "Memorial" in Moscow for writing a stimulating afterword, "Augustów Roundup: Crime with No Statute of Limitation." I am extremely grateful to Danuta and Zbigniew Kaszlej, two historians from Augustów, for providing the invaluable historical consultation to this publication. I would also like to thank Wojciech Walulik—a dedicated local patriot, a former principal of the Lyceum No. 2 in Augustów and mayor of Augustów[2]—for all his help and faith in my creative potential. It was he who persuaded me to write this book. I also thank the gracious, dear President of the Association for the Memory of the 1945 Augustów Roundup Victims, Monsignor Stanisław Wysocki, and all others who contributed to the creation of this very much-needed publication.

From the Translator
Historical Backdrop to the Augustów Roundup

The narrative of World War II has numerous, multilayered perspectives and shades. The picture of Nazi Germany and its fanatical leader wreaking havoc and carrying out murder on several continents is part of the common knowledge. So is the heroic triumph of the Allied forces led by the United States, Great Britain, and the Soviet Union that followed. In order to learn about many insidious nuances of those horrific years, however, one has to make an effort and dig deeper by examining various accounts, resources, and records. As many readers may not be familiar with the events that led to the crime of the Augustów Roundup, so vividly presented in this book, they will appreciate some general background that will paint a bigger, more multifaceted picture of those times. It will hopefully help them better understand and make a more informed judgment about this terrible crime.

Thanks to the Molotov-Ribbentrop pact signed in August of 1939, just days prior to the outbreak of World War II, Adolf Hitler and Josef Stalin were initially allies. Immersed in the center of the murderous regimes of Hitler and Stalin was Poland—a newly created state reborn after a 123-year partition and barely a nation for two decades. The Poles persistently fought back against the Nazi-German blitzkrieg that began promptly on September 1, 1939. Roughly two weeks later, on September 17, Stalin's Red Army attacked from the East. While trying to defend massive military invasions on two opposite fronts on a landmass half the size of the state of Texas, the Polish government decided to relocate to Paris before settling in London. Major military operations in Poland ceased during the first week of October, nearly five weeks after the initial September 1 invasion. However, unlike many other European nations whose governments collaborated with Nazi occupiers in one form or another, the Polish government, although defeated on paper, never officially declared surrender.

With the Polish army defeated, the underground resistance movement began operations almost seamlessly with the establishment of the

Home Army (in Polish: Armia Krajowa, or AK). After all, the Poles were used to resisting any and all forms of occupation, persecution, and slaughter. The remnants of Polish military troops regrouped in the vast forests spread throughout the country, forming sizeable insurgence units and subsequently utilizing guerrilla warfare tactics for the entirety of the occupation, up until the ill-fated Warsaw Uprising of 1944 (not to be confused with the Ghetto Uprising of 1943). The Polish Underground would become the most extensive and most effective resistance movement out of all occupied countries during World War II.

In the territories occupied by Germany, the Polish intelligentsia—lawyers, doctors, teachers, priests, and the like—were quickly selected for elimination and sent to forced labor camps (by spring of 1942, converted to death camps mostly for the Jews, Roma people, and other minorities). On the Russian side, mass deportations of Poles to Siberia began in earnest.

Then, in defiance of the Molotov-Ribbentrop pact, Hitler suddenly attacked the Soviet Union in 1941. Russia was stunned and quickly overrun, yet managed—against all odds—to finally halt and defeat the Nazi behemoth in the Battle of Stalingrad on August 23, 1942, and forced Hitler to a hasty withdrawal of German troops from the advancing Red Army. All this time, the British Prime Minister, Winston Churchill and U.S. President Franklin Delano Roosevelt tirelessly courted Stalin and succeeded in persuading him to join the Allied cause, which was perceived as holding Poland and the entirety of Eastern Europe as the juicy carrot.

As the Germans were retreating across Poland, the Polish Underground began to encounter Soviet partisan groups. The tensions were palpable, as Poles keenly remembered the recent Siberian deportations and the newly uncovered Katyń Forest massacre of Polish officers. They were well aware that Stalin was another totalitarian aggressor in many ways like Hitler. However, Churchill and FDR were so keen on ridding the world of the Nazi-German regime that they turned a convenient blind eye to the true face of their new ally and the rising political tensions between the Polish and Soviet governments.

Meanwhile, the Red Army marched across Poland to the Vistula River banks directly towards Warsaw, where they halted only to mercilessly watch the Polish capital city be destroyed and its residents butchered in the aftermath of the Warsaw Uprising of 1944. After the Germans finally left, leaving behind a city razed to the ground and over 200,000 inhabitants killed, the Russians entered Warsaw, proclaiming Poland "liberated." The Red Army would continue to march through Poland en route to Berlin, raping and killing Polish civilians as they pleased.

Stalin next ordered the Soviet Secret Police (or NKVD) to initiate a systematic cleansing of the members of the Polish Underground. The

Home Army was officially disbanded, and the Polish insurgents, who had been fighting for Poland's independence since 1939, were ordered to come forward and surrender their arms to the newly installed Polish communist government (in essence, a "puppet" government controlled by the Kremlin in Moscow). Those who followed the order were promptly arrested and incarcerated in Soviet prisons. In most cases, they were brutally tortured and ultimately executed. The Polish soldiers fighting in major Allied campaigns abroad (such as the Polish II Corps in Italy) knew that they could not return to their country, where they would face certain imprisonment or even death.

At the infamous Yalta Conference on February 4–11, 1945, FDR and Churchill gave up Poland and the rest of Eastern Europe, and the so-called "Soviet Bloc" was formed. Poland existed on the map, but, in truth, it was controlled by the Soviet Union. One occupier was replaced with another. Polish soldiers forced to remain abroad were barred from participating in London's Allied Victory Parade in 1946 for fear of aggravating Stalin. The communist rule would not be overthrown in Poland until 1989, in the aftermath of the Solidarity movement created in 1981 and led by Lech Wałęsa nearly *50 years* after the V-E Day of May 8, 1945.

Many Polish insurgents, members of the former Home Army, knew that surrender to the newly formed communist authorities in Poland meant certain death, so they remained hidden in the woods, refusing to surrender. They continued guerrilla warfare against the communist government, fighting for a free and independent Poland. The Russians labeled them as "bandits." Most of these individuals were young men and women in their teens and 20s who lived in the forests year-round in all sorts of inclement weather. During particularly harsh winters, they had to march in each other's footsteps to prevent their traces in the snow from being discovered.

Armed conflict between the two sides began almost immediately—in May of 1945, Polish insurgents defeated NKVD agents in the Battle of Kuryłówka in southeastern Poland. The reprisal roughly a month later was swift and brutal as the Soviet authorities conducted one of their biggest counterinsurgency operations, the Augustów Roundup, which is the subject of this book. Considered "the largest crime committed by the Soviets on Polish lands after World War II," this assault resulted in the loss of thousands of lives, and for their relatives—years of grieving. Like the forced Soviet deportations to Siberia of millions of Poles as well as the Katyń and Smoleńsk Forest massacres, the crime of the Augustów Roundup remained relatively unknown because Stalin and the Communists disseminated false information to the West for nearly 50 years after the conclusion of the war. It was only after the instigation of the "glasnost" period in the late 1980s and the downfall of Communism that authentic documents were brought to public light to prove Soviet crimes. The undying patriotism, integrity, and, most of all, the ultimate sacrifice of thousands of Polish men and women for a free and independent Poland could finally be recognized.

Further Reading

Adamczyk, Wesley. *When God Looked the Other Way*
Atkin, Ronald. *Pillar of Fire: Dunkirk 1940*
Dallas, Gregor. *1945: The War That Never Ended*
Davies, Norman. *God's Playground: A History of Poland* (Volume II)
Davies, Norman. *No Simple Victory*
Davies, Norman. *Rising '44: The Battle for Warsaw*
Groom, Winston. *The Allies*
Leffler, Melvyn. *Cambridge History of the Cold War* (Volume I)
Lukas, Richard. *The Forgotten Holocaust*

Marian Tananis (Sejny)
"Traitors are the worst"

Marian Tananis welcomes me in his small apartment located in one of the mass housing areas in Sejny. He has this aura of refinement that is quite rare today. Right from the start, he cautions me: "I made an exception to tell my story about the Augustów Roundup. My heart cannot bear it any longer. I am the last one left in this corner of Augustów forests. All my friends have died."

Born in 1929, gray, slim, with a somber expression in his eyes, he has this aura of dignity and pride characteristic of the pre-war Polish elite. Elegant: blue-gray shirt, a shade darker tie with light stripes, classic pants and suspenders. His only life companion, a well-fed mongrel, Pusio, barks with dissatisfaction, sensing that his master will be busy for several hours.

"We brought it on ourselves. We were too bold manifesting our power in the Augustów Primeval Forest"[1]; with his hand gestures, he tries to chase away unpleasant memories.

His father, Antoni Tananis—a Piłsudski[2] follower who served in the Legions and was severely injured while fighting with the Bolsheviks as a

Marian Tananis in his apartment in Sejny.

volunteer—was a forester by profession. In the Polish Republic, reborn after 1918, he became a hunter in the Białowieża Forest. Marian's grandfather Leonard Tananis was also a forester in the borderland forests. During the 12 years of service in the tsarist army, he earned the title of an assistant surgeon, and after leaving the military service ran his own medical practice. He also delivered babies. Therefore, Marian's mother, Leokadia Tananis, née Waluś, who came from the Podhale region, gave birth to her children in the care of her father-in-law. Marian Tananis came into the world in the house of his grandfather in the village of Lipiny, in Augustów County.

Antoni Tananis, a hunter from the Białowieża Forest, lived with his family in idyllic Narewka, Hajnowka County. There, the Tananises raised two children: Marian and Walentyna. Near the very picturesque Narewka on the edge of the Białowieża Forest Danuta Siedzikówna, alias "Inka," was born and grew up.[3] She was a liaison girl for Major Łupaszka,[4] commander of the 5th Wilno Brigade of the Home Army.

The home of the Tananises in the Białowieża Forest was very patriotic—Polish to the core.

"As a son of the famous hunter, I had a carefree childhood, growing up in the remarkably scenic Białowieża Forest and soaking up local sentiments. I well remember hunting parties and the meetings which hosted distinguished guests, not only Polish, but also from Germany, France, Great Britain, and Soviet Russia. In my childhood, I met many celebrities including president of the Republic of Poland Ignacy Mościcki[5] and Hermann Goering.[6] They often stayed with us in Narewka," recalls the 84-year-old Marian Tananis. As a young boy, he served as a record keeper of many celebrities, and one of the things he remembers to this day is that Goering used to come to their house to enjoy specially prepared fried eggs.

After the outbreak of World War II and the occupation of this area by the Soviets, his father—being a hunter and Piłsudski follower—knew he had to flee Narewka to avoid the Soviets. He didn't have too many options as Poland was occupied by her two neighbors. The only choice for him was going to the territories under German occupation, because, although during the September 1939 defense campaign the counties of Suwałki and Augustów were first occupied by the Red Army (Augustów—September 23; Suwałki—September 24, 1939), the invaders soon split them between each other. Following the German-Soviet agreement on borders and friendship, signed on September 28, 1939, in Moscow, Suwałki County was eventually allocated to the Third Reich (Wehrmacht troops marched into Suwałki on October 12, and on October 26, 1939, by decree of Adolf Hitler, the county was incorporated into the Third Reich as Suel Ostpreussen province). In turn, under the resolution of the Supreme Council of the Soviet Union of November 2, 1939, Augustów County was annexed by the Soviet Union as the Augustów area of the Byelorussian Soviet Socialist Republic (BSSR).

Marian's father, forester Antoni Tananis, managed to get to Augustów, which remained under Soviet occupation for fewer than two years, until the German invasion of the Soviet Union in June 1941. In Augustów, he obtained permission to resettle with his family in the lands occupied by the Germans. Marian Tananis well remembers the hell of their resettlement: the way was through Brest, Łódź, and Pabianice, where, after three weeks of waiting in the former military barracks, in April 1940, the Tananises received documents written in German necessary to reach Suwałki (on the German side).

They stayed with their family in the village of Płaska at the home of Anthony Tananis's father-in-law, Piotr Waluś, who, at that time, supplied wood to the nearby sawmills. In order to survive, the hunter from Białowieża transported timber from the forest. Together with his wife, Leokadia, he also helped around the farm. Not for long. Germans began to bring in German settlers, and "foreign" Poles from the East became their primary enemies.

"My father was accused of being an enemy of the Third Reich. Again, we had to flee. While crossing the Soviet-German border, my father was shot by a guard in the lungs and died in September 1941. He was thirty-nine years old," recalls the son, who was 12 at that time.

Antoni Tananis, a father, hunter from the Białowieża Forest, and fervent supporter of Piłsudski, was buried in Mikaszówka. The mother and daughter, Walentyna, remained in Płaska. The orphaned Marian became a little wanderer. He first spent some time with his grandparents (the Waluś family in Płaska), then at the Tananises in Krasnopol or at the house of his father's old colleagues, the foresters in the Białowieża Forest. He always dreamed of going to the forest to join the Polish Underground to fight for independence.

The first resistance structures against Germans in the counties of Suwałki and Augustów began to form in the fall of 1939. The formation of the underground was kind of a grassroots movement, although the leading role was played by elites (usually reserve officers). The units carried out intelligence and propaganda activities; they built the organizational structure of the underground, collected weapons, and conducted acts of sabotage or even military actions. On April 28, 1940, for example, on the Kalety-Sejny route near Lake Pomerania, a group "Żwirki," under Corporal Witold Pilecki,[7] disarmed the Grenzschutz officers who were transporting weapons, ammunition, and uniforms.

The Polish Underground in Augustów County, unlike Suwałki County, led dynamic operations directed against the Soviet power and the

Poles who collaborated with NKVD (People's Commissariat for Internal Affairs).[8] In the summer of 1940, the operation carried out by the execution squad of Augustów underground was an absolute phenomenon in the whole country—they eliminated at least 20 people hostile to the quest for Polish independence. This operation, of course, was met with a counteraction from the NKVD-NKGB (Soviet security organs). The peculiarity of the Soviet repressive activities (such as the risk of deportation) and the local terrain conditions (broad areas of forest and swamp) resulted in a quick formation of insurgence units in Augustów County.

The outbreak of the war between the two Polish occupiers in June 1941 resulted in the seizure of Soviet-occupied land by the Germans. It consolidated the operations of the Polish Underground in the counties of Suwałki and Augustów. Local independence structures focused mainly on organizational work, intelligence, and propaganda. Sabotage actions slowly gained momentum. Battles with the German gendarmerie were carried out, military posts were destroyed, and dangerous agents of the occupying apparatus were liquidated.

Although on February 14, 1942, the Union of Armed Struggle was renamed to the Home Army; the underground structures used the code name PZP, for Polski Związek Powstańczy (Polish Uprising Union) for almost the whole time of the Nazi occupation in this area.

In late April of 1944, a Soviet sabotage-vigilance group under the command of Major NKGB Włodzimierz Cwietyński, alias "Orłow," appeared in the area of the Augustów Primeval Forest. Reinforced by the prisoners who escaped from German captivity, it soon formed a formidable insurgency unit. In May 1944, it made contact with the local command of the Home Army, and an agreement on military cooperation against the Germans followed. Unfortunately, the collaboration with the Soviet insurgents contributed to the uncovering of the organizational structures of the Polish Underground army and consequently in the repression against Home Army soldiers.

In the summer of 1944, during the retreat of German troops and the advance of the Red Army to the eastern Polish lands, the underground in both counties took part in an extensive sabotage operation, "Burza" ("Storm"). After a joint fight with the Poles against the Germans, the Soviets, sadly, revealed their real attitude towards the Polish Underground.

When Marian Tananis turned 16, his dreams came true: He became a member of the Home Army, which at that time turned into the Citizens' Home Army (AKO). This organization was in every respect—ideological, organizational, and personnel—a continuation of the Home Army.[9]

Along with several colleagues. Tananis took the oath of the Home Army on April 22, 1945, at Mały Borek, a beautiful wild spot, in front of the commander of the AKO Augustów District, Sgt. Władysław Stefanowski, alias "Grom" ("Thunder"). He remembers standing at attention, holding a rifle in his right hand over his heart, and saying:

> Before God Almighty and Mary, the Blessed Virgin, Queen of the Polish Crown, I pledge allegiance to my Homeland, the Republic of Poland. I pledge to guard Her honor steadfastly and fight for Her liberation with all my strength, to the extent of sacrificing my own life. I pledge unconditional obedience to the President of Poland, the Commander-in-Chief of the Republic of Poland, and the Home Army Commander whom he has appointed. I pledge to stay resolute in keeping all secrets no matter what should happen to me.

The 16-year-old Marian also remembers what "Grom," who was administering the oath, told the insurgents about their fundamental mission: Home Army soldiers should not allow Poland to be flooded with Communism. He also recalls the text of the Polish Underground Anthem, at least the first two stanzas, which they sang in the Augustów Primeval Forest:

> The dawn of freedom is blazing
> For Poland and all that she'll be.
> Our might will conquer the slavery,
> New world emerges today.
> The hour of vengeance is striking
> For our wrongs, tears, and blood.
> To arms, O, Jesus and Mary,
> Our soldiers are summoned to fight.
>
> For our freedom and yours,
> O, Brothers, let's draw our swords.
> No death or hardship can scare us,
> The victorious eagle shall soar.
> The hour of vengeance is striking
> For our wrongs, tears, and blood.
> To arms, O, Jesus and Mary,
> Our soldiers are summoned to fight.

Today—in Sejny—he recalls: "The Home Army accepted me without any reservation because they knew my father very well. Besides, I was well-built and looked a few years older than I was. I got a military uniform and the allocation to the armed patrol of the forest in a unit under 'Grom's' command. I was given the nickname 'Murka.'"

Boys his age, mainly scouts, were many in the Augustów Primeval Forest. The AKO branch under the command of Sgt. Władysław Stefanowski, alias "Grom,"[10] was created in April 1945 and was one of the largest in the area. Just before the Augustów Roundup, it consisted of 120–150 soldiers. First, it gathered on the Lebiedzianka River in Balinka. In

July 1945, "Grom" moved his unit deep into the Augustów Primeval Forest by Lake Brożane. According to Mr. Tananis, this idea was pushed by Lt. Joseph Sulżyński, alias "Brzoza" ("Birch"), the commander of a large Suwałki District branch of AKO.[11]

"'Grom' was swayed by Brzoza, although he never trusted him. The part of the Augustów Primeval Forest that was free from the Soviets was shrinking, though. He probably had no choice," explains Tananis.

The water in Lake Brożane—in some places 40 meters deep—seemed bottomless and was so pure that one could drink straight from the lake. Water lilies and all kinds of flowers and grass bloomed on the water; there was an abundance of birds, insects, fish, amphibians, reptiles, and the entire lake was surrounded by the beautiful, old-growth forest. For anyone who had ever seen Lake Brożane, its beauty was unforgettable. From the north, Lake Brożane was surrounded by difficult-to-cross marshes and wild terrain, and on the other side of the lake, there was a sacred spot of exceptional beauty. During the times of the partitions of Poland,[12] it was chosen as headquarters of the forestry authorities; a few farm buildings and a warden's cottage were located there. In 1942–1945, the Home Army insurgent's units' "Żwirki" was stationed nearby on Lake Płaskie. There was also a school for officers and noncommissioned officers from which Commander Witold Pilecki, alias "Żwirko," graduated.

Marian Tananis participated in many military patrols of the Augustów Primeval Forest, which was divided by "Grom" into three parts. Each three-man patrol had its section to inspect, observe, and provide reports. Tananis's patrol was charged with frequent assessments of the following roads: the Płaska-Gorczyca-Mołowiste and Sucha Rzeczka-Czarny Bród-Żyliny routes as well as all the roads through the woods leading to the Augustów, Lipsk, and Grodno highways.

"We had excellent German bicycles. They allowed us to move fast, to almost glide," reminisces the former soldier of the underground.

The armed operations took place mostly in the woods near the Augustów-Grodno highway.

"To these days, the shoulder of this road hides the bones of many Polish soldiers." The former insurgent speaks slowly, trying hard to focus. He often seems embarrassed that his memory is failing.

The fighting between the Germans and the Soviets was ruthless. Polish insurgents of the Augustów Primeval Forest preferred to support the Soviet "liberation" army, with whom they fought together against the German Nazis. But soon, the Soviets showed their real intent.

The former "cursed soldier"[13] closes his eyes and tries to concentrate: "In April 1945, there came a substantial supply of weapons. I do not know from where, but I remember the new Czech machine guns, the so-called

'Bergmans.' The holiday of the Constitution of May 3 [1791] was approaching. 'Grom' wanted to celebrate that day, strengthen his people, and show off our power. In the forest near the village of Płaska, he organized a parade of three hundred Home Army soldiers, combined with the weapons show. The Soviets found out about it. They communicated to Beria[14] in Moscow that they would not be able to get rid of the 'gangs' on their own. As a result, thousands of Red Army soldiers and the NKVD personnel were dropped on this tiny piece of land. A celebration of the Constitution of May 3 was 'Grom's' greatest folly," observes Tananis, not without bitterness.

Traitors were the worst. To give an example, Tananis starts talking about Włodzimierz Cwietyński, who has been mentioned before:

> He was a Pole. He bragged about his Polish roots, at least to us. He said that his father, a fighter of the January Uprising [of 1863], was sentenced to exile in Russia, and it was there that Włodzimierz Cwietyński was born. The Home Army soldiers liked him—he spoke good Polish—and considered him their comrade in the forest. He turned out to be a commander of a special surveillance-sabotage unit of the NKVD. The Soviet insurgents under Major Włodzimierz Cwietyński, alias 'Orłow,' penetrated forests and disintegrated Polish insurgents [by giving weapons in exchange for information]. Acting under the orders of Beria, they gathered intelligence on the Polish Underground. Many consider 'Orłow' as one of the foremost perpetrators of the subsequent misfortunes. He was the one who led to the Home Army structures being exposed, not only in the Augustów Primeval Forest.

In his recollections, Marian Tananis goes back to Brzoza:

> Next, let's take Lieutenant Józef Sulżyński, alias "Brzoza"—a Pole, too. He was the commander of a large Home Army unit in the Augustów Primeval Forest. Today, they say that he fought on Lake Brożane, like people from "Grom's" unit. That's not true; he didn't fight even for one hour. "Brzoza" withdrew his troops from the lake earlier, because—as the Polish Underground learned later—he collaborated with the NKVD and UB.[15] In his unit, there were also eleven well-armed deserters from the German army. "Brzoza" was a traitor; he denounced many of our colleagues from the Home Army. After he was exposed, the Home Army authorities sentenced him to death.[16]

At the sound of the name "Brzoza," this old, but still tough, face of a former insurgent from Sejny shrinks from pain, because, in his opinion, "Brzoza" finished off "Grom's" unit in which Tananis served.

After a break, Tananis continues his story of the traitors. One can see that even today the subject is extremely painful for him: "Or take Jan Szostak,[17] also a Home Army soldier. He was a regular church-goer and prayed earnestly. However, at some point, he became friendly with 'Orłow.' He stopped being a Catholic and became a bandit, a real bandit, capable of brutally murdering his closest colleagues from the underground. On top of that, he did it with a smile on his lips. During the Roundup, he accompanied the NKVD and helped in drafting the lists of the victims. Just like Judas."

After the war, his "accomplishments" were recognized: Szostak led the District Office of Public Security in Augustów (Powiatowy Urząd Bezpieczeństwa Publicznego) where he became an executioner and exercised the reign of terror. After being promoted, he moved to Białystok where he made every effort to chase the Polish patriots. Following the October thaw of 1956,[18] he transitioned to a new career as a folk sculptor in Augustów. He was quite successful and could never complain about the lack of money. However, at the end of his life, after a few attempts on his life, he grew scared. Although many years have passed since his death (and his funeral was grand), people still remember the pains inflicted by him. At the Augustów cemetery, Szostak's body has been thrown out of the grave three times because "the Polish soil does not want to accept his body." The Augustów citizens hope that now he is paying for his crimes in hell.

Among other Poles who keenly supported Russians during the Roundup was also Mirosław Milewski (1928–2008), who, beginning in 1944, worked in Stalin's security apparatus. He started at the Office of Security in Augustów and took part in the pacification of the Augustów Primeval Forest. The People's Republic of Poland mightily rewarded him for his assistance in the liquidation of the liberation underground forces. He went through all career levels: He became a general in a Security Bureau, Minister of the Interior (1980–1981), and secretary of the Central Committee of the Communist Party (1981–1985). He was also one of the close associates of Gen. Wojciech Jaruzelski.[19] His name is associated with numerous scandals and crimes against Poles, including the operation "Iron"[20] or murder of Fr. Jerzy Popiełuszko.[21] In 1985, however, he was removed from all state positions in the party and forced to retire. After the overthrow of the communist system, he was arrested in 1990, but not for long. He lived in peace and prosperity in Warsaw until his old age without suffering any punishment. Although judicial proceedings were waged against him before the court in Giżycko, Milewski died before a final ruling.

"Traitors are the worst," Tananis, speaking in Sejny, emphasizes emphatically. "Traitors are not humans."

The end of the war was not greeted by the soldiers of the Home Army and Citizens' Home Army with joy. Aware of the acts of their fellow traitors and the NKVD, they knew Poland was jeopardized under the wings of the Soviet Union. They did not expect, however, that the upcoming summer of 1945, after the "liberation," would bring the most tragic event and that the Augustów Primeval Forest, which people associated with lakes, beautiful forests, and summer recreation, would also become known as a place of the biggest crime committed in Polish territory after the war. Even today, only a few people, even among the locals, are aware that in July 1945, just a few weeks after the end of World War II in Europe, a massive military operation was carried out in the Augustów Primeval Forest and on its edges in the three counties of Augustów, Suwałki, and Sejny as well as the northern part of Sokółka County. It had brought persecution and sudden, mysterious death of hundreds or—in light of recent research—even thousands of innocent residents.

When the Roundup started, "Grom's" unit numbered about 200 soldiers. It included soldiers from the unit under Sgt. Wacław Sobolewski, alias "Sęk."[22]

Tananis and his young colleagues were still part of a one-of-its-kind infiltration unit. They not only reported to the commander about any strangers showing up in the forest but also delivered intelligence and orders. They carried arms, too. But above all, they observed the area.

The underground fighters from the wilderness did not know that, starting on the first days of July 1945, regular troops of the Red Army, numbering approximately 45,000 soldiers, would enter their territory. These troops were made up of the Third Belorussian Front and the units of the 62nd Division of NKVD Internal Troops (including the 385th Infantry Regiment of the Internal Troops of the NKVD) and were supported by the members of the Internal Security, Citizens' Militia, and the Polish section First Infantry Regiment of the Praga District in Warsaw.[23] Nor did they know that these units would carry out a wide-ranging pacification in the Augustów Primeval Forest and the adjacent area. This operation would be named the Augustów Roundup, "Little Katyń" or "Another Katyń."

The command of the Polish Underground of the Augustów Primeval Forest could not imagine that soon, on this soil, over 7,000 people would be detained and imprisoned in dozens of places. They could not imagine that the Soviets would use barns, pigsties, and sheds that belonged to local farmers to create the so-called "filtration" camps and that methods developed by the Stalinist apparatus of cruelty and terror would be employed to interrogate, beat, and torture the detainees, sometimes even by bounding them with barbed wire or keeping them in the flooded pits under the open sky. They could not imagine that only some Poles would return to their homes and that 592 of them would remain lost without a trace. This figure has been quoted so far. However, some recent findings show that the number of the Roundup victims was higher.[24]

The summer of 1945 was exceptionally beautiful. July was scorching hot. The Soviets began to comb the Augustów Primeval Forest more thoroughly than they would normally do. They walked in the line formation, meticulously examining the thickets and bushes, the surrounding hamlets, fields, and villages. They arrested the men who were mostly members of the Polish liberation underground forces, though many managed to avoid the Roundup thanks to the proficient AKO intelligence. Virtually everyone was detained, even those who had just returned from the forced labor camps in Prussia. They were taken from their homes, meetings or while they were in the middle of their work in the fields or the woods—virtually from anyplace. They were told it was only for questioning, but they never came back. They disappeared without a trace.

The whole operation was handled by the Soviet military counterintelligence SMERSH[25] and led by Gen. Viktor Abakumov,[26] who sent his deputy Ivan Gorgonov[27] to the nearby town of Olecko. Based on the reports from Gorgonov and Zelenin,[28] Abakumov generated encrypted reports to the Head of NKVD, Lavrentiy Beria. (Two of these reports became known recently, thanks to Nikita Petrov.[29]) The liquidation of Polish liberation underground forces was also aided by Polish informers. Besides, some, even the toughest insurgents, could not withstand inhumane interrogation and cruel treatment in Soviet torture chambers and often squealed on their pals from the Home Army.

Marian Tananis experienced his first setback at the beginning of the Roundup. While carrying out his duties, he found himself in the middle of the Augustów Primeval Forest. He knew the forest by heart, as his own pocket. To this day, he can flawlessly list the names of its villages, lakes, and rivers. He can picture Lake Brożane or Sajno and the villages of Mikaszówka, Mały Borek, Płaska or Strzelcowizna; he knows how and where the Czarna Hańcza River flows. Just as "Grom" taught them: "The forest is everything to you."

The former underground fighter, "Murka," continues:

> On July 12, 1945, during the surveillance work in the section of Small Borek-Płaska, together with my colleague Eugeniusz Gołębiowski, we suddenly saw a line of the Soviet troops, combing the forest. Next moment, another line emerged from the woods. We were trapped. We spotted hay bales in the meadow and buried our weapons; we took up scythes and rakes and pretended to be working in the fields. An NKVD officer apparently believed us, because he ordered three soldiers with machine guns to take us to the site No. 2. If we had been sent to point No. 1—the barn and cellar of the Werner family in Paniewo, from where all the captured were to be quickly deported—nobody would have heard from us again, just as they never did from the others detained in No.1 site.
>
> Site No. 2 was a meager, badly roofed and sheathed barn that belonged to Józef Wiśniewski, also from Paniewo. It was densely surrounded by

Soviet soldiers. When the NKVD squad escorting Tananis and Gołębiowski commanded to open the door of the barn to push them inside, it turned out that there were already several dozens of people imprisoned there. Most of them were known to the young insurgents from "Grom's" unit.

Tananis says:

> People from Płaska and other villages were continually being brought to the barn. When the night came, there were 93 of us in the barn. Our hearts ached with terrible pain because the shots from machine guns, rifles, and bursting grenades reached us from Lake Brożane. We could well imagine what was going on its dark marshes. We guessed that these were battles of life-and-death. For three days, we heard the sounds of fighting. Then all went quiet.

The young guides were kept in the barn without food or even water, just like everyone else. If none of the close ones had brought the detainees any food, they were dying of hunger. One day, Marian Tananis's mother reached out to the all-powerful master of that camp. She handed food to her son but was not allowed to see him. On the fifth day of their arrest, 11 new prisoners were brought in, including Kostek Hańczuk, who told them exactly what had happened over Lake Brożane.

Two young guides from the Home Army unit under "Grom" were kept in the barn together with other detainees for almost two weeks.

"I can't say we were beaten there, but the interrogation was indeed brutal. In other filtration camps, truly terrible things were happening," says the former insurgent, who, through the holes in the old barn where he was imprisoned, could see what the Soviets were doing. He heard discussions about whether they should be shot. After all, "the bandits do not fit into the new times and must die."

"That barn will remain forever in my memory. It's no longer there; it was dismantled," sighs former "Murka."

Beating, terrorizing, rape, and torture were standard practices during the July raid. For example, the wife of one of the rangers, whom Tananis knew and with whom he spoke after the tragedy, was raped in Mały Borek by over a dozen Red Army soldiers. In front of her husband. The soldiers were taking turns to rape her on the door taken off from the barn until she lost consciousness. She woke up naked, covered with blood and surrounded by flies. Afterwards, she didn't want to live. She lost a lot of weight and soon died.

Tananis still remembers Kazia Dobrowolska (the guides worked with her), who was a liaison girl in "Grom's" unit. Her husband, Kazimierz, was a communications officer before the war. She took care of the Home Army documents. She was imprisoned in Werner's barn and severely beaten.

Then, she vanished without a trace. She was killed, just as the son of a forester, Fabian Stefanowski, was mercilessly beaten, or Eugeniusz Hańczuk and many others who were murdered—so effectively that to this day no one knows where their bones are buried. Just like other families of the missing, Kazimierz Dobrowolski searched for his wife, Kazia, all his life to no avail.

"At Werner's house [as survivors told me] the Soviets were hiding 'Brzoza.'" He helped them identify the soldiers of the "Polish Underground," the former insurgent shows a hand-drawn operational map of the area. He drew villages and marked and numbered filtration points; he pointed out five lakes, several locks, the Augustów Canal, and his journey as a prisoner.

On July 23, 1945, Tananis was driven out of the Wiśniewskis' barn, along with more than 100 other arrested men, and moved to another "filtration" barn that belonged to Mr. Godlewski and was located at the end of the village of Płaska. They were escorted by strong, armed NKVD combatants, who were treating them like desperados. There were about 170 Polish prisoners there. Many were quickly moved to Augustów or, according to Tananis, further, closer to Grodno. At Godlewski's house, all were subjected to harsh interrogations. Prisoners were beaten and tortured, often for the mere fact that the NKVD interrogators did not understand the Polish language.

A barn in the village of Płaska that belonged to the Godlewski family, where Marian Tananis was imprisoned and interrogated.

The Godlewski's house in the village of Płaska, where Marian Tananis was imprisoned and interrogated, looks different today. The old one burned, and, in 1971, they built a new one in the same place.

"We came back from these interrogations to the nearby Godlewski's barn increasingly battered," says Tananis. "During the last days, two officers, who spoke Polish well [they were probably Poles], arrived at the yard outside the barn. As usual, they asked about the Home Army, weapons, and commanders. They asked me what I did. I replied that I was a student at a vocational school in Suwałki that I wanted to be a tractor driver, and I had never seen any insurgents." Tananis says that the last interrogations lasted day and night. By the end of his stay in the barn, there were precisely 93 prisoners.

Godlewski's barn in Płaska still stands today, although with several wings added. Tananis even took its picture. The house—a place of brutal interrogation of Poles—still stands there. A cross to commemorate this human tragedy has been erected in front of the house.

After the next few days, the Soviets announced they would again change the place of the confinement. The detainees were awakened early morning, and, after the list was read out, arranged in a column in groups of four. The NKVD officers rode in front and at the end of the column, while all the arrested were in the middle as if they were going to an execution. They were herded from Godlewski's barn in Płaska, from one direction to the other. Prisoners were convinced they would be shot to death. The area was dangerous—mines were everywhere, and, in Augustów, bridges were torn. There was no way to escape.

First, they came to Czarny Bród, then to Lipowiec, where they were held in a pine cone drying room. Here, three officers spoke Polish well, although they had Soviet uniforms. There, Marian Tananis met his grandfather Piotr Waluś, who was also imprisoned. He also met with his mother, who brought him food. Like other women, she went to the NKVD with a request to release her son. Some women tried to bribe the NKVD officers with moonshine or, sometimes, with their bodies, hoping their men would be released.

From Lipowiec, Tananis was led together with his colleague Eugeniusz Gołębiowski by three NKVD soldiers into the Soviet camp in the village of Białobrzegi, where they heard: "The operation is over. You have to go back." They turned back and arrived in the downtown of Augustów.

They were imprisoned in the basement of the then-familiar, now the infamous, building of the District Office of Public Security (PUBP), the so-called "Turk's House," which haunted from above the Netta River. Its dungeons were temporarily empty because the prisoners had just been removed to be shot. In the Augustów basement, Tananis spent only one, horrible night. He and his friend were lucky—in this "hell," they were interrogated by Milewski, not by Jan Szostak, who knew them from the forest underground operations and who (they were told) had just left for Grodno with the transport of prisoners. They lied to Milewski and said they had been looting the area.

On August 7, 1945, the 16-year-old insurgent went back to the woods.

"The forest is everything to you." These were "Grom's" words Tananis had on his mind while rushing, as if on wings, from the Augustów PUBP office back to the forest. He walked for over six hours. He was hungry—he ate only some young carrots from one of the vegetable beds and some poppy seeds from another.

"It turned out that our unit was gone. It had been completely decimated on Lake Brożane. Dozens of my colleagues had been murdered. 'Grom' perished. Many of his soldiers, my colleagues, had been captured and nobody heard from them again." The former insurgent, alias "Murka," lowers his sad eyes.

Even today, the memory is still very traumatic for him because on the very same day he fell into the hands of the Soviets—on July 12, 1945—the biggest battle of the Augustów Roundup took place on Lake Brożane. Seven thousand Red Army soldiers approached the woods adjacent to the lake from several directions. The Soviets directed a massive attack at about 200 insurgents. The battle was one-sided—the NKVD soldiers outnumbered the Polish insurgents and were much better armed with heavy machine guns, grenades, and mortars. Besides, the Soviets had a guaranteed, constant supply of ammunition. Even so, the battle lasted three days.

The notorious building of the District Public Security Office (PUBP) in Augustów on the Netta River, the so-called "Turks' House" where Marian Tananis was twice imprisoned. The residents still find it intimidating.

As long as the soldiers of Citizens' Home Army had enough ammunition, the Russians were afraid to move away from their permanent positions and enter into the woods. The liberation fighters who were trying to escape into the open or to the lake were showered with the heavy machine guns, which had been set at strategic positions.

"Hardly anyone survived the massacre on Lake Brożane—only locals who knew the forest well," recalls Tananis. "Most of the soldiers who served under 'Grom' came from the Vilnius region, and during the battle, about 75 underground fighters were slaughtered. The Soviets finished off the wounded and took their corpses closer to Belarus. The rest were taken alive and transported to an unknown place—no one ever heard from them since. Most likely, "Grom's" younger brother, an insurgent Lucjan Stefanowski, died on Lake Brożane, too."

Marian Tananis heard these stories from a few survivors from "Grom's" unit. To this day, he cannot let off the idea that "Grom," whom he called "the only man of principle I knew, a great patriot, a very righteous, brave, and noble man," had allowed himself to be apprehended and killed by the Soviets. They say that first he stumbled while jumping on the lake from islet to islet. He was wounded. Then, as Marian Tananis was told, the Soviets finished him off, like the other wounded, and transported his body somewhere, removing all the traces.

"And all that happened because 'Grom' gave in to 'Brzoza's' persuasions and moved his unit to Lake Brożane." Tananis finds it impossible to forgive. "The fact is that we all knew that they did not like each other; they never knew how to communicate. 'Grom' called 'Brzoza' a 'Soviet scum.' I heard it myself. However, 'Brzoza' succeeded in convincing 'Grom' that on the lake, it would be easier for them to defeat the Soviets together. Later, this turned out to be a trap: 'Brzoza' collaborated with the Polish secret police and the NKVD. He did not take up the fight at Lake Brożane and withdrew his soldiers."

"Traitors are the worst," the former member of the Home Army, now an elderly man, keeps repeating, realizing that his survival was a miracle.

He now remembers the images from those days better than the events of yesterday, especially the people.

"I can still see these noble, brave, homeland-loving soldiers—their faces, moves, and their loyalty to the commander." The former insurgent wipes off some tears.

He knew "Grom's" sister Jadwiga Rewińska, née Stefanowska. She told him that before the Roundup, she had seen her brother a couple of times. He had arrived at the family home in Augustów in uniform and armed. He said he was fighting for a different Poland, and now, instead of the German occupation, there was a Soviet one. She also heard that her younger brother Lucjan Stefanowski joined his brother Władek, alias Grom. There has been no trace left of him, either.

The soldiers who were stationed in the forest wanted revenge for Brożane. They decided to create a new unit in Srzelcowizna to prove that the Roundup did not destroy the entire, patriotic underground. For additional safety, Marian Tananis got a second code name: "Burak" ("Beet").

"Just imagine: In only three weeks, we created a new, heavily armed unit that was ready for revenge," Marian Tananis smiles. He immediately lights up by mere recollection, and his voice becomes more resonant. Once again, they began getting under the Soviets' skin by carrying out diversionary operations.

According to historian Danuta Kaszlej, the creation of a new armed unit was facilitated by the impact of the July raid. The fear after the display of supremacy and impunity of the terror apparatus during the Augustów Roundup was huge. Survivors were still ruthlessly hunted. The NKVD, along with Polish secret police, continued to raid the region. The underground soldiers who did not leave the area or hide were forming new units because, after their cover was blown, the forest was for them the only shelter, the only chance for self-defense. In this situation, they did not have much of a choice—it was either the forest or the communist secret police dungeons and death sentence, which at the time was the most likely scenario. They preferred to die fighting. By creating partisan divisions from 1945–1947, they still hoped to last until the change of fortune.

A few weeks following the horror at Lake Brożane and having come to terms with the suffering and defeat in the fight against the Soviets, Marian Tananis, along with three armed insurgents—Rogalewski, Gołębiowski, and Dzimitrowicz—ventured to visit the place of the tragedy over Lake Brożane. They took with them shovels, blankets, and sheets.

"We wanted to bury our colleagues with dignity and to see and analyze the course of the massacre," explains Burak. "It turned out that on the lake, there were no traces of the battle: not a single body, no weapons or even splinters! Everything had been thoroughly cleaned in the 45 days since the battle."

They discovered, however, a dirt road leading to the east (toward Giedzie and Kalety) that bore traces of vehicles. They followed the way almost to the border with Lithuania and Belarus. They noticed that some passing zones had been plowed by tires. At one spot, Gołębiowski found an eagle with a crown, the one you would find on insurgents' hats. Then, they took the oath to remain silent about the crime on Lake Brożane, at least until the time when it would be possible to tell the whole truth about it. They swore that the fellow soldiers who had been killed would forever remain in their minds and hearts.

Only recently has Marian Tananis decided to speak up about the tragedy on Lake Brożane. From time to time, he visits the tragic lake and its surroundings. He recalls the time of the Roundup, its greatest battle fought by soldiers from "Grom's" unit—his unit. He keeps making notes and talks to journalists. With the help of his discoveries, the archaeologists from Warsaw, who were brought by the newly formed organization in Augustów, the Association "Leśni" for Exploring Places of Struggle and Martyrdom and the War Graves, have already begun to comb the lake, eager to find traces of the battle: weapons, human remains, and their belongings. Since the mid-90s, Danuta and Zbigniew Kaszlej (from 2006, as part of the Historical Club of the Home Army in Augustów) together with the Association "Leśni" (starting in 2012) have been gathering materials about this little-known battle. They are making an effort to erect a Lake Brożane monument commemorating the Soviet crime against the soldiers of the Polish Underground so that the memory they deserve shall be restored.[30]

"Lake Brożane looks completely different today because, during the time of the People's Republic of Poland, all traces of the crime were obliterated," states Tananis. "Many trees pierced with bullets were cut down. The land by the lake was drained. Sand and gravel had been spread around the edges of the lake, creating a convenient place for camping."

On June 14, 2014, during a ceremony commemorating the tragic skirmish on Lake Brożane, a historian from Augustów, Zbigniew Kaszlej stated in his speech that soldiers from the units commanded by "Grom" and "Brzoza" fought on Lake Brożane.

Retreating from the Red Army corps that were carrying out the Roundup, both units met in the vicinity of Strzelcowizna, about ten kilometers from Lake Brożane. They were traced by the Soviets and slowly pushed towards Lake Brożane where, on July 12, 1945, the final battle of soldiers from Citizens' Home Army of the Augustów and Suwałki districts took place. The outcome was predictable. Bolesław Rogalewski, alias "Sosenka," an insurgent from "Brzoza's" unit who fought over Lake Brożane, told the historian a very significant piece of information: "[The Soviets] were getting the supply of the ammunition, and we were not." According to some documents, the battle lasted several days. "Sosenka" claimed it was five days. However, according to the historian (considering the disproportion of forces and resources), the fight must have lasted only a day or two, and then, the Soviets started to search for insurgents in the vicinity of the lake.

According to some reports, a part of "Brzoza's" unit managed to break away from the ambush. The historian has spoken with several

A ceremony of unveiling the cross over Lake Brożane in the Augustów Primeval Forest, dedicated to the soldiers from Augustów and Suwałki, members of the Home Army and the Citizens' Home Army from units of Sgt. Władysław Stefanowski, alias "Grom," and a second lieutenant Józef Sulżynski, alias "Brzoza," who, on July 12, 1945, during the Augustów Roundup, took up the battle on Lake Brożane with the overwhelming Soviet forces. The creation of the monument was initiated by the Association "Leśni" for Exploring Places of Struggle and Martyrdom and the War Graves and supported by local authorities and residents.

participants of the battle and was given different accounts. Some insurgents survived by climbing the trees and waited high up in the branches until the Soviets departed. Others sat in the lake waters, and, when they heard Soviet patrols, they put reed straws into their mouths and ducked down. Still others said that "Brzoza," leader of the unit, did not fight on Lake Brożane, only some of his soldiers did. After so many years, when participants of the battle over Lake Brożane are dead, it is difficult to make a clear determination.

The cryptogram written by General Abakumov to Beria on July 24, 1945 (disclosed in 2012 by Nikita Petrov of the Association "Memorial" in Moscow), identifies the arrest of "Grom" and his 50 soldiers. There is also a report from Second Lieutenant Mossakowski, the branch manager of PUBP in Suwałki, who, on July 16, 1945, during the Roundup, communicated that on Lake Brożane, the Soviet troops met "bandit groups"—led by "Grom" and "Brzoza"—which actively resisted. Four officers from the Home Army "gang" were killed, and 57 "bandits" were captured. The document states that a total of 58 pieces of handguns and automatic machine guns were taken. The last sentence in Mossakowski's report reads: "The detainees and confiscated weapons are in the hands of the Soviet military counterintelligence SMERSH."

Oral testimonies supplement these documents. The historian spoke with Franciszek Miluc, alias "Karp" ("Carp"), who was captured in the Roundup and was held in a barn in Białowierśnie. He confirms

A photograph of Władysław Stefanowski, alias "Grom," pinned to the cross, taken at the unveiling ceremony.

that the Soviets brought about 30 soldiers detained at Lake Brożane to the barn in Białowierśnie. They were transported from there and killed together with the Roundup victims detained in other places. Moreover, "Sosenka" confirmed that "Grom" did not die on Lake Brożane. He was questioned by counterintelligence SMERSH in Giby. This testimony is consistent with the information provided in cryptogram by Abakumov to Beria on July 24, 1945. No matter if Władysław Stefanowski, alias "Grom," was killed in a battle over Lake Brożane or was passed on to SMERSH and tortured in Giby—he was still killed in the Augustów Roundup. On the other hand, his name does not appear on the lists of Roundup victims published by the Institute of National Remembrance.

Silent witnesses of the events of July 1945 found in the area: a holy medal and a military button, which probably belonged to the insurgents who fought there.

The fate of Józef Sulżyński, alias "Brzoza," was quite different. He survived the Roundup, surrendered during the operation "Radosław" in September 1945 and for that reason (not for treason as claimed by "Brzoza's" insurgents) received a death sentence by the Polish Underground that was not carried out. After the war, he left for the Recovered Territories,[31] where he worked in Giżycko, then in Ełk. Secret police documents confirm he had been under surveillance until 1956. He died in Warsaw in November 1995.[32]

Anyhow, let's go back to the protagonist of this chapter, insurgent Marian Tananis. On January 21, 1946, during one of the clashes in the forest, Marian was wounded in his side. Despite the repressions in northeastern Poland, which was occupied by the Soviets, the Polish Underground continued its liberation operations, which were carried out until the mid–1950s by the Home Army and, after its termination, by the Citizens'

Home Army and later, the "Freedom and Independence" Association. The wounded Tananis was interrogated by the NKVD in the police headquarters in Lipsk, along with other "bandits." Then, the Soviets brought him and other captured Home Army soldiers again to the dungeons of the District Office of Public Security in Augustów. This time, the Augustów executioner, Jan Szostak, was present. He recognized Marian and reminded him that he had recently eluded them after having been kept in this very building.

"You won't get off this time! You will be tried by our authority," he said ominously. He threatened Marian with a court-martial and the death sentence.

Tananis recalls today, not without pain:

> This time, they tortured us. We were beaten only for being Home Army members. Brutally. I was also brutalized by Jan Szostak himself. For the two weeks of my imprisonment in the basement of the District Office of Public Security in Augustów, horrible things took place.

These days, he has scars and disfigurements from having his nails pulled off and fingers broken. Even more painful was the beating of his feet with chains.

Rulings were issued quickly. After having been transported to Białystok, Tananis learned that he should be court-martialed and sentenced to death. He wasn't even 17. He was tried by the Military District Court and on April 26, 1946, and sentenced to 15 years of imprisonment in Wronki.[33] Under the amnesty, however, his sentence was reduced to seven years and three months.

In Wronki, he served six and a half years. How does he remember the infamous prison? Like a nightmare. Unimaginable. In two-person cells, six prisoners were placed without beds. Anyway, he spent most of the time in solitary confinement in a dark enclosure. The rest of the sentence he spent working in the quarries.

Outside, it is a beautiful, warm day in late May. It is a Holy Day of Corpus Christi, and the town enjoys a Eucharistic procession with girls dressed in white, strewing flower petals before the Blessed Sacrament. In the center of Sejny, in front of four altars, crowds pray in two languages, Polish and Lithuanian. You can hear a lilt, distinctive for the Eastern Borderland.

Pusio barks all the time.

After serving his sentence in the Wronki prison and quarries, Tananis was released on February 26, 1953. Still, he was not free. He was allowed to work but only at coal mines. First, he got an employment card to work at the uranium mine in Kowary in Lower Silesia. After three months, he ran

SĄD WOJEWÓDZKI
III Wydział Karny
ul. M.C. Skłodowskiej 1
15-950 BIAŁYSTOK
tel. 227-17

syg.akt... R 262)46

Białystok dn. 14.12.1992r.

Z a ś w i a d c z e n i e

Sąd Wojewódzki w Białymstoku Wydział III Karny zaświadcza,

że Pan .Tananis Marian s. Antoniego. wyrokiem b.Wojskowego
Sądu Rejonowego w Białymstoku z dnia 26.04.1946r.
skazany został z art. 87 kkWP, art.46 § 1 kkWP, art.3 dekr.z 16.11.45r
15(piętnastu)
na karę .... lat więzienia.

W więzieniu przebywał od dnia 26.02.1946r.

do dnia 26.02.1953r.

Powyższe należy traktować jako skazanie za działalność polityczną związaną z walką o suwerenność i niepodległość bYtu Państwa Polskiego.

Zaświadczenie wydano na prośbę .Tananisa Mariana.-

bt

Z up.
Prezesa Sądu Wojewódzkiego w Białymstoku
Przewodniczący Wydziału III Karnego
Sądu Wojewódzkiego w Białymstoku

Janina Do...cka-Szerel

Za zgodność z oryginałem

A certificate from the Białystok Regional Court stating that Marian Tananis was sentenced to 15 years in prison by the Military District Court in 1946.

away to Upper Silesia. There, he worked at four coal mines, including the coal mine "Wujek."

"In the coal mines, I worked along—and under the same slave rules—with other former soldiers, as well as the penal mine battalions and the outcasts, who were satisfying the Stand-in Military Service. I was subjected to the most camouflaged methods of repression directed towards the 'enemies of the regime.' We were surrounded by the aura of contempt."

Tananis remembers that the nation, deprived of Polish patriotic, intellectual elites eliminated during World War II by the actions of Germans and Soviets, was extremely divided after the war.

"Even my own family viewed me as a criminal. However, I survived, and also upheld the dignity of a soldier." Marian stands up quite energetically to silence Pusio, who barks all the time.

As an "enemy of the Polish nation," Marian Tananis was not allowed to go to school. Despite the restrictions, though, he managed to finish evening classes at a mining high school in Silesia and then completed engineering studies without being enrolled in the Academy of Mining and Metallurgy. How? "Somehow, fate helped me," he smiles.

He became an engineer, a specialist in occupational health and safety. He worked at a coal mine with 2,500 employees. He got married and became a father to two daughters. His younger and only sister, Walentyna, who visited him after he had served his sentence, also got married in Silesia. She met her husband there and stayed. Since her brother had been a member of the Polish Underground, she was under regular surveillance and was persecuted by the secret police. She is still alive.

Marian Tananis worked in Silesia until 1982, that is until he contracted silicosis, an incurable occupational disease. He took advantage of earlier retirement and returned to "his" forest during martial law, declared in Poland in 1981. He settled down with his family near the Augustów Primeval Forest in Sejny.

Today, the former insurgent Marian Tananis lives alone. His wife is no longer alive. Daughters lead their own lives—one of them resides in Sejny; the second one got the family apartment in Silesia. The former soldier of the resistance, whose only company is his pet dog, has hired domestic help. In 1993, as a veteran and a victim of the war and postwar repressions, he received 10,000 Polish Zlotys[34] (he was asking for 420,000 PLN) as compensation for the harm he suffered.

Tananis goes to another room. He brings a document by a Russian commander of the military counterintelligence SMERSH, Gen. Viktor Abakumov to the head of the NKVD in Moscow, Lavrentiy Beria, on July 21, 1945, discovered by Nikita Petrov in 1990 in KGB archives and published in 2011. Tananis got a copy from Monsignor Stanisław Wysocki, head of the Association for the Memory of the 1945 Augustów Roundup Victims.

Tananis hands me the document without uttering a word.

Following your command, on the morning of July 20, I ordered a plane to carry an assistant to the head of GUKR SMERSH, major general Gorgonov, to the city of Treuburg [Olecko], along [with] a group of counter-espionage officers to carry out the liquidation of bandits arrested in the Augustów Primeval Forest.

After arriving, Gorgonov and chief of the UKR SMERSH of the Third Belorussian Front Lieutenant General Zelenin provided the following report: From July 12 to 19, the forces of the Third Belorussian Front combed these woods and arrested 7,049 people. After they were interrogated, 5,115 people were released; out of the remaining 1,934 detainees, 844 people were identified and arrested as bandits, including 252 Lithuanians, who had dealings with bandit groups in Lithuania and were handed over to the local powers of the NKVD-NKGB of Lithuania; 1,090 people are being checked, of whom 262 are Lithuanians, and for that reason, they have been transferred to the authorities of the NKVD-NKGB. Thus, the number of arrested on July 21, 1945, amounts to a total of 592 people plus 828 detainees, who are being checked. From the bandits arrested in the forest hideouts, the following were seized: 11 mortars, 31 machine guns, 123 automatic pistols, rifles, pistols and grenades, and 2 radio stations.

If you deem appropriate to carry out operations in this state of affairs, we intend to carry out the liquidation of the bandits in the following manner:

1. Liquidate all detected bandits in the number of 592. For this purpose, we will commit an operational team and a battalion of troops from SMERSH of the Third Belorussian Front, whom we have already brought in connection with the counterintelligence activities. The operational staff and the battalion's personnel will be fully briefed on the rules of the liquidation of the bandits.

2. During the operation, all necessary measures will be taken to prevent the escape of any of the bandits. For this purpose, in addition to the excellent instructions given to the staff and operational battalion, the forest plots on which the operation will be carried out will be surrounded, and, as a preventive measure, the area will be combed.

3. The responsibility for carrying out the liquidation will be divided between the assistant chief of the Main Directorate SMERSH, Major General Gorgonov and head of the Counterintelligence of the Third Belorussian Front, Lieutenant General Zelenin. Comrades Gorgonov and Zelenin are good and experienced Cheka[35] officers, who will execute the task. The other detained 828 people will be verified during a 5-day period, and all confirmed bandits will be liquidated in the same way. The number of confirmed bandits from this group of detainees will be reported to you. Awaiting your orders.

Abakumov

Tananis comments with a smile: "For Beria, they would have done anything. This cable states that on July 20, 1945, a special team of officers SMERSH, led by gen. Ivan Gorgonov, arrived from Moscow to Olecko to perform 'the liquidation of the bandits detained in the Augustów Primeval Forest.' The liquidation was led by gen. Gorgonov and the head of the SMERSH of the Third Belorussian Front, gen. Zelenin. The number of 592 people, mentioned in Abakumov's cable, corresponds almost exactly to the number of inhabitants of our region who disappeared during the Augustów Roundup."

According to Nikita Petrov, who regularly visits Augustów, works with researchers, and meets with the locals, the Augustów Roundup was carried out under the personal order of Joseph Stalin. The Russian historian links this massacre with the pre-planned passing of a special train through Poland on route from Moscow to Berlin, with Stalin on board (on July 17, 1945, the Potsdam Conference[36] began in Berlin with Stalin's participation), which intensified the activities of the NKVD and the Red Army against the Polish Underground fighting for Poland's independence.

Where were the victims of the Roundup taken? How were they murdered? Where is their resting place? So many questions come to mind. Tananis is pondering upon these questions: "In my opinion, they are in Belarus, in the woods or in the forts near Grodno. Beria sent his best executioners and Chekists to Olecko, so the crime was even more perfect than in Katyń. And he succeeded. To this day, we do not know where and how the victims died or where they were buried."

Marian Tananis, next to Fr. Stanislaw Wysocki, during one of the Augustów Roundup commemorations.

Indeed, it is believed that the Polish insurgents apprehended during the Augustów Roundup were taken to the vicinity of Grodno and murdered in the so-called Forts of Grodno, where previously the NKVD had carried out other mass executions. The villages of Kaleta and Naumowicze in the Grodno region in Belarus are often indicated as possible sites of the execution.

But there are also other hypotheses. An eminent historian, Professor Krzysztof Jasiewicz of the Polish Academy of Sciences, has concluded that the murder was committed in the area of Lake Gołdap, or, which he considers more likely, in the vicinity of the village of Rominty, now Krasnolesie, in the northern part of the Romincka Forest (in former East Prussia, about ten kilometers from the Polish border and 25 km from the Lithuanian border). Hermann Goering's hunting manor was located there.

Professor Natalia Lebedeva[37] from the Institute of History of the Russian Academy of Sciences proposed a theory that the Poles could have been sent to a secret camp and subjected to experiments with chemical or biological weapons.

"Is it worthwhile to remind people about the Augustów Roundup?" I turn to Tananis.

"It is, I think, but only if we tell the truth. I have talked a lot about this crime; I have written a lot. Journalists and the media, however, are guilty of manipulation. Besides, these days, my health no longer allows me to speak up."

Some publications make him laugh. The bastards have been turned into heroes, and the Home Army soldiers, so far, have not been thanked for the fight for independent Poland. Nowadays, instead of them, young girls are being bestowed medals. Tananis, a soldier of the liberation underground in the Augustów Primeval Forest, was only honored with the Cross of Valor in 2006.

"Well, if the prime minister says that for him, Polishness is a problem, one cannot be surprised. Again, we are, as a nation, in the hands of our neighbors, who decide about our existence," he says helplessly.

"Under these circumstances, how do you assess your life?"

"I do not regret anything," he replies firmly, with conviction, despite bitter reflection. "I could not stand on the other side. I hope to see another explanation for this terrible crime. Nikita Petrov said at a meeting that he needed only two more documents from the Moscow archives. And then, everything will be clear."

* * *

At this point, it is worth discussing the state of affairs regarding the explanation of the Augustów Roundup. Although 70 years have passed since those tragic events, and the residents of the Suwałki region have been afraid of talking about it (at least until recently), all this time the families of the victims of the Augustów Roundup have kept the memory of this highly concealed crime alive, even though quietly. They have also searched for their loved ones, not only in Poland and Russia but also through the Red Cross in Geneva. Many waited till the end of their lives hoping that the missing would somehow show up, especially during the last return of the prisoners of Soviet camps in 1956. They wished to know—and it continues to this day—how their relatives died and where their bodies were buried. Nevertheless, the victims of the Soviet terror have never been found.

As early as November 1945, the residents of Giby sent a delegation to the President of the Polish People's Republic Bolesław Bierut,[38] to find out about the fate of the missing residents. They wanted to know what happened to their loved ones, who were told they were being taken only to have their documents checked. They left in the middle of their chores and duties to disappear without a trace. Sending a delegation did not help. Nor did writing a petition.

At the end of the 1950s, two deputies, Jan Kłoczko and Antoni Palczak, also tried to inquire about events from a dozen or so years before. Both of these initiatives, however, encountered an impenetrable barrier.

In 1987, the Citizens Committee for the Search for the Residents of Suwałki Region Who Went Missing in July 1945[39] was founded. At that time, the exhumation of graves started in the forest at Wielki Bór near Giby. The hopes for finding the bodies of the Roundup victims there were high. However, after the exhumations in 1987 and 1989, it turned out that these were the bodies of German soldiers. In 1991, a monument in the shape of a cross, designed by Professor Andrzej Strumiłło,[40] was erected on the symbolic grave of the lost in Giby. The names of the victims were engraved on the cross. Every year, on the third Sunday of July, the commemoration of the anniversary of the Roundup takes place in Giby.

The authorities of the Polish People's Republic never officially confirmed the fact that the Augustów Roundup ever happened. The government spokesman Jerzy Urban denied the very fact of the disappearance of Polish citizens. In 1992, the Prosecutor's Office in Suwałki undertook an investigation. It was later suspended, though.

Since 1992, the requests for legal assistance have been sent to Russia. It is worth pointing out that on January 4, 1995, the Military Prosecutor's Office of the Russian Federation sent a letter to the Embassy of the Republic of Poland in Moscow stating that as a result of the pacification of the territories of northeastern Poland and parts of the territory of present Lithuania, about 7,000 people were temporarily detained "in order to detect and dispose of the anti-Soviet organization, the Home Army." It also confirmed the arrest of some people from this group by the SMERSH authorities of the Third Belarusian Front. This group numbered 592 people, and their fate, according to the letter, is unknown. Moreover, 575 people "were indicted and subjected to criminal investigations," but "there were no charges brought against those Polish citizens, and criminal cases were not referred to the court." In the letter, the Russian side also declared that in the state archives of the Russian Federation, no information about the fate of detainees was available, and those responsible for carrying out this military operation were dead.

Nine years later, in 2003, the Russian authorities stated that there were no documents confirming the shooting of civilians in the Suwałki Region in 1945. Although it was acknowledged that the 62nd Division of the Internal Forces of the NKVD was active in this area, the requests for copies of this unit's battle logs remained unanswered.

In mid-July 2006, the Russian authorities refused once again to respond to the Polish request for legal assistance in pursuing this case, citing the statute of limitations. In 2009, Poland submitted to Russia another, more extensive application for legal aid.

In 2001, the investigation was undertaken by the Białystok branch of the Institute of National Remembrance (IPN), which is still going on today. Initially, the IPN prosecutors classified the Augustów Roundup as a communist crime, but since July 2009, it has been recognized as a crime against humanity. In June 2011, the IPN sent a request to the Russian side for a copy of a specific document on the Augustów Roundup that was published by Russian historian Nikita Petrov. In August 2011, the General Prosecutor's Office of the Russian Federation reported that besides the information provided to Poland in 1995 and 2003, nothing else was available.

In addition, on September 23, 2010, the IPN in Białystok drafted and directed an appeal for legal assistance to the Republic of Belarus to carry out a search in the local archives, which would determine whether, in the area of the former fortress Grodno and in the neighboring villages, in July or early August 1945, any action indicating the liquidation and burial of about 600 people may have been carried out. In response, the General Prosecutor's Office of the Republic of Belarus stated that the above-mentioned legal aid could not be granted because it would be contrary to the basic legal principles in force in their territory. The IPN in Białystok sent a similar request to the Prosecutor General of the Republic of Lithuania on January 23, 2009. The Lithuanian side sent a copy of the documents to the Polish side, but they had already been obtained in the course of a search in the Central Military Archive in Rembertów, Poland.

In December 2011, the IPN in Białystok issued a new request to the

Russian prosecutor's office for legal aid, this time to hand over a copy of the second cryptogram from Gen. Viktor Abakumov to the Head of NKVD, Lavrentiy Beria (No. 25871), stored in the Central Archives of the Federal Security Service in Moscow. In the summer of 2013, Zbigniew Kulikowski, a prosecutor of the Białystok IPN, declared that according to the Russian Prosecutor General's Office, meeting the Polish requests for legal aid "does not seem feasible."

During the IPN investigation, however, it was determined that the following people were responsible for the liquidation of the detained Polish citizens, members of the Home Army: Major General Ivan Ivanovich Gorgonov, the head of the First Division of the Military Board of the Counterintelligence SMERSH at the People's Defense Commission of the Soviet Union (d. 1994), and Lieutenant General Pavel Vasiljevich Zelenin, the head of SMERSH at the LKO of the Soviet Union of the Third Belarusian Front (d. 1965). So far, during the investigation, approximately 700 witnesses have been interrogated. In 2013 and 2014, DNA samples were collected from members of the families of the victims of the Augustów Roundup. The investigation continues, but in order to reconstruct the fate of the missing persons and indicate the location of their burial, it is necessary to obtain the information stored in the Russian archives.

In addition to the formal investigation, the Białystok branch of the Institute of National Remembrance is conducting an educational campaign. In July 2010, on the 65th anniversary of the Augustów Roundup, it prepared an exhibition devoted to this unexplained crime. It was on display in the building of Sejm [lower house of the Polish parliament] in Warsaw and later in Suwałki, Augustów, and Węgorzewo as well as other towns. During the 11th Cavalry picnic in Suwałki (June 9, 2011), an historical show, "Augustów Roundup: July 1945," was presented in collaboration with the Regional Museum in Suwałki.

The Augustów Roundup was also the subject of seven sessions of the Home Army Historical Club at the Lyceum No. 2 in Augustów. The club is led by Danuta Kaszlej, a teacher at this high school. The first session was held in 2007 with the participation of five members of the Citizens Committee for the Search for the Residents of Suwałki Region Who Went Missing in July 1945. (Each session gathered over 100 people.) The Historical Club also organized a project, "Augustów Roundup: When There Are No Graves, Let's Preserve the Memory," which included workshops, meetings with teachers and the youth, three excursions covering the Augustów Roundup area, annual commemorations, memos, and resolutions.

The Association for the Memory of the 1945 Augustów Roundup Victims, led by Monsignor Stanisław Wysocki (his testimony is presented in another chapter), was founded in 2009. From July 21–24, 2013, on the 68th anniversary of the genocide in Augustów, Suwałki, Sejny, and Sokółka, the association organized a three-day Catholic mystery play in cooperation with the Historical Club of Home Army and the Lyceum No. 2 in Augustów as a tribute to the victims of the Augustów Roundup. The program of the ceremonies, held in Augustów, Sztabin, Krasnybór, Suwałki, Sejny, Biała Woda, Giby, and other places in the Augustów Primeval Forest, was vibrant and included historical lectures, Masses, a motorcyclist rally, concerts, and shows.

At the initiative of various civic organizations, more events were organized in 2014, including the following: the unveiling of a plaque at Jasna Góra Monastery in Częstochowa dedicated to the victims of the Augustów Roundup (May 3, 2014); the raising of a symbolic cross commemorating the decisive clash of the Home Army with the Soviets on Lake Brożane near Augustów (June 14, 2014); a solemn Mass at St. John's Cathedral in Warsaw followed by an academic conference at the Royal Castle with Polish historians and Nikita Petrov from the Association "Memorial"[41] in Moscow (July 27, 2014).

President Bronisław Komorowski[42] is also familiar with the issues surrounding the Augustów Roundup—he even promised to help find an explanation but, so far, without success. The subject of the crime was also addressed in the Polish parliament—an exhibition about the Augustów Roundup was held on Warsaw's Wiejska Street, and a special resolution was adopted (more on this later in the book).

Moreover, on October 22, 2014, a letter from the Institute of Political Studies (IPS) of the Polish Academy of Sciences (sponsored by the IPS Permanent Representative for the Augustów Roundup, Professor Krzysztof Jasiewicz, and signed by 14,000 people under the petition "To the Supreme Powers of the Republic of Poland") was delivered to then-Speaker of the Sejm of the Republic of Poland, Radosław Sikorski. The petition advocates the "intensification of efforts to establish the burial site of about 2,000 Polish citizens murdered in the summer of 1945 by a special NKVD battalion, SMERSH during the so-called Augustów Roundup." An appeal for more vigorous actions of the Polish state was signed by several Polish scholars (105 professors, 136 scholars with postdoctoral degrees, and 145 PhDs), and members of the clergy (219 priests, including two cardinals and five bishops), and many others.

People in Poland and beyond who are engaged in the matters pertaining to this still little-known crime are getting ready for the 70th anniversary of the Augustów Roundup in 2015. The former insurgent Marian Tananis, one of the few survivors, hopes to still be alive at the time of this anniversary.[43]

Sejny, May 2013–October 2014

Krystyna Świerzbińska (Augustów)

*"When we came back from Siberia,
my father was gone"*

She was only two and a half years old, but she remembers how she cried on the train while her father was being taken away. She screamed, "Daddy! I want my Daddy! I want my little bed!"

The wagon—with no compartments, designed for carrying cattle—was dirty and crowded with people to the limit. Through June 1941, the Soviets were deporting Poles to Siberia. This operation was the fourth wave of the so-called great deportations.[1] This transport had been prepared before Nazi Germany invaded its former ally, the Soviet Union, so when the train from Augustów took off, Hitler had already attacked Stalin. As a result, the cattle wagons crammed with Poles were being bombed by the German Air Force.

Little Krysia[2] also remembered that "Daddy waved goodbye" before the murderers took him from

Krystyna Świerzbińska outside her Augustów apartment.

the wagon, away from his family. This was the last time she ever saw her father.

Today, Krystyna Świerzbińska[3] (b. 1939) is 75-years-old, lonely, and sick. She keeps collecting all the materials concerning the Augustów Roundup—recently published books, articles, lists of the missing, reports, and documents. She has even saved the identity card of her father, Klemens Świerzbiński, from his bachelorhood. She has also kept the only letter from her father that reached the family in Siberia as well as several family photos taken before World War II.

"These are my relics," she sighs, touching them with reverence.

She wants to show them all. Therefore, she gets up to reach the bookcase in her neat, sunny, one-bedroom apartment in Augustów, not without difficulty—"because of the aching spine, the legs have no use." Despite the illness and traumatic life experiences, she has kept her warmhearted and peaceful state of mind. Her blue eyes look kindly from beneath her gray hair; one can feel that East European openness to the world. She has never been afraid to talk about the Augustów Roundup. Today, she speaks quietly, almost casually, without emotion. The years that have passed have made her feel at ease with those extraordinary events in her life.

The Soviets came to the Świerzbińskis' home in Jaziewo, a village located in the Augustów Primeval Forest near the Biebrza Basin and the Augustów Canal, on the night of June 20, 1941. During World War II, the area around Jaziewo witnessed an intense insurgent activity of the Polish Underground. Klemens Świerzbiński, a farmer, was known in the surrounding villages as a handy, smart, and hardworking man who knew carpentry, could fix shoes, and, on top of that, could play the violin. His over 20-hectare[4] farm was run in an exemplary fashion. He also owned a nice, large house. He owed much to his father, also named Klemens Świerzbiński, who in the interwar period worked in America and returned with precious dollars. For some time, he was also the mayor of the local municipal government.

The Soviets took the entire Świerzbiński family—crying and lamenting—straight from their beds: the parents of the little Krysia, Klemens and Franciszka Świerzbiński (they were a happy couple, married fewer than four years before); her grandfather and grandmother Klemens and Pelagia Świerzbiński (already an elderly couple); Auntie Monika Świerzbińska (then 15-years-old); and Auntie Romualda Kugiel, the mother's sister. The

Opposite: The Świerzbiński family before the outbreak of World War II. Sitting, from the left: Pelagia and Klemens Świerzbiński with a few-months-old-granddaughter Krysia. Standing: Franciszka (their daughter-in-law, Krysia's mother), Monika (Klemens's sister), and Klemens Świerzbiński (Krysia's father).

Krystyna Świerzbińska (Augustów)

Soviets seized the horses from the farm and took the prisoners first to Jastrzębna where they stayed overnight, and, on the next day, by train to Augustów.

The father of the two-year-old Krysia had already been loaded with his family into a cattle car in Augustów when suddenly the Soviets opened the door, and one of them asked if Klemens Świerzbiński was there. When

Klemens Świerzbiński during his military service in the Second Polish Republic.

Photograph of Krystyna's father, Klemens Świerzbiński (probably first row, sitting on the ground, second from left), during his military service.

he confirmed, he was taken away along with other men separated from the transport and imprisoned in an Augustów prison. They were liberated by Germans, who, on June 22, 1941, attacked their former ally. Klemens Świerzbiński was lucky—in another detention center formed by the Eastern occupier, in the so-called Augustów Canal Commission, the fleeing Russians had managed to murder almost all the detainees. Krysia's father was one of the first to see this massacre.

In the summer of 1941, after leaving the Augustów prison, Klemens Świerzbiński returned to their farm in Jaziewo without his family. For a short time he lived alone, then moved in with his brother in the neighboring village. He joined the Home Army, was a corporal, and participated in underground diversionary operations [against German occupiers]. He waited impatiently for any sign of life from his family deported to Siberia. Through the entire German occupation of Poland, which he survived by living on his farm, he did not receive any news.

Krystyna Świerzbińska recollects their three-week journey to Siberia. From this trip, during which they were given bread and water only sporadically, she only remembers the floor flooded with blood trickling from people wounded by bombs.

They were unloaded near Krasnoyarsk[5] into the wilderness, where only four houses stood. They lived in dugouts and worked hard. To warm the dugouts, they had to walk for almost 20 kilometers[6] to the near forest

Klemens Świerzbiński's ID.

to pick up wood, and to get water, four kilometers. In winter, the temperature fell to negative 50° C,[7] and the soil cracked. Summers were short, and the nights were frigid. Franciszka Świerzbińska, the mother of the little Krysia, milked and washed cows in a nearby kolkhoz, combed and milked the sheep, and worked in the fields. Her grandfather, the one who had been to America, did not withstand the exile and died near Krasnoyarsk, even though he had been asking God to have his body laid in the Polish soil. Aunt Monica, whose gorgeous hair was now full of lice and its eggs, was taken deep into the taiga for timber logging. Aunt Romualda was sentenced to death after a Russian woman overheard her saying, "We owe our fate to Stalin," while working in a kolkhoz. Later, the sentence was converted to ten years of imprisonment. She was released from a prison in Irkutsk and returned to Poland 53 years later, in 1994, with her husband, also a deportee to Siberia. She died in Augustów in 2009.

However, little Krysia grew to like the Siberian land. From the local children she learned the Russian language and spoke it better than Polish. She still remembers it well, thanks to her excellent memory, which even today can be admired.

"On the fertile Siberian steppes, lilies and many flowers bloomed in summer—and large wild strawberries, and other fruits and vegetables. To this day, I remember the smell of bird cherry trees," she continues with nostalgia, stressing that the people there were kind to them.

They kept sending letters to her father, Klemens Świerzbiński. For a long time they had not received any replies. Finally, one of the letters somehow got to her father's sister, who lived in the village of Jaminy. After two months, they received a response. Klemens Świerzbiński wrote, in violet ink, in November 1944. In Krystyna's family archives, the letter has kept this color to this day.

> Dear Wife and Dear Krysia, Mother and Father, and Dear Sister,
>
> I got a message that you are alive! There was nothing more cheerful in my life; it is my comfort.
> I am alive and healthy by the grace of God, and I wish you lots of such health.
> I have filled out and sent an application for your release, so if you get a message, get ready to come home as soon as possible.
> I have not been hungry yet, but my life is miserable. I have no place; I have no rest; I always think of you, whether you eat and sleep well. Please describe what you do, what you are busy with, whether you are all together or separated—how are you there?
> Do not stint anything, sell anything you can do to save your lives, and when we meet, these are just material things. I had such wealth and lost it. I am alive, but without you and our family, this is the worst life in the world. ...
> How is my daughter growing? Perhaps she goes to school already? Perhaps you can take a photo, send it, and let me look at you because, in my dreams, I don't see both of you. I thought you were not alive, but God is watching over us.
> Do you have the cross I brought from the forest? Take care of it and bring it home because God will help you. He has helped already—you are all alive.
> At this point, I shall finish my writing. With God's will, we will soon see each other.
>
> With my sincere love,
> Your dearest Klimek[8]

Upon receiving this and two more letters, the uplifted Świerzbiński family began the process of seeking a return from the exile in Siberia to Poland, which lasted for many months. One day, they heard on the Soviet radio that in the Augustów Primeval Forrest, many Polish bandits had been caught. They did not suspect that Klemens was among them, but his wife Franciszka "shivered." She said, "Klimek is gone for sure." Just before their departure from Siberia, a letter came from Poland with the news that Klemens had been taken by the Soviets and deported, just like his family.

They returned from deportation after five years, in April 1946—three women and the seven-year-old Krysia—with the cross that Klemens had brought from the Augustów Primeval Forest. They watched over it as Krysia's father commanded so that God would help with his return.

They learned about the July 1945 Roundup from their neighbors. They believed, however, that Klemens would come back from the exile, as they did from faraway Siberia. They could not comprehend that one of their neighbors, Mirosław Milewski, had helped the Soviets with the whole operation. Milewski (1928–2008) came from nearby Lipsk, but after losing his family, he took refuge in their village of Jaziewo and was treated like one of the locals. He turned out to be particularly active in arresting his neighbors. Later, starting in 1944, he worked in the communist security apparatus, holding the highest posts. He has never been formally held accountable nor charged with the crimes and brutality towards his countrymen.

Franciszka and her daughter Krysia—the so-called "Sybiraks"[9]—found temporary lodging with Franciszka's uncle, Honoriusz Kugiel. Her grandmother and Aunt Monika stayed close by with their family. From the conspicuous buildings of the Świerzbińskis' farm, only a cellar and a small granary were left. With the family and neighbors' help, a window was cut out, a stove was built, the walls were whitewashed, and the floor was laid in the granary. Neighbors helped them find a table with two chairs and two beds. In this tiny room, Franciszka Świerzbińska and her daughter Krystyna would live for 49 years! Alone, they struggled with running the farm, breeding several cows, flocks of pigs and hens. They used the services of the local state-owned farms, but Krystyna, when she grew up and took over the farm, did not sleep for more than three to four hours a day.

It was under these conditions—in this primitive granary, with no amenities—that Krysia completed evening classes at an agriculture high school in Dojlidy near Białystok. She also got married, but unfortunately, the man was lazy and a drunkard. They broke up after four years. In this tiny room, her mother Franciszka Świerzbińska died in 1995.

All this time both women, Franciszka and Krysia, were waiting for Klemens—the husband and father. In their dreams and wishes, too. Meanwhile, they investigated the circumstances of his disappearance. They managed to find a lot of facts, some of which have been confirmed since then, for example, in the testimony of a Jaziewo resident, Helena Matyskieła.

It turned out that the Soviets and their Polish allies from the District Office of Public Security (PUBP) in Augustów, totaling several hundred troops, appeared in Jaziewo on July 10, 1945, at noon. They surrounded the village by setting up the posts at the mouth of each road at a distance of several dozen feet from one soldier to another. The camp, with trucks covered with tarps, was set up on the road leading to Mogilnica. They entrenched the artillery posts near the barns that belonged to the Olszewski and

Opposite: Klemens Świerzbiński's letter to the family in exile, dated November 1944. No.1.

Sejwyber dnia 2 X 944

Kochana Żono i Krysia droga Matko i Ciocie i droga Siostro, dostałem wiadomość że żyjecie, barzo mnie uradowało że dostałem taką wiadomość nie weselszą w życiu jeszcze nie miałem ta moja pociecha jestem żywy i zorazy z łaski Boża Boga i życze wam takiego zdrowia, Podołem zadowić by was odesłano do domu więc jeśli dostaniecie wiadomość to się starajcie żeby mogli jak naprędzej przyjechać do domu sprzedaj wszystko co masz do życia masz moje Garnitury i jakie rzeczy nowe i pościel co tylko masz to sprzedawaj aby mogła dostać się do domu, bo ja nie mogę nic wam dopomóc co się tyczy do ubrać to ja mam wszystko spać będziem mi poduszek mam dwie pierzyny i mam poduszki żyje u Bredka moje budynki spalone i rozbite w sierniu jak stół w front to do o domu nie mogę się dostać, sprzedałem jedno krowe na życie, a jedną krowę i jednego konia mam i tak żyje z tem przeżywam było by barzo dobrze żeby byli razem Kochana Froniu się starajcie że by mogli przyjechać do domu, a tody jeszcze nie byłem, ale życie moje nie zadowolnione niemam miejsca, niemam spoczynku zawsze myślę o was czy wy podjecie i jakie wy możecie wyspanie i spać czy wy robicie jakie macie zajęcie, tylko patrzy do w kupu wasz z łaską możesz sprzedawać tylko

Zostaw tem jak wujek Ciotka nie żyje
Elijasz się ożenił o kredytka nil niem
nie wszystko byłoby w porządku
tylko przyjedziecie do domu. A czy
Romcia żyje przy was czy odzielnie i czy wy
wszyscy razem cała rodzina jak otrzymasz
list mój to opisz wszystko czy wy razem
czy wy po osobno to wszystko opisz jak wam
tam jest, nie żałuj niczego sprzedawaj
co tylko możesz, aby ratowali sobie
życie a jak się spotkamy to jest zbyta
rzecz ja miałem takie bogactwo i
stworzenie że można, a bez Ciebie i
i swojej rodziny najgorsze życie na świecie
kończym kończę swoje pisanie jak otrzym-
-acie list naszych miast pisz do mnie
Janaszów. Józef córka utopia i niema
że wszyscy żyjecie. Ten list otrzymała Bronia
i dała mi odezw. (Romek nie żyje i Bomek.)
Bronia jedna została. Żaty kończę już
mój list aby Boże stwórco się zobaczyli razem
pozostaję twój najstarszy Klimek
szczerze się kochający jak się hodują
moja córka może do szkoły chodzi może
będzie mogła zrobić zajęcia to piszcie
niech ja popatrzę na was bo roku mnie
się nie śnicie myślałem że nie żyjecie
ale Bóg nad nami czy ten krzyż macie
co złoto przy córce to jego pilnujcie i przy-
-wieźcie jego do domu to jak Pan Bóg do pomoże
uratować z lasu my wszyscy zginem i Klimek
zonaty do czekał z córką Czesiek ma jedno córkę
do uczenia do rolnego z żona... Klimek Sw...

A barn in Jastrzębna Druga that belonged to the Koszycki family, which served as one of the detention places for the 16 men arrested in Jaziewo.

Kalinowski families. Field kitchens were set up at the Murawskis and at the fire station. Several remaining trucks stood in the Świerzbińskis' yard and near the property of the Juchniewicz family, where a store was later established. A car with a megaphone was set up in the Putynskis' yard. Lively music and Stalin's speeches were aired on the radio.

The Soviets stayed in Jaziewo for about a week. Their headquarters were at the Kozłowskis' house, with a colonel as a highest-ranking officer, while the officers of the PUBP from Augustów found accommodations in the neighboring house that belonged to Wacław Ziemba. They drank lots of moonshine, and when intoxicated, they shot the guns into the ceiling. The wooden ceiling at Ziemba's house has bullets holes to this day.

Every day at dawn, the "visitors" rode around the fields in search of fugitives who could be hiding in the fields. However, they tried to be friendly to the villagers. On Friday, July 13, the Soviet soldiers walked from home to home and invited all grown-up men to attend a meeting the next day. "Завтра мы уезжаем" ("We are leaving tomorrow"), they assured.[10]

On July 14, 1945, several men from Jaziewo responded. When they reached the fire station, they were surrounded by a tightening cordon, so

Opposite: Klemens Świerzbiński's letter to the family in exile, dated November 1944. No.2.

no one could turn back. They were all detained in the yard and the barn at the Kozłowskis' property. The area was densely encircled by the Soviets. Some women were allowed to hand over only a two-day food supply to their close ones. Klemens Świerzbiński, whose family had been sent to Siberia, was given food by Helena Matyskieła.

The men arrested in the neighboring villages of Wrotki and Mogilnica were brought to Jaziewo. After two days of interrogations in the Kozłowskis' barn in Jaziewo, the Soviets rushed the men under a strict escort to Kopiec. Desperate women, with children in their arms, who accompanied their fathers, husbands, and sons to their march, were assured by the NKVD that the men would return home after a few days. In Kopiec, the prisoners spent the night, and the next day, they were driven further, to Jastrzębna Druga, where for a few days—in the Koszyckis' barn and in the Granackis' basement—some families were allowed to see their loved ones for the last time.

After the interrogations in Jastrzębna Druga, men were divided—some of those arrested in Jaziewo were later seen in Sztabin in the barn that belonged to the Szyc family, located near Rybacz, close to the municipal building. They were subjected to further "investigations" and divisions. Families who brought food to Sztabin saw their men in bloody shirts—obviously the result of the beatings. Some of the "bandits" were sentenced to death and transported at night by car.

However, some of the men captured in Jaziewo were most likely taken from Jastrzębna Druga directly to Augustów, bypassing Sztabin. Probably at this stage of the interrogations, they were classified as "bandits."

A monument dedicated to the victims of the Augustów Roundup, including 16 men from Jaziewo, was erected in 1995 at the parish cemetery in Jaminy.

To this day many families think that all 16 Jaziewo men were taken (via Sztabin or not) to the infamous "Turk House" (the PUBP headquarters). However, some women who wanted to give them food heard from the Soviet prisoner guards (who "were wearing red caps with red bands, navy blue trousers, and held whips in their hands, used for hitting their boots") that their men were not there. They learned that the night before, the residents of Augustów witnessed the prisoners being marched through the city. They walked in columns of four and were carrying shovels on their shoulders. The Soviets marched on both sides of the street and were shooting into the air, so the locals were afraid of approaching the windows. Later, people in Augustów claimed that all Polish detainees were shot in the Augustów Primeval Forest near the village of Płaska.

Out of the 16 men arrested during the July operation, 15 were arrested at the Jaziewo meeting. Jan Janik, on the other hand, was arrested in neighboring Mogilnica, also at a village meeting. Most of them fought in the Home Army. Some of the Home Army members suspected deceit and did not go to the meeting on July 14. In this way, they escaped the arrest, hid, and waited out the critical time of the Roundup. The 16 missing inhabitants of Jaziewo were: Mieczysław Andruszkiewicz, Jan Bielawski, Stanisław Dziądziak, Antoni Guziejko, Eugeniusz Haraburda, Jan Janik, Leon Karp, Czesław Kozakiewicz, Adam Kugiel, Edward Kunda, Kazimierz Kułakowski, Stanislaw Matyskieła, Ludwik Suchwałko, Franciszek Szmygel, Klemens Świerzbiński (Krysia's father, b. 1904), and Jan Usnarski.

The fate of those 16 men captured at the meeting on July 14, 1945, in Jaziewo has never been explained. What remained was the despair of the mothers and wives and the orphaned children. Up to this day, they cannot even light a candle on their grave. However, in 1995, the families had a symbolic monument erected at the Jaminy cemetery, with the inscription: "Victims of the NKVD and UB[11] crime of July 14, 1945. They died for the freedom of our homeland and for a better tomorrow." Underneath, the names of all 16 victims are listed.

The 17th victim of the Roundup in Jaziewo, Stanisław Panasewicz, the son of Benjamin, escaped from the Soviets to Jagłowo, to his sister in Karpowicze. In the darkness, he fell into a river and drowned. After a few days, the family found his body near the passage over the Brzozówka River.

When Krystyna Świerzbińska, the daughter of the captured Klemens Świerzbiński, who disappeared without a trace, turned 17, she took matters into her own hands. Through letters and requests, the teenage girl started looking for her father and all 16 victims of the Roundup in Jaziewo. For many years, she wrote to local, regional, and central governments as well as to party officials, the Red Cross, and media agencies, asking for help in locating men of Jaziewo who went missing on July 14, 1945. Each time, she listed them all. Unfortunately, no answer ever came. Here is an excerpt from one of her letters to [then Polish Communist Party leader] Władysław Gomułka, dated 1966:

> Poland is about to commemorate the 21st anniversary of the liberation of our land. Monuments have been built for fallen heroes, so each city and every village can celebrate with joy. However, we have to observe the 21st anniversary of the disappearance of our fathers, husbands, and brothers, with mourning, regret, and heartache. We have appealed dozens of times to various Polish offices and institutions for help with the search—always unsuccessfully. And yet, these are our Polish brothers! How can one forget about them?
>
> We turn to all the officials who hold the highest offices in Poland for assistance in finding our people. There are thousands of them, but we give only the names of people from our village.
>
> Let the tears of the crying orphans, widows, and mothers, who, for so many years, have been waiting for the return of their beloved ones, finally disappear.

Krystyna Świerzbińska has kept all these letters in her Augustów apartment. She moved there in 1997, two years after the death of her mother, Franciszka Świerzbińska. The land that belonged to her parents was sold together with the livestock; the rest was given to a distant family. The money from selling her possessions and from the compensation for her father's death Krystyna used for purchasing a two-bedroom, sunny, comfortable apartment with a garage in the residential area in the city on the Netta River. She also bought a small Fiat car and refreshed her driving skills. She originally learned to drive at the agriculture high school, where she got her driver's license.

"What was I supposed to do in Jaziewo, alone and sick? I used to drive back for a few more years—to mow the grass and grow the garden. I like flowers and my own vegetables." She also talks about going on pilgrimages, even around Europe. This is the whole joy of her life.

In her Augustów apartment, however, she dreams about her Jaziewo daily. It is only in her dreams that she takes care of animals, collects eggs from hens, and grows vegetables and flowers. And in her mind's eyes, she still sees her mother, standing. "Kind and good looking were my parents. Why couldn't we be together?" she asks.

How does she assess her fate? It hit her hard. But she has been courageous, strong, and efficient, and despite the misery and injustice of this world, she has tried to stay positive. While meeting people, she has always "locked her poverty in a closet."

She no longer believes in the explanation of the Augustów Roundup crime, unless there is a miracle, and the Russians will hand over documents from their archives. She doubts it, though, because "Putin, unlike the Polish authorities, is not afraid of anyone."

One of the letters Krystyna Świerzbińska wrote to the highest authorities of the People's Republic of Poland.

She tells her extraordinary story to warn the next generations. Recently, on February 25, 2014, she shared the story with the prosecutor from the Institute of National Remembrance (IPN) in Białystok, who took a sample from inside of her mouth for DNA testing—in a noninvasive way, using a sterile swab. This will help determine the identity of the Augustów

Roundup victims. The families of the missing and the historians dealing with this crime demand that the IPN check the locations indicated by the witnesses, and then—if the investigations result in the discovery of remains—carry out the exhumations in several places in the Augustów Primeval Forest (especially along the Giby-Rygol road), where those murdered in July 1945 could have been buried.

Perhaps only then will Krystyna Świerzbińska be able to see the secret of the postwar "Little Katyń" explained. Maybe she will still be able to know the resting place of her father Klemens, a corporal of the Home Army. For the time being, from the branch of the Commission for the Prosecution of Crimes against the Polish Nation of the Institute of National Remembrance in Białystok, she has received the status of a victim.

Augustów, August 17, 2013–March 8, 2014

Fr. Stanisław Wysocki (Suwałki)

"Our farm was an oasis for the insurgency"

The dark, lively eyes watch closely from under the thick eyebrows to examine whether the interviewer can be trusted. This does not come as a surprise. After all, prelate Stanisław Wysocki—a charismatic long-time youth priest, Solidarity Chaplain in the Łomża District, builder of churches and, in recent years, an uncompromising spokesman for

Fr. Stanisław Wysocki.

revealing the truth about the greatest crime committed by the Soviets against the Poles after the end of World War II, considered by the Suwałki region people as "Another Katyń"—has been hit hard by the totalitarian system. It already started when he was a child. In the Augustów Roundup, he lost his father, two older sisters, and his sister's fiancé, and he was only seven years old. During the time of the Polish People's Republic, he experienced horrific persecution and even two attempts on his life.

However, by the second meeting with the author, Father Wysocki's watchful and intense eyes become friendly and welcome her warmly at the threshold of his apartment in Suwałki. He lives in an apartment in one of the residential complexes on the Czarna Hańcza River that belongs to his niece, a doctor. The place overflows with exotic orchids; the summer sun peeks through the window. On the balcony, a white-and-red flag flutters in the wind.

"In my traditional Polish family, which was naturally very much involved in the Home Army, both totalitarian regimes of the 20th century—Russian and German—have been reflected as if in the mirror," says the priest and asks where to start our conversation.

Stanisław Wysocki was born on March 1, 1938, in the village of Biała Woda near Suwałki, in then Jeleniewo municipal district. He remembers his father, Ludwik Wysocki, as an extremely busy man. About his mother, Józefa, née Jarząbska, he recalls that she was not only a good mother and wife but also a very patriotic and entrepreneurial person. The family of nine (including seven children) owned a farm that stood on 30 hectares[1] of land. It was the most prosperous family in the village, and their house, beautifully situated by the forests and hills in Biała Woda, was spacious, hospitable, and affluent.

During the German occupation, their farm, now near Suwałki Vista Park, became a refuge and an oasis for anti–Nazi resistance. Usually, a dozen or so soldiers of the Polish Underground resided in their house. Fr. Wysocki well remembers the resistance soldiers' conversations or when they were leaving at night to carry out sabotage operations.

"I would hang around—just like a child does—and watch their uniforms and weapons. Before every operation, they always prayed, kneeling before the holy image in our large room. My mother led the prayers. And when the soldiers returned, they talked to her about the events of the day." The priest narrates the events precisely as if those images from the past were right in front of his eyes.

His father, Ludwik Wysocki, ran the farm. He provided for the family and the insurgents but also participated indirectly in underground activities. He was a sworn member of the Home Army and helped Russian escapees from German captivity survive. He met them one day in their field as they ate pods of peas. He brought them home and fed them. Besides, any time the members of the Wysocki family went to Suwałki, they took with them some bread for the Russians imprisoned in a German camp over the Czarna Hańcza River.

The arrest of his father by the Gestapo stuck forever in his memory. The Germans came to Biała Woda with a dog. (Fortunately, there were no Home Army soldiers in the house.) They took his father and tortured him in Suwałki. He returned after a few days. The priest remembers that his father's back was all black-and-blue from torture. Mother did not hide the sight from the children. She said, "See what the enemy did to your father."

"It stuck in our memory, and I've been carrying this image to this day," the priest recalls. "Soon, the Germans took our father again. This time he did not return quickly. He was convicted and sentenced to prison in Konigsberg. As a prisoner, he worked in an ammunition factory. He returned from Konigsberg at the end of the German occupation."

In May 1944, two months before the implementation of the anti–German operation "Burza" ("Storm"), the units of the Home Army entered into military cooperation with Soviet diversionary intelligence groups (particularly with the "Orłow" unit). However, during the course of the "Burza" operation and the subsequent maneuvers undertaken by the Red Army, the Poles were left with no illusions. The Home Army troops mobilized for this operation were later disassembled by the Soviets, disarmed, and interned. They were then incorporated into the Polish People's Army. However, many officers and soldiers were arrested and deported to Siberia.

Stanisław Wysocki's father, Ludwik Wysocki.

In the second half of 1944, the entire region and the Polish Underground in the Suwałki and Augustów districts suddenly found themselves in a new reality—under actual Soviet occupation. After the Germans, the Soviet Union and the newly appointed communist authorities became a new adversary in the fight for a sovereign state. The Polish insurgency, even though severely decimated by the Soviets, was supported by the local population and fought with a new enemy, the Soviets.

After the war with Germany ended in May of 1945, nothing had changed in the Wysockis' household in Biała Woda. Only the enemy changed: from Germans to Soviets, the new occupants of these beautiful lands. The Wysockis' farm secretly housed the headquarters of the Suwałki Region of the Home Army, with then commanding officer Captain Mieczysław Ostrowski, alias "Kropidło."

People in that area were also well aware that the liberation from the five-year German occupation did not bring the desired freedom but more cruel enslavement. On November 30, 1944, the inspector of the Suwałki Region, Major Franciszek Szabunia, alias "Zemsta" ("Revenge"), was already reporting to the Home Army District Command in Białystok: "Arrests, terror, and roundups ravaged and ruined the area of the insurgency structures. The five-year German occupation did not do as much evil ... as the Soviets do now. The NKVD has accurate tallies of all insurgents, reserve commanders, and even citizens collaborating with the Home Army."[2]

After January 19, 1945, following the official dissolution of the Home Army by General Leopold Okulicki,[3] insurgence activities continued in the Suwałki region. The commander of the Białystok District, Lt. Col. Władysław Liniarski, alias "Mścisław," announced on February 18, 1945, the creation of the Citizens' Home Army (AKO, for Armia Krajowa Obywatelska). He argued: "The war continues. As long as there is one occupying *soldat*[4] or a *bojec*[5] on the Polish land, the war shall continue. Until the last NKVD member leaves our borders, the war shall continue."[6]

In spite of persecution, terror, arrests, and deportations, the AKO of the Suwałki District rebuilt its forces, and at the end of April 1945, it had 1,500 members. The AKO of the Augustów District had around 500. They focused on communication, propaganda (appeals and leaflets), and armed struggle, mostly in self-defense. AKO patrols and units also kept order and protected civilians from repression and robberies committed by Soviet soldiers. For example, they administered whipping as a punishment for illegal logging of the forest or carried out death sentences for cooperation with the Soviet security apparatus.

The intense activities of the Citizens' Home Army, such as liquidating municipal offices or disarming the checkpoints of the communist Citizens' Militia, aimed mainly at the organs of the communist power, and, together with the support of the local population, led in May 1945 to the breakdown of the local administration of the security apparatus. In the spring of 1945, the AKO was prevalent in both districts; the communist forces remained only in the cities of Suwałki and Augustów. At one of the Augustów rallies, one NKVD major shouted: "You, bastards! You don't like the Lublin Committee?[7] You are all Home Army bandits. If the Polish Peoples' Army does not quiet you down, we will bring an 18-million Soviet army that will teach you the lesson and restore order."[8]

And soon, in the two districts—Suwałki and Augustów—more and more Soviet troops began to gather. Also, a network of informers among Poles developed intensely. The local communist authorities turned out to be helpless, so the liquidation of the Polish Underground in the area was taken over by the Soviets. The decision to prepare a massive pacification operation using the Soviet army probably took place in Białystok on May 16, 1945, during a meeting of the command of internal troops of the NKVD (operating in the Białystok region) with the authorities of the People's Republic of Poland.

Residents of the Suwałki and Augustów districts observed intensification of the NKVD troops as early as at the end of May 1945. The Soviets, with the support of Internal Security Corps (KBW) soldiers and the District Office of Public Security (PUBP) in Augustów, carried out a spectacular operation in the famous sanctuary of the Studzieniczna on the lake bearing the same name, surrounded by Augustów Primeval Forest, a few kilometers from Augustów. It was a roundup of people who gathered at a large religious fair on May 20, 1945. NKVD soldiers demolished the altar with the miraculous image of Our Lady of Studzieniczna in the chapel of the Blessed Virgin Mary and made numerous arrests among the participants of the ceremony.

However, the most tragic act of the drama was yet to come.

Wysocki's house in Biała Woda, which served as the last office of the Home Army/Citizens' Home Army Suwałki Region headquarters in July 1945.

The Wysockis' household in Biała Woda continued to participate in the operations against the Soviets, just as they had against Germans before. The entire family was involved, even the grandmother of Fr. Stanisław Wysocki, Apolonia Jarząbska, née Kolenkiewicz, a person of high integrity whose authority was respected by the grandchildren and who had a significant influence on Stanisław's upbringing to become a priest. Grandma was very pious and well-read and had a remarkable memory. She came from Gawrych Rudy; she was a cousin of the famous aviation hero, General Witold Urbanowicz,[9] commander of Squadron 303. She died in 1962 when her grandson Stanisław was in the seminary. He could not come to her funeral at that time, which he regrets to this day.

Also, all the Wysocki children were involved in the fight against the enemies of an independent Poland since their earliest years. As young scouts, they watched the roads and reported on the activities to their parents and to the Home Army soldiers, who rested during the day, to alert them if anybody was heading for their home. Very active were Fr. Stanisław's two older sisters: the petite Kazimiera—the oldest, born in 1923—and Aniela, five years younger than Kazimiera, a Home Army liaison girl. With apparent nostalgia, Fr. Wysocki shows the family photo album—kept in his niece's sunny apartment in Suwałki, where he lives—with the black-and-white photos of his sisters. All family memorabilia are meticulously collected in the apartment, which is tastefully decorated in a patriotic-and-religious fashion.

The day of July 27, 1945, which turned out to be so tragic for the Wysocki family, was warm, and the air felt refreshed after light summer rain. Ludwik Wysocki ordered an afternoon raking of hay at a nearby meadow. The insurgents joined the family members in the work. All of a sudden, just before sunset, the NKVD soldiers showed up. Members of the Home Army (a dozen or so) were having a council meeting at the house but managed to get out of the barn at the last minute. They had been warned by the priest's older brother Roman Wysocki, a young scout, who yelled, "Russians are coming!" The boy was brutally kicked by several Soviets because they saw him close the doors of the barn behind the insurgents. "You warned the bandits!" shouted an NKVD soldier, beating Roman, who would feel their kicks for the rest of his life.

"I remember that moment: the Russians drove up to our yard, and the Home Army soldiers fled into the forest, just behind our barn. In the yard, an NKVD soldier shot some 'shining bullets' in the air, which could have caused fire," reports then seven-year-old Father Stanisław, pointing to the places of the tragic event, while visiting Biała Woda. His memory is amazing. He recalls that precisely at that time, he had just brought, together with two older sisters, the cows from a nearby pasture to a drinking pond.

"At home, in the middle of the kitchen, we found a second, armed NKVD soldier. The whole family stood by the wall. I was told to join them, along with the sisters. I stood by my father. Grandma was not there," he relates with great precision.

He also remembers that among the Russians, there was one young and elegant Pole.

The priest-to-be was surprised when the Pole, who entered the kitchen from the adjoining room (where the NKVD soldiers were conferring), instead of saying, "Praised be Jesus Christ," which was customary at that time, only uttered, "Good evening to you all!" He approached the younger sister Aniela, the Home Army liaison girl, who was studying at a trade school in Suwałki, and asked what she had been doing on Gałaja Street in that city. His sister, deeply frightened by the traitor's words, fainted. Who was that young person? Probably a student from the same school, though it is still unknown to this day.

"He helped the Russians, who came to arrest members of my family affiliated with the Home Army—my father and two sisters. In addition, they found in the house the fiancée of one of them, also an insurgent. They also discovered the headquarters of the Home Army–Citizens' Home Army of the Suwałki district set up in our Biała Woda house, including its commander Ostrowski," Fr. Wysocki analyzes the dramatic situation.

The priest's youngest brother, Alojzy Wysocki, who now manages the family estate in Biała Woda, was two at that time and does not remember the tragic event but adds, "This is like living in the Bieszczady Mountains.[10] Our farmhouse, located at the end the houses scattered on the hills of Biała Woda, even today, is hard to reach. Even with GPS. The Soviets would not have found us without the help of the Polish traitor."

There is one more thing that Stanisław, who is five years older than Alojzy, remembers about that tragic day: While standing in the kitchen against the wall, he and all the younger siblings started to cry. The father ordered them to be silent. At the same time, the mother made a step forward and announced that she had to make supper for the children. Then, she calmly began to peel potatoes. The armed NKVD soldier who was guarding them did not protest.

On that day, the Soviets arrested five people: the owner of the farm and head of the family, Ludwik Wysocki; his two daughters, who both were members of the Home Army—the 22-year-old Kazimiera and the 17-year-old Aniela as well as Kazimiera's fiancée Aleksandr Gliniecki, also a Home Army member. They also ordered Zofia Gugnowska and their neighbor, grandma Krzywicka, both of whom stopped by to "borrow some bread," to board their vehicle. From the barn, they also took bicycles that belonged to the Home Army soldiers, and their equipment, including a radio station.

A few hours after leaving Biała Woda, the Russians sent more forces to the village. They surrounded the Wysockis' buildings and waited for the insurgents who had escaped earlier and had hidden in German bunkers located in the surrounding hills. In the family house, where mother, Józefa Wysocka, stayed together with five of her younger children, aged between two and 15, the NKVD set up their headquarters for a week. The priest remembers their atrocious behavior; they even tried to rape his mother. She was saved by praying and staying calm.

"It was a Judgment Day for us. We suffered a lot of pain and humiliation. We thought we would not survive," Fr. Wysocki recalls those traumatic days.

Father Wysocki's sister, Kazimiera, age 22, was murdered in the Augustów Roundup.

"They searched everywhere. They took our clothes, shoes, explaining that they would be no longer needed, neither for us nor the detainees," remembers Teresa Wysocka, the priest's sister, who was 12 at that time.

The Soviets kept visiting them for weeks. Later, as a "family of bandits," the Wysockis were similarly "taken care of" by the Polish secret police.

What happened to their loved ones who were arrested in the Augustów Roundup on July 27, 1945? According to Gugnowska's account, they were taken from Biała Woda to some barracks in Suwałki. (She was released on the second day because, during the investigation, she was judged "insane"; she was the only

Father Wysocki's sister, Aniela, age 17, was murdered in the Augustów Roundup.

one who was let go.) There, they were interrogated and sorted. According to Gugnowska, who was held with two other women, Kazimiera Wysocka was most likely tortured to death by the Russians during the interrogation in the barracks, and her younger sister Aniela Wysocka and their father Ludwik Wysocki were deported by the Soviets to an unknown location. Gugnowska met Aniela in the car transporting prisoners to a school on Hamerszmit Street, and Aniela managed to whisper, "Tell them you don't know anything." Every trace of them was lost in the same way as of approximately 2,000 other victims of the Augustów Roundup. The number provided by Fr. Wysocki is based on the documents from the Moscow archives that Nikita Petrov from the Association "Memorial" in Moscow had discovered in the early 1990s.

Stanisław's mother, a beautiful and energetic woman, searched for her husband and two daughters for the rest of her life, with the help of Apolonia Jarząbska, her mother and the priest's beloved grandmother. She

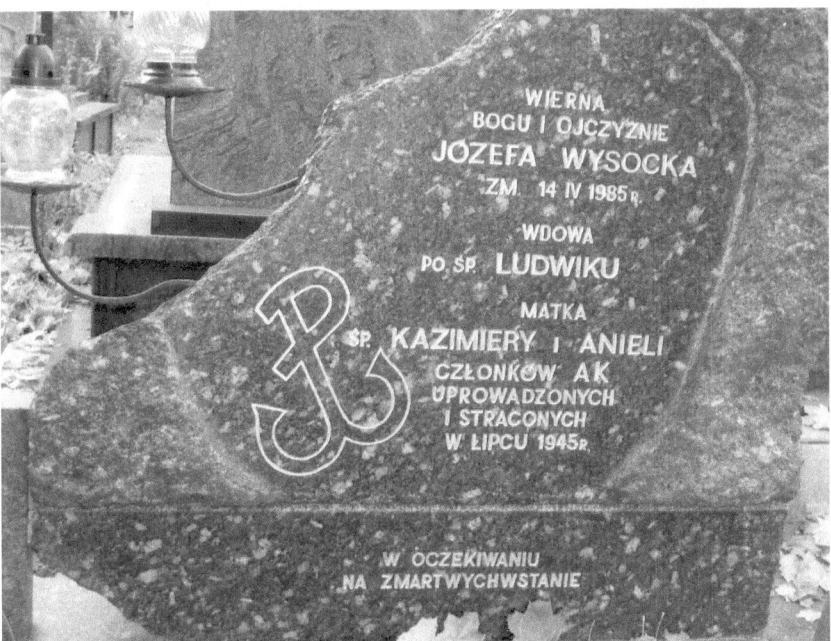

A grave of Fr. Stanisław Wysocki's mother, Józefa Wysocka, née Jarząbska, at a Suwałki cemetery, with an image of an anchor, a symbol of the "Fighting Poland." She lost her husband and two daughters in the Augustów Roundup. Inscription on the grave: "Faithful to God and Homeland, Józefa Wysocka died on April 14, 1985. Widow of Ludwik, mother of Kazimiera and Aniela, soldiers of the Home Army, imprisoned and executed in July 1945. Awaiting Resurrection."

reached out to authorities and public offices, sent letters to the International Red Cross and the communist authorities in Poland and the Soviet Union, including Stalin himself. Even in her 70s, Józefa Wysocka personally intervened in the Soviet embassy in Warsaw, also unsuccessfully. She was told there that "they were murdered in the Augustów Primeval Forest." This was hard for her to hear and bear because her last hope for the return of her loved ones was shattered.

"It is impossible to describe all those years of longing for our lost family members. The same goes for the poverty, persecution, and hostility from the communist authorities and their allies towards us," says Father Stanisław, who as a boy of seven witnessed his father and two older sisters being led to their death by the Russians. "For many years, we were harassed and persecuted as 'bandits' family.' There were also enemies in the immediate vicinity."

The sixth child of the Wysockis, Stanisław was supposed to be the future landlord of Biała Woda. However, God had a different plan for him and wanted him to graduate from the Higher Theological Seminary in Łomża.[11]

"While at the Seminary, he already distinguished himself by his commitment and openness to others," points out Fr. Wysocki's colleague, Archbishop Józef Michalik, metropolitan bishop of the Diocese of Przemyśl and president of the Polish Bishops Conference. On May 23, 1964, they both received priestly ordination in a group of 16 deacons, from Bishop Czesław Falkowski, the ordinary of the Diocese of Łomża.

"He is a highly righteous man, always sensitive to the truth, trustworthy, and caring, which is especially evident in his ministry work. Young people admired him. They found a common language, and he has kept in touch with them to this day" says Adam Kruczek.[12]

Fr. Wysocki served as a priest in many places. The first two years of his priesthood he spent in the Czerwin parish and later in Sejny.

In 1974, Bishop Mikołaj Sasinowski[13] transferred him to Łomża and appointed him rector of the seminary church, entrusting him with the mission of youth ministry. That is how the Seminary Church of the Assumption of the Blessed Virgin Mary (located on Sienkiewicza Street 1 in Łomża) established the famous Youth Church, headed by the charismatic priest Stanisław Wysocki.

Even today, the prelate Wysocki still lights up when he talks about "his" young people and the time he spent with them. With the members of the Youth Church community, he organized prayer groups, art sessions, and discussion meetings; they went on kayak trips and camps, participated in retreats, and met with the guest artists, virtually from all over Poland. They closely cooperated with St. Anna's Church in Warsaw. His

Fr. Wysocki at the Church of the Assumption of the Blessed Virgin Mary in Łomża meets with his students after 30 years (June 29, 2013).

student ministry even attracted the Communist Party notables' children, who participated in the meetings but kept it a secret from their parents.

"We did a good job with the youths. It is hard to believe now." Fr. Stanisław Wysocki still has that spark in his eyes while talking about it today.

The Communist regime, furious about the priest's successes and a wide range of endeavors, launched an attack. The security apparatus from the Militia Headquarters in Łomża harassed the clergyman in various ways, such as by constant surveillance, numerous interrogations, and attempts to discredit him in the eyes of Bishop Mikołaj Sasinowski by disseminating false charges. These schemes were based on three methods: provocation, shame, and blackmail. The priest was stalked and harassed with provocateurs (often women). But never did Fr. Stanisław let himself be fooled. Never were the secret police agents able to humiliate him, especially because the priest had abstained from alcohol since his youth—the invitations to a glass of vodka or meal at a restaurant always failed.

When, in 1980, the Independent Self-Governing Labor Union "Solidarity" was created in Poland, the Church of the Assumption of the Blessed Virgin Mary in Łomża hosted the first "Solidarity" meeting of that region, and Fr. Stanisław Wysocki became the free union's chaplain (along with coordinator Fr. Piotr Zabielski). The patriotic Masses for the homeland, celebrated in Łomża by Fr. Wysocki, started to attract more and more crowds. It was not only young people who participated but also the workforce from Łomża because Fr. Wysocki celebrated many services in various workplaces. The excitement around the "Solidarity" movement lasted over a year and was suddenly interrupted by martial law, which General Wojciech Jaruzelski and his communist administration declared on December 13, 1981.

"But even during the martial law, especially at the retreats, the Youth Church in Łomża was full, from the evening until the curfew, which was at 10 p.m. We continued to organize many interesting meetings and trips with young people," recalls the patriotic and brave priest.

The chaplain of the Łomża "Solidarity" also supported the repressed members of the "Solidarity" Union. He even hid, in his apartment, the chairman of the local "Solidarity," Marian Chojnowski, wanted by the secret police. That did not escape the attention of the communists. After the introduction of martial law, the persistent and repressive actions against Fr. Wysocki intensified.

"Sometimes, it seemed to me that I would not endure," Fr. Wysocki sighs at the memory of those dark times of the Polish People's Republic.

However, he does not want to reveal everything—some of his persecutors are still alive. They never received any punishment or reprimand and live on high pensions today.

The pressure put by the communist regime on ecclesiastical authorities also increased. In 1982, Bishop Mikołaj Sasinowski decided to move Chaplain Wysocki to a parish in Puchały, located 12 kilometers away. In exchange for his transfer, the communist authorities promised the bishop to grant permission to build a new church in Łomża.

The security forces, however, did not leave the priest alone in Puchały. He survived two attempts on his life. The new Bishop of Łomża, Juliusz Paetz,[14] wanted to bring Fr. Wysocki back to young people, who fervently demanded him. But this bishop also had to succumb to the regime. In the Puchały parish, the priest worked for ten years.

Still, those extremely challenging years and the clerical work of Fr. Wysocki were fruitful. His relationship with the youth has endured and remains strong. Many of his students, who live all over the country, keep in touch with him, visit him, and adhere to the principles he instilled in them. On June 29, 2012, 30 years after the end of Fr. Stanisław Wysocki's service in the youth ministry, a thanksgiving Mass was celebrated in the seminary church in Łomża, the so-called "small church," where he led the ministry known as the Youth Church from 1974 to 1982. Nearly 150 people from every corner of Poland and even two from America turned up to show their appreciation. All who came were associated with the youth community founded by Fr. Wysocki in Łomża—now mature, many educated, many holding important positions. When they met with their chaplain, they all felt young and carefree, though still responsible, just as in the times when the legendary Fr. Stanisław was their leader. The ceremony was beautiful, as is recorded by the entries on the internet.

After leaving Łomża, prelate Fr. Wysocki made a name for himself by building churches and monuments. First, after moving from Łomża to Puchały, he contributed to the reconstruction of a beautiful Gothic church, especially its new décor. In this parish, he also took over and completed the construction and furnishing of a smaller church for farmers in Pruszki Wielkie.

Then, in 1992, he undertook priestly work in the newly established Diocese of Ełk, where he became pastor of the cathedral parish of St. Wojciech, the Bishop and Martyr and the Transfiguration of the Lord in Ełk. He renovated the Ełk cathedral and adapted it to the needs of the new diocese. Thanks to his initiative, the monument dedicated to the Martyrdom of the Polish Nation was erected there. In 1999, he prepared the beautification of the whole town as well as set up the altar and the whole square where the celebrations of John Paul II's visit were to take place. The greeting delivered by the Holy Father himself on the steps of the Ełk cathedral and the common prayer are particularly engraved in the priest's memory.

In 2004, after working in Ełk for 12 years, Fr. Wysocki took over another parish, St. John the Baptist's Church in Augustów. As a pastor, he again united the community, and through his personality and selfless service to his homeland and the Church, earned universal admiration. In Augustów, he created and led numerous ministries for adults and adolescents. In a joint effort with some committed Catholics, a Siberian Monument was erected in front of the new church [in memory of 1.2 million Poles deported by Soviets to Siberia in 1940–1941].

Fr. Stanisław Wysocki retired in 2009. He lives in his native Suwałki but remains active, both as a spiritual leader and member of his community. He has become more involved in national affairs, especially in the matters pertaining to the Augustów Roundup. In 2009, he initiated the founding of the Association for the Memory of the 1945 Augustów Roundup Victims, over which he presides to date. Fr. Wysocki has endured a lifelong sense of pain and injustice after having lost the closest members of his family in the Augustów Roundup—his father and two sisters—in a mysterious way, without a trace and without judgment.

"He often talked about it, which indicates that these memories are still present in him and affect his views on the affairs of the Motherland and the Church," points out Fr. Jacek Uchan, PhD, Director of the General Pastoral Department in the Diocese of Ełk.

A monument dedicated to the Poles deported by Soviets to Siberia erected at the Church of St. John the Baptist in Augustów, one of many that Fr. Stanisław Wysocki helped build during his pastoral work.

Archbishop Fr. Józef Michalik adds: "It is with great dedication that Fr. Stanisław Wysocki tries to reveal the truth about the Augustów Roundup. He has found many people who are helping him, which is wonderful. One of the successes is that he found allies in the Russian Federation, for example, Dr. Nikita Petrov. It shows that there are honorable people among the Russians, too, ready to take a risk in order to expose the truth."

However, Fr. Wysocki's pursuit to reveal communist crimes during the Augustów Roundup turned out to be dangerous. On December 10, 2011, in the center of Suwałki, a ruthless assault was carried out on the old clergyman. The priest was taken to the hospital. As usual, the "unknown" perpetrators were never found, and, as usual, his efforts were "inconvenient" for someone. The priest, though, has a sense of mission and duty to the country, to the Church, and to his family, and he keeps on bearing testimony.

On July 24, 2013, when the Parliamentary Club of Law and Justice and the Białystok branch of the Institute of National Remembrance organized an exhibition about the Augustów Roundup at the Sejm [the lower house of the parliament] of the Republic of Poland in Warsaw, the tireless priest spoke on behalf of the families of the victims of the Augustów Roundup—members of the Association for the Memory of the 1945 Augustów Roundup Victims. During a press conference and a scholarly conference, "Do Not Let the Dead Fall," he pleaded to the Polish authorities for an appeal to the powers of the Russian Federation to open their archives to Russian and Polish historians. The exhibit about the Augustów Roundup in such a prominent place as the Sejm, along with the historical session, had a great educational impact. A painful and bloody card of the nation's recent history was revealed to the parliamentarians, all participants of the event, and the visitors to the exhibition. Several press articles appeared afterward, but the knowledge of the crime is still insufficient.

In the same year—also with a significant input from prelate Wysocki—a draft resolution on the commemoration of the victims of the Augustów Roundup was submitted. The draft waited a long time for the Sejm to approve it—until July 25, 2014. The resolution was adopted but with significant changes. Its parliamentary petitioner, Jarosław Zieliński from the Law and Justice party, announced that a very important fragment was removed from the draft of the resolution by the Civic Platform party and its allies, with the objection of the Law and Justice party, which read:

> The Sejm of the Republic of Poland asks the government to take vigorous efforts to fully explain the circumstances of the pacification of July 1945 aimed at our compatriots, who showed an unwavering attitude towards Poland's independence.

Zieliński has not yet received an answer to the question of what the current [as of 2015] government of the coalition of the Civic Platform and the Polish People's Party has done to access archival documents available to the Russian Federation and to find out the truth about the Augustów Roundup.

The cleric from Suwałki continues an effort to adequately commemorate the victims of this crime in the public space, especially in towns and municipal districts covered by the pacification operation of the Augustów Roundup. He is fighting to make sure that this painful part of history will find a place in the school curricula and the collective consciousness of Poles through symbolic acts of commemoration: installing commemorative plates and naming streets, squares, parks, and institutions such as schools and culture centers after the Augustów Roundup.

The priest is also among the families of the victims of the Augustów Roundup who sent their petitions to the Central Archives of the Federal Security Services of the Russian Federation, requesting copies of the interrogation protocols, photographs, and personal documents belonging to their loved ones who disappeared in July 1945.

"During the detention, each person was carrying personal items and documents such as a personal ID. When they were called for an interrogation, from which many did not return, the identity was verified on the basis of these documents," emphasized Fr. Stanisław Wysocki.

In response, the Central Archives informed him that the records of the date and place of the arrest of his father, Ludwik Wysocki, and his sisters, Kazimiera and Aniela, do in fact exist. Fr. Stanisław thanked it for the information and, in the next letter to the Central Archives, asked for documents about his relatives (photos, souvenirs) and the reports of interrogations, but the reply stated that they were missing from the Moscow archives.

"I am working with lawyers and I will continue to write to the Russian Central Archives. I am sure that such documentation exists," says the president of the Association for the Memory of the 1945 Augustów Roundup Victims.

Recently, Fr. Stanisław Wysocki visited Jasna Góra in Częstochowa with another petition. On October 13, 2013, during the Appeal of Jasna Góra,[15] he again pleaded to the highest authorities of the Republic of Poland to intervene with the powers of the Russian Federation to help find the death pits of the victims of the Augustów Roundup and then allow for the exhumation of their remains and a proper Christian burial. As a spokesman for the disclosure of the truth about the greatest crime committed by the Soviets on Poles at the end of World War II, he stated:

> We have come from Augustów, Sejny, Sokólka, Suwałki, and the surrounding lands, where the Augustów Primeval Forest bears the difficult history of these Polish territories, and where the roadside crosses lead to places soaked with the blood of our martyrs. We hear them calling: 'Our Land! Do not hide our blood—our cries need to be heard!...
>
> We stand before you, oh, Mother—our only hope—on behalf of the families of the Association for the Memory of the 1945 Augustów Roundup Victims. We stand here, in Jasna Góra, where the beat of Poland's heart is the loudest and most sincere, where the law is law, justice is justice. We stand here to confess our endless pain. ...
>
> We bring our request to you, our Lady of Consolation! We beg you, our Queen, do not leave us, for all have failed us in our expectations to have the truth unveiled!
>
> Our Beloved Mother, 68 years ago, in July 1945, this land was raided and Home Army soldiers arrested, the soldiers who remained faithful to God, Honor, and Homeland to the very end. To this date, the truth about them has been concealed from us. The Augustów Roundup of 1945, which took place two months after the end of World War II, was another genocide committed against the Poles. ... The conspiracy of silence implemented by the communist regime continues to this day. Just like the Katyń massacre, the crime of the Augustów Roundup, too, cannot see the light of day.

As an eyewitness to these tragic events, and as a priest, I am pleading with the Almighty, and all of you gathered here, in this holy place, to call upon all people of goodwill to arise at this hour of the Appeal of Jasna Góra, and join us in demanding, crying, and begging for the truth about those events, and, above all, persistently conveying this truth to the young generation of Poles, who—as our beloved compatriot, Blessed John Paul II said—is to take over the spiritual legacy, whose name is Poland.

A few months later, on May 3, 2014, a momentous plaque-epitaph, "In honor of the victims of the Augustów Roundup," was unveiled at Jasna Góra in Częstochowa. It was funded by the families of the victims of the crime as well as people and institutions of goodwill, and it was placed in the Chapel of the Miraculous Image of Our Lady of Częstochowa. The ceremony was attended by the event's initiator, the tireless prelate Stanisław Wysocki, members of the Association for the Memory of the 1945 Augustów Roundup Victims, and other residents of the Augustów, Sejny, Suwałki, and Sokółka districts. They all participated in the Holy Mass in honor of the Motherland and the victims of the Augustów Roundup and their families. It was accompanied by a procession of 17 flags and celebrated in front of the miraculous image of the Blessed Virgin Mary by Archbishop Józef Michalik, Metropolitan Bishop of Przemyśl, assisted by Archbishop Wojciech Ziemba, Metropolitan Bishop of Warmia, and Bishop Jerzy Mazur, Bishop of Ełk, as well as many other clerics. Father Stanisław's voice of conscience resounded again:

> Blessed Mary, thank you for accepting this epitaph—a permanent tribute to approximately two thousand of our murdered fathers, brothers, and sisters—to your shrine. Yet, we do not know the full truth about their fate—where they were executed and where they were thrown into the pits of death.
>
> We give thanks to You, Holy Mother and the Queen, for the Guardians of your Holy Place—the Pauline Fathers, who took this painful chapter of the history of our homeland under their care.
>
> Through You, Mary, we thank our friend, Professor Nikita Petrov and his colleagues from the International Association "Memorial" in Moscow for their uncompromising work to discover the full truth about the victims of the Augustów Roundup.
>
> We also thank the professors—the signatories of the Augustów Roundup Appeal and a dozen thousand or so supporters, who backed the Appeal on the internet pleading for Polish memory.
>
> Oh, Mary, standing under Your Son's Cross! You know that the full truth comes through suffering and the cross, so please support us in our persistent pursuit of the truth. Let me—a witness and son of Ludwik and a brother of my two sisters, Kazimiera and the seventeen-year-old Aniela—put in a request on behalf of all victims of the Augustów Roundup:
>
> To all pilgrims of Jasna Góra—when you stop by the epitaph, remember that we are calling: "Our Land! Do not hide our blood—our cries need to be heard."

A plaque in tribute to the victims of the Augustów Roundup unveiled on May 3, 2014, at Jasna Góra in Częstochowa. Inscription on the plaque: "'Our Land! Do not hide our blood—our cries need to be heard!' In tribute to the victims of the Augustów Roundup of July 1945: soldiers of the Home Army and citizens of Augustów, Sejny, Sokółka, and Suwałki, and those living behind the 'Curzon Line'—murdered under Stalin's order by the NKVD "Smiersz" and Polish secret police and Militia—around 2,000 in number, faithful to God and Homeland to the very end. [From] The families of victims and residents of the Augustów Roundup areas. "Mary, the Queen of the Polish Crown, protect Poland, our Homeland! Jasna Góra, 2014."

> Remember that we were murdered just because we were Poles, faithful to God and Homeland till the very end!

"This Mass was very significant for the contemporary history of Poland. The truth about the Augustów Roundup was inscribed in the place which is extremely important to the spiritual life of Poles, that is Jasna Góra. To understand the Poles, as St. John Paul II used to say, you need to listen closely to Jasna Góra and feel how the heart of the nation beats in the Mother's heart," says the participant of the Mass, Father Dariusz Cichor from Jasna Góra, member of the Pauline Order who, together with Father Nikodem Kilnar, helped organize this celebration. He is originally from Augustów, and his grandfather Mieczysław Cichor was also a victim of this crime.

Other events of the Association for the Memory of the 1945 Augustów Roundup Victims led by Fr. Wysocki prove how dynamic the organization is. In 2014 he organized several celebrations in Sejny. Together with Barbara Kuklewicz, a teacher from a high school in Sejny, Teresa Tur, a teacher from Junior High School No. 1 in Sejny, named after John Paul II, and Lucyna Fidrych, director of an elementary school in Karolina, he prepared a patriotic-and-religious mystery "in honor of the victims of the Augustów Roundup" (June 14, 2014).

He also organized patriotic-and-religious celebrations in Studzieniczna on the day of the Most Holy Trinity (June 15, 2014). Dariusz Cichor, OSPPE, a delegate from Jasna Góra, was the presider of the Holy Mass, whose intention was for the victims of Augustów Roundup and their families. He also delivered the homily. The Mass was enriched by the participation of the Honorary Guard of the Marshal Józef Piłsudski 14th Artillery Brigade from Suwałki, under Colonel Waldemar Siedlecki's command. The Studzieniczna celebrations also included Commander Wiktor Wegrzyn and motorcyclists from the Association of the International Katyń Rally, students and teachers from the Lyceum No. 2 in Augustów, named after Polonia, and Poles Around the World and its principal Wojciech Walulik, members of the Home Army Historical Club in Augustów with its president, Danuta Kaszlej, members of the Association "Leśni" for Exploring Places of Struggle and Martyrdom and the War Graves, scouts, and school delegations from the municipal government of Augustów with a procession of flags, and the City Brass Orchestra in Suwałki under the baton of Beata Michniewicz, and many local residents.

Together with his organization, Father Wysocki organized a special national ceremony in Warsaw (July 27, 2014)—a Mass at St. John's Cathedral celebrated by Bishop Romuald Kamiński from Ełk, assisted by several priests, including Fr. Stanisław Wysocki. It was also attended by representatives of state and local governments, members of the World Association of the Home Army Soldiers, the Association of the Home Army Soldiers "Łagiernicy," teachers, educators and students, scouts from the Scouting Association of the Republic of Poland, the families of the Augustów Roundup victims, and even a procession of flags from local governments and schools from the area, where the Augustów Roundup took place. Thanks to Fr. Edward Żmijewski, who is always ready to serve where the homeland's bells resound, the liturgy in the Warsaw cathedral was enriched with the performance by the "Victoria" Orchestra from Warsaw-Rembertów with the soloists of the Grand Theatre in Warsaw. In this capital city's majestic temple, which for centuries has been a place of constant prayer for the homeland, Fr. Stanisław Wysocki appealed once more for the truth, asking for clarification of "the genocide committed in Augustów by the NKVD in July of 1945."

Immediately after this sublime service, a conference was held at the

Fr. Wysocki with motorcyclists and the Commander of the International Katyń Rally, Wiktor Węgrzyn, in Sejny, during a mystery, "In honor of the victims of the Augustów Roundup," which had a patriotic and religious character. June 14, 2014.

Mass at St. John the Baptist Basilica in Warsaw on July 27, 2014. Left to right: Father Piotr Kępa, Father Dariusz Cichor, Bishop Romuald Kamiński, Rev. Stanisław Wysocki, and Rev. Maciej Melaniuk.

Royal Castle in Warsaw. It was attended by many notable Polish historians: prof. Krzysztof Jasiewicz from the Institute of Political Studies of the Polish Academy of Sciences (the conference chair), prof. Grzegorz Nowik (ISP PAN), prof. Barbara Bojaryn-Kazberuk, director of the IPN Branch in Białystok, and Zbigniew Kulikowski, prosecutor of the Białystok Branch of the Commission for the Prosecution of Crimes against the Polish Nation. A special guest of the conference was Professor Nikita Petrov, vice president of the Association "Memorial" in Moscow, who flew to Warsaw especially for this meeting. During this conference, he electrified everybody by announcing the results of his latest research on the Augustów Roundup, as he pointed to a probable place of burial of the victims of the crime—a small town of Kalety, on the Belarusian side of the Augustów Primeval Forest.

"Fr. Stanisław, I think, possesses the qualities of holiness, both as a man and as a priest. He is exceptionally charming, noble, and capable of uniting people around him. He is a good spirit for our whole family." Prof. Krzysztof Jasiewicz from the Institute of Political Studies of the Polish Academy of Sciences in Warsaw talks about him with pride. The scholar's grandfather, Leon Kolenkiewicz from Gawrych Rudy, was the brother of the prelate's beloved grandmother, Apolonia Jarząbska, née Kolenkiewicz.

In light of the newly discovered events, does Fr. Stanisław Wysocki—a bearer of the wounds of Nazism and Communism and an uncompromising spokesperson for the disclosure of the truth about the Augustów

Fr. Stanisław Wysocki and Nikita Petrov from the Association "Memorial" in Moscow at the Royal Castle Conference in Warsaw on July 27, 2014.

A symbolic burial place at Fr. Wysocki's home in Biała Woda, dedicated to his father Ludwik Wysocki and two sisters Kazimiera and Aniela, all murdered during the Augustów Roundup. It was funded by the surviving members of the Wysocki family.

Roundup, also called "Another Katyń"—believe that this crime will ever be explained?

"There are only a few following documents needed: records about the places of the execution and burial of the victims' bodies, and a full list of the murdered. So I hope that this terrible crime will be explained. It is only a matter of time," says the shepherd from the Diocese of Ełk.

His sisters, Teresa and Wanda, who live in the Suwałki region, and the youngest brother, Alojzy Wysocki, who manages the farm in Biała Woda, are also waiting. Their families are waiting, too. They are waiting for justice. They would also like to see the exhumation and funerals of the loved ones who disappeared without a trace. For now, the grave of Józefa Wysocka at the parish cemetery in Suwałki, which displays an emblem of the Polish Underground, stands lonely—with a free plot next to it.

The family has built a symbolic necropolis at the entrance to the hospitable Wysocki family home in Biała Woda, which is located in a valley. Fr. Stanisław's youngest brother, Alojzy Wysocki, breeds recreational horses there and continues to manage meadows and pastures. Next to a huge, heart-shaped boulder and a tall statue of the Pensive Christ, carved by a local folk artist, a white-and-red flag is fluttering. To commemorate the three victims of the Augustów Roundup from this family, three oak trees were planted nearby. The inscription on the stone serves as a reminder: "On the memorable day of July 27, 1945, the NKVD and Polish secret police (UB) abducted from our patrimony and tortured father Ludwik and the two sisters Kazimiera and Aniela, soldiers of the Home Army. For us, the memory of them is the most sacred. The Family."

Next to it, there is the same meadow. The same two old, mighty apple trees grow sweet apples (mainly for the fawns that live in the vicinity). The same pear tree, also planted by the proprietor, Ludwik Wysocki, still bears the same fruit. The same hills surround the property, and the same forest now whispers about those tragic events. Just as in the past, the farm is a home for storks, though surely their younger generations.

"We are anxiously awaiting the explanations of what happened not only to our father, Ludwik Wysocki, and Kazia and Aniela. The entire big family of the Augustów Roundup is waiting. We wish for all those who died to be inscribed in the pantheon of Polish heroes," says Fr. Stanisław Wysocki.

However, time is inexorable. In 2014, the priest celebrated the 50th anniversary of his ordination. Witnesses of the Augustów Roundup move to the other side of the light. Human memory is short, and imperial Russia is not willing to help with the explanation of the 1945 crime. Moreover, a recent statement by Yuri Bondarenko, the director of the Center of Russian-Polish Dialogue and Agreement of the Russian Federation, brought even more pain to the president of the Association for the Memory of the 1945 Augustów Roundup Victims. The statement read: "Warsaw is not being creative on this issue."

Suwałki, August 17, 2013–October 12, 2014

Tadeusz Jagłowski (Augustów)

"Our parents waited for their son's return until their death"

Tadeusz welcomes his guest with tea, plum cake, and a regional *kołacz*, baked over the open fire, in his Augustów house, surrounded by a lovely garden. Another delicacy here is *kartacze*—oblong potato dumplings stuffed with meat. In the bordering country of Lithuania, they are called *cepeliny*.

"My wife, Ryta, makes the best *kartacze*. But I help her a little because they are very labor-intensive," says Tadeusz Jagłowski energetically. He loves this dish. He is slim, focused, and willing to talk.

Tadeusz Jagłowski.

Tadeusz Jagłowski (Augustów)

He was born on October 29, 1931, in the village of Kopiec, the municipality of Sztabin, in the Augustów District, about 20 kilometers from Augustów and over 50 kilometers from Suwałki. His family has cultivated land in this region for generations. The Kopiec village was established at the beginning of the 19th century when some of the light forest lands were turned into farmland and opened to a new settlement. The village of Kopiec was surrounded by the Augustów Primeval Forest on the one side and the Netta River and the Augustów Canal on the other. The village had about 80 peasant farms.

Stanisław and Eugenia Jagłowski managed 20 hectares[1] of land, where, in the past, only trees had rustled. Therefore, the soil was sandy and infertile, as one might expect in vast forests. They primarily farmed rye, oats, and potatoes as well as barley, but only here and there.

The pursuit for Poland's independence and support for Catholic traditions were always powerful in their home. In the interwar period, the father, Stanisław Jagłowski, belonged to the Polish Peasants' Party,[2] and after German invasion—to its underground equivalent, established in 1940. His mother, Eugenia Jagłowska, warmly sympathized with this movement. The house was full of the local press (which, during World War II, became illegal), and peasant traditions and customs were respected. During World War II, the whole family supported the resistance movement, just like the majority in the area.

The Jagłowski family had five children: three sons and two daughters. During the German occupation, the eldest son, Piotr Jagłowski, was deported to East Prussia as a forced laborer. After a year, he managed to escape from the German imprisonment. Upon return, however, he did not stay at his home in Kopiec for long, and in late 1942, he joined the resistance movement in the Augustów Primeval Forest. First, he was a member of the Peasants' Guards "Chłostra"—the only independent military organization in the municipality of Sztabin—later renamed the Peasants' Battalions. His commander was Władysław Pycz, alias "Twardy" ("Tough"), a blacksmith from Krasnoborki, and his deputy was Ignacy Andracki, alias "Topór" ("Axe"), later "Filtry" "(Filters") from the village of Wrotki.

The Peasants' Battalions (in Polish: "Bataliony Chłopskie") was an armed underground organization with about 160,000 members, mostly Polish peasants, which operated during World War II in the General Government and Greater Poland Voivodship. It was the second-largest armed formation during the occupation, after the Home Army.

The Peasants' Battalions were formed against the wishes of the Union of Armed Struggle (first the management directed their members to join the UAS), and its goal was to give the farmers a decisive voice on the structure and character of the underground and to create a chance to decide or co-decide on the social and political shape of the future state. The organization was established in August 1940 as the Peasants' Guard under the code name of the "Chłostra." In the spring of 1941, it was renamed to the Peasants' Battalions, although the official approval by their authorities took place in May 1944. The organization was a military division of the Polish Peasants' Party. The principal power was exercised by the central management of the peasant's authorities, represented by Józef Niećko, and regionally by threesome units of the Polish Peasants' Party "Roch." Villagers formed the core of the organization. From October 8, 1940, to the end of the war, Franciszek Kamiński was its commander. The central press body was called *Żywią i Bronią* ("Nourish and Protect").

The primary purpose of the Peasants' Battalions was to defend the population of the Polish rural areas against the occupants' terror and economic exploitation. In order to counteract the enemy's destructive economy, the following sabotage actions were organized: the burning of sawmills and timber depots, immobilizing distilleries and dairy farms, destroying warehouses, destroying quota records and files in labor offices and municipalities, dispersing cattle drives, rescuing political prisoners and peasants taken to forced labor camps in Germany, launching assaults on properties under German management, punishing officials who were too eager to fulfill their duties as well as liquidating informers and gangs of thieves.

During World War II, soldiers of the Peasants' Battalions carried out over 3,000 combat operations of a different kind, including approximately 900 battles and skirmishes, over 200 attacks on the enemy transport, and about 800 operations against the administrative and political apparatus. The most important operations carried out by soldiers of the Peasants' Battalions include fighting in defense of the pacified Zamość region in 1942–1943, especially the battles of Wojda and Zaboreczno, fighting in defense of the so-called Republic of Pińczów, as well as the sinking of the Tannenberg ship, blowing up an ammunition train near Gołębie, destroying prisons in Krasnystaw, Radomsko, Siedlce, and Pińczów, and fighting on the Baranowsko-Sandomierz front.

"In the nearby forests, there were about thirty soldiers of the Peasants' Battalions," recalls Tadeusz Jagłowski, while sipping his tea. "The residents of the surrounding villages provided them with food, such as meat, milk, eggs, bread, potatoes, and vegetables—at the beginning, free of charge. It was only in the spring of 1943, after some units of the Peasants' Battalions merged with the Home Army when farmers began to receive payment for this help—in hard currency, i.e., US dollars. At that time, the insurgents also received better uniforms and weapons."

After escaping from East Prussia and joining the insurgents, Tadeusz

Jagłowski's brother Piotr, got his uniform and a gun, too. Starting in the fall of 1942, he participated in subversive actions: first, against the Germans, and in 1945, against the Soviets.

Besides Piotr Jagłowski, two of his younger brothers—Konstanty (b. 1928) and Tadeusz (b. 1931)—were also active in the Polish Underground. Konstanty's responsibility in the underground was to provide the commanders—Pycz and Andracki—with the intelligence about the activities of the German gendarmerie. The younger Tadeusz was a liaison soldier—he passed orders, documents, reports, and information about meetings and carried supplies of medications.

"When I took the oath in June 1943, I was only twelve years old. They accepted me because they knew my family. I was given the nickname 'Kret' ['Mole'] and assigned to the unit under Witold Siarkowski, alias 'Mewa' ['Seagull'],[3] from the same village of Kopiec. Both my father and brothers were still members of the Peasants' Battalions. Soon, the Battalions merged with the Home Army and we were all soldiers of the Home Army, under the command of the Home Army officer, Stanisław Świątkowski, alias 'Zapała,'[4]" says Tadeusz Jagłowski.

Their sister Stanisława, was also a member of the Home Army. She performed many different tasks: washed and mended insurgents' uniforms, prepared medications and delivered them to the sick fighters. She also worked as a nurse. At the Jagłowski family, only the youngest, Apolonia, born in 1936, was still too young for the insurgency.

In addition, the Jagłowskis' house in Kopiec was a contact point for the so-called "burnt" fighters, whose cover had been blown. They could no longer stay in their homes or places of residence, and, to avoid arrest, they had to move and hide frequently. The insurgents stayed at the Jagłowskis' during the day. They were fed, and women washed their underwear, repaired uniforms, and prepared medications from forest resin, lime tree flowers, and herbs.

"Many times, my parents' household was a shelter for the sick and the constantly moving 'burned' soldiers," recalls Tadeusz, the only son of the Jagłowski family still alive today. "I remember these best: Stanisław Orłowski, alias 'Piorun,' from Fiedorowizna, Leon Kunda, alias 'Nieznany,' from Jamin, and Tadeusz Zięcina, alias 'Falcon,' from Krasnoborki."

In April 1945, Piotr Jagłowski, at that time in the rank of second lieutenant, returned from the Augustów Forest to his home in Kopiec. He managed to show the insurgents' hut and his weapons to his brothers.

"I even held his long rifle and grenades, set on wooden handles," recalls the youngest son, Tadeusz.

On July 12, 1945, between 2 and 3 a.m., they heard a loud knocking on the door. The Jagłowski family were suddenly awakened from sleep. When the head of the family came to the door and asked, "Who is there?" he heard a voice shouting in Russian, "Open up!" Stanisław Jagłowski knew Russian because he had served in the tsarist army. He opened the door. He was violently pushed away by three armed Soviet members of the NKVD. They ordered the whole family to stand against the wall, with legs apart and hands raised behind their heads. They carried out a thorough search of the house, throwing straw mattresses out of beds and clothes from the closets, and knocking the furniture over.

"Give us your weapons!" they shouted.

"I do not have any weapons: I am a farmer," Stanisław Jagłowski tried to explain.

The search lasted quite a long time because all utility rooms were searched—the barn, the stable, and pigsties. In the end, one of the Soviets took out his papers and asked which of them was Piotr Jagłowski, born in 1925. The father pointed to the eldest son. At that time, Piotr was precisely 20 years and six months old. They twisted his hands to the back and tied them with a telephone wire. His brother Konstanty, three years younger, stood next to him. "Is he a bandit too?" the question was in Russian. "There are no bandits here," the father replied. Still, they also bound Konstanty, tying his hands from behind. Both brothers were pushed outside and tied together with a cable, connected in a "brotherly" embrace.

"My sister Stanisława, and I were not home at that time. We stayed for the night with relatives in a neighboring village. It was the time of summer vacation." Tadeusz Jagłowski still does not know whether he would have met a similar fate.

The captured Jagłowski brothers, Piotr and Konstanty, were transported by the Soviets to the Tomaszewskis' barn in the same village. There were more "suspects" there. On that day, the Soviets arrested 12 men from the village of Kopiec alone. On the third day, they were moved from the Tomaszewskis' barn to the so-called "Turk's House" in Augustów, the PUBP[5] headquarters, where they were brutally interrogated, at night, for several days. Of the 14 men arrested on July 12, 1945, only two were released: Konstanty Jagłowski and Eugeniusz Duchiński. They returned to their village at the end of July 1945.

"My brother's whole body was grayish-purple." Tadeusz Jagłowski remembers this very well. "Konstanty told us that they had been tortured, beaten, and starved. They slept on the cement floor, close one to another, without any space to move. They used barrels for relieving themselves. An officer with Jewish background, in the rank of captain, interrogated them. He had several Soviet soldiers at his disposal; at his nod, they tortured the soldiers of the Polish Underground. The local Poles were not allowed to be present at the interrogations, but some helped identify the captured. My

The former location of the District Public Security Office (PUBP) in Augustów, which to this day is called "Turk's House." Tadeusz Jagłowski's two brothers—Piotr, aged 20 (murdered in the Augustów Roundup), and Konstanty, aged 17 (after brutal tortures, he became incapacitated)—and sister, Stanisława Jagłowska (a Home Army nurse) were imprisoned there by the NKVD.

brother did not meet Jan Szostak personally; he only saw him during his arrest."

Tadeusz Jagłowski knows from Konstanty's account that in the "Turk's House," the Soviets compared the brothers' testimonies. Piotr admitted that he was in the Home Army, while Konstanty, whose name did not exist in the underground documentation, was saved by his older brother, Piotr Jagłowski. In order to protect his brother Konstanty, Piotr said to the Soviets, "This was a clandestine organization. No one in my family knew about me being a member of the Home Army, not even my parents."

That is why Konstanty, after brutal interrogations and cruel tortures, was released—as one of only two from the village of Kopiec. The remaining 12 captured Poles were deported at the end of July 1945 to an unknown destination. They were: Zygmunt Dobrowolski, Jan Duchiński, Piotr Jagłowski, Antoni Kamiński, Lucjan Małkowski, Izydor Roszkowski, Stanisław Roszkowski, Stanisław Rutkowski, Witold Siarkowski, Zygmunt Siwicki, Stanisław Szyszkiewicz, and Konstanty Żukowski.

Tadeusz Jagłowski also remembers what his freed brother said about the car transporting the prisoners—it came back after about two hours for the next batch of the arrested. Everyone who was imprisoned in the "Turk's House" wanted to leave as soon as possible. Though surrounded by NKVD bayonets, they were confident that they would be taken to Soviet labor camps (like many from their land) or would be imprisoned in Communist Poland. They were not aware, probably until the last minute, that they were being transported to a quick death. They did not know that no one taken from the Augustów PUBP headquarters would be coming back. Perhaps this lack of knowledge was the fate's last grace for them.

They could not imagine, of course, that for so many years no one would even know the place where they were killed or buried—that this would be a perfect crime.

The 17-year-old Konstanty Jagłowski, who was allowed to return home, never recovered from the arrest and torture during the Augustów Roundup. Severely crippled, he received benefits for disabled veterans of category two and later of category one.[6] After the war, he helped run the family farm, which was heavily damaged because, at the end of the war, the front line ran through the municipality. He lived in the village of Kopiec until his death at the age of 70.

His sister, a young Home Army nurse, Stanisława Jagłowska, was arrested in March 1946. She was also held in the casemates of the infamous PUBP headquarters in Augustów. In the "Turk's House," she was imprisoned for eight days, which seemed like an eternity. She was released thanks to an intervention of their parents' friend, the first secretary of the county's Communist Committee in Augustów.

Tadeusz Jagłowski remembers well how his family of farmers reacted bitterly to the falsified referendum of 1946.[7] He did not vote himself but remembers the communist-recommended vote: three times for "yes." He also knows that after the referendum, there was a supposedly "low" level of support for the opposition (for the Polish Peasants' Party as well as more radical groups). He remembers that not only Stanisław Mikołajczyk[8] but also representatives of the United States and Great Britain protested against forged results. The propaganda of the Eastern bloc took advantage of this, calling the leader of the Polish Peasants' Party a traitor, who allowed foreign powers to interfere in Poland's domestic affairs. Stanisław Mikołajczyk had to flee to the West.

The new regime made Jagłowski's life even more difficult after the war was over.

"We were treated as second-class citizens, the 'filthy dwarfs of reaction'—all of us, not just my family but members of the entire Polish Underground," says Tadeusz, the youngest son of the Jagłowski family. "Still quite recently, it was not possible even to mention the Augustów Roundup. It was a taboo subject, just like Katyń. People who happened to mention the Roundup were interrogated and persecuted; they forever became an enemy of the nation."

Because of their former affiliation with the pro-independence underground, their education in the Polish People's Republic was hindered. Although Tadeusz Jagłowski never admitted that his brother Piotr disappeared without a trace in July 1945, he still had to take the matriculation exam in the distant Grajewo. His high school teacher from Augustów, Helena Mikołajewska, said that pigs might fly before he earned a high school diploma in Augustów. He asked, "Why? I'm not the best student, but not the last, either." "You still don't understand, do you?" the teacher replied. "Here, in Augustów, you will never pass the final exams," she said mysteriously. She probably wanted to warn him to prepare him for failure. Many generations of students—before and after the war—remembered this teacher as a Polish patriot.

In order to finish high school, Tadeusz Jagłowski left Augustów and moved to Ełk. It turned out, however, that the school was still too close. He was treated there as badly as in his neighborhood at the Netta River. Only in Grajewo did he finish high school, although remotely. He faced a similar situation with higher education and managed to complete only partial studies in agriculture in Olsztyn.

It was not easy for him to get a job, any job. First, he managed to get modest employment at the Road Construction Enterprise in faraway Warsaw, then in Biała Podlaska and Ostrów Mazowiecka. In 1952, Tadeusz Jagłowski returned to his family farm, but, two years later, he was drafted to the People's Army of Poland. He served in Trzebiatów, in the Pomerania region, in antiaircraft artillery. After two years, he returned to Augustów, to the same job at the Road Construction Enterprise. In 1962, he was promoted to the head of the bookkeeping department. Later he was employed in a dairy farm as a manager of nutrition counseling, then in the meat department as one of the managers for four districts—Augustów, Suwałki, Sejny, and Dąbrowa Białostocka. In total, he worked in People's Poland for over 48 years.

"After the war, we were looking for my brother Piotr, all the time," he remembers. "We all missed him very much, and we still miss him. We were waiting for him. Even now, it seems to me that he is still alive, somewhere there. Because we do not know if he was really murdered, we do not know the place of his death; we have not been able to bury him and to light a candle or ponder upon his grave."

The parents could never get over the loss of their firstborn son. They waited for him until they both died. The father died early, though, in 1958, and the mother in 1973 at the age of 78.

After the war and quite recently, too, Tadeusz Jagłowski has been sending letters to the International Red Cross and to the authorities of the Polish People's Republic and Russia. He asked for information about the 12 citizens from his village missing since July 1945 and to declassify the Augustów Roundup records in the Moscow archives. Almost all the letters remained unanswered, although some, such as from the Embassy of the Soviet Union in Warsaw, gave some hope for the return of the missing men. But the announcement of the Polish Red Cross, in May 1960, stating, "The issue of searching for the missing men from the village of Kopiec in the Soviet Union is considered closed," left no doubt—Tadeusz Jagłowski would never find his brother Piotr and other residents of the Kopiec village.

In the Third Polish Republic, after 2000, he wrote to the Institute of National Remembrance and the Archives of New Records, but these institutions replied that they were expecting some information from Russia. Therefore, he started searching for the traces of his missing brother in Russia by contacting the Embassy of the Russian Federation in Warsaw.

Recently, through the Embassy of the Russian Federation, he has been in correspondence with the Federal Security Service (FSS) of the Russian Federation, the Office of Registration, and Archival Resources of the State. In a letter dated June 18, 2013, he was informed that the "materials from the Central Archives of the FSS contain the following data: Jagłowski, Piotr Stanisławowicz,[9] born in 1928 (according to the files), born and living in the village of Kopiec in the Augustów County, Białystok Province, was detained on July 12, 1945, because he was accused of being a member of the Home Army. The archival materials do not contain anything regarding prosecution, sentencing, vindication or any further fate." It was signed by the First Deputy Manager, A.V. Vasiliev.

However, in a letter from the FSS of the Russian Federation, the Office of State Registration and Archives, dated November 25, 2013, Tadeusz Jagłowski was informed, in response to an inquiry from September 26, "The Central Archives of the Federal Security Service of Russia contain no trace of an archival case of criminal proceedings against Piotr Jagłowski."

"This is just a nasty reality. The authorities have always dismissed me, both Polish and Russian," says Tadeusz Jagłowski with sadness, announcing that he will never cease his search. He believes that the memory of the fighters and the sacrifice of their lives forever remain an obligation for the present and future generations.

He is an active member of the management of the World Union of Soldiers of the Home Army. He was its president, then treasurer, and now he is serving a third term as the chairman of the Audit Commission of the Union's Augustów branch. He has been recognized with such honors

Tadeusz Jagłowski (Augustów)

Федеральная служба безопасности
Российской Федерации Москва,
10100. ул. Большая Лубянка, д. 2
Начальнику УРАФ ФСБ РФ
Василию Степановичу Христофорову

от

Тадеуш Ягловски
16-300 Аугустув
ул. Новомейска, 27
Польша

Tadeusz Jagłowski
ul. Nowomiejska 27
16-300 Augustów
Польша / Polska

Глубокоуважаемый Василий Степанович!

В июле 1945 года Ягловски Пётр, 1925 г.р., проживающий по адресу: Копец, гмина Штабин, повет Аугустув, Польша, был задержан в ходе облавы проведенной силами 3 Белорусского фронта в Августовских лесах на территории Польши. С тех пор о нем больше не было никаких сведений.

Прошу Вас сообщить о том, есть ли о нем какие-либо сведения в Вашем архиве, был ли оформлен арест и сохранилось ли в Вашем архиве его индивидуальное архивно-следственное дело или дело на задержанного.

Прошу Вас сообщить, какова дальнейшая судьба и состоялся ли акт реабилитации Ягловского Пётра по факту необоснованного задержания, ареста и содержания под стражей.

С уважением,

Tadeusz Jagłowski

Augustów 08.04.2013

A letter Tadeusz Jagłowski sent to Russian authorities asking about his missing brother Piotr and other missing Polish citizens from his village. No. 1.

Федеральная служба
безопасности
Российской Федерации
Москва, 10100.
ул. Большая Лубянка, д. 2

Начальнику УРАФ ФСБ РФ
Василию Степановичу Христофорову

От: TADEUSZ JAGŁOWSKI
16-300 AUGUSTÓW
UL. NOWOMIEJSKA 27
POLSKA

Глубокоуважаемый Василий Степанович!

От всей души я хочу выразить Вам преогромную благодарность за полученные сведения о моём(моей) BRACIE PIOTRZE JAGŁOWSKIM SYN STANISŁAWA URODZONY 1925 ROKU W ŻORSU POWIAT AUGUSTÓW WOJEWÓDZTWO BIAŁYSTOK ZATRZYMANY 12 LIPCA 1945 ROKU

Глубокоуважаемый Василий Степанович!

Благодаря за оказанную помощь в поисках моих самых близких я осмеливаюсь обратиться к Вам с очередной просьбой. Смогли ли бы Вы переслать мне копии документов (напр.: фотографии, протоколы допросов, личных документов итп.) касающихся BRATA PIOTRA JAGŁOWSKIEGO

Сердечно благодарю за доброжелательное отнесение к моей очередной просьбе.

Со словами глубокого уважения

Tadeusz Jagłowski

Сувалки, 26 сентября 2013

A letter Tadeusz Jagłowski sent to Russian authorities asking about his missing brother Piotr and other missing Polish citizens from his village. No. 2.

Tadeusz Jagłowski (Augustów)

Tadeusz Jagłowski
16-300 Augustów
ul. Nowomiejska 27
Polska

Augustów 23.09.2013

AMBASADA

FEDERACJI ROSYJSKIEJ w RP

Wydział Konsularny

00761 W-wa ul. Belwederska 25 bl "c"

Stosownie do pisma Waszego NR 10/A-R-1649 z dnia 18 czerwca 2013r pragnę wyjaśnić:

12 lipca 1945 funkcjonariusze NKWD aresztowało dwóch moich braci Jagłowskiego Piotra urodzonego w 1925 roku i Jagłowskiego Konstantego urodzonego w 1928 roku. Prawdopodobnie funkcjonariusze przesłuchujący ich (moich braci) pomylili daty urodzenia przypisując datę urodzenia Konstantego Piotrowi, a datę urodzenia Piotra Konstantemu.

Jagłowskiego Konstantego zwolniono z aresztu 30 lipca 1945 r. ale jestem przekonany, że jego akta z okresu przebywania i przesłuchania w areszcie są w Centralnym Archiwum FSB Rosji.

Wobec powyższego proszę o sprostowanie daty urodzenia Piotra Jagłowskiego.

Ponadto dziękuję za skromną informację dotyczącą Jagłowskiego Piotra i proszę o dalsze poszukiwanie materiałów w Centralnym Archiwum FSB Rosji o dalszym jego losie.

Z poważaniem

Tadeusz Jagłowski

A letter Tadeusz Jagłowski sent to Russian authorities asking about his missing brother Piotr and other missing Polish citizens from his village. No. 3.

as the Cross of the Home Army and the Badge of the Fights for Independence Veteran, and actively stands up for equal rights for the members of the Union.

"As veterans, we are still underappreciated," continues the social activist of the World Union of Soldiers of the Home Army. "Even now, we

Аугустув, 23.09.2013 г.

Тадеуш Ягловски
[Tadeusz Jagłowski]
16-300 Аугустув
ул. Новомейска, 27
Польша

ПОСОЛЬСТВО
РОССИЙСКОЙ ФЕДЕРАЦИИ в РП
Консульский отдел
00-761 Варшава, ул. Бельведерска 25С

В связи с Вашим письмом № 10/A-R-1649 от 18 июня 2013 г. хочу выяснить следующее:

июля 1945 сотрудники НКВД арестовали двух моих братьев Ягловского Петра [Jagłowski Piotr], 1925 года рождения и Ягловского Константина [Jagłowski Konstanty], 1928 года рождения. По свей вероятности сотрудники, которые их (моих братьев) допрашивали перепутали даты рождения приписывая дату рождения Константина Петру, а дату рождения Петра Константину.

Ягловского Константина освободили из-под ареста 30 июля 1945 г. но я уверенный, что его документы из периода пребывания и допроса в аресте находятся в Центральном Архиве ФСБ России.

Учитывая вышеуказанное исправьте, пожалуйста, дату рождения Петра Ягловского.

Кроме того, благодарю за скромную информацию касающуюся Ягловского Петра и прошу поищите ещё материалов в Центральном Архиве ФСБ России о дальнейшей его судьбе.

С уважением,

Tadeusz Jagłowski

A letter Tadeusz Jagłowski sent to Russian authorities asking about his missing brother Piotr and other missing Polish citizens from his village. No. 4.

still get unnoticed. Nobody ever thanked us for the fight for independent Poland. I have sent, for example, several letters to all prime ministers and presidents of the Third Polish Republic, asking for expanded benefits for veterans, including free medication, to which the veterans of the communist system have the rights. No prime minister or president ever helped us, the former members of the Home Army."

He closely monitors the efforts to explain the Augustów Roundup. Every year in July, he attends the festivities in Giby. However, his fragile

Tadeusz Jagłowski (first from the left) was a flag bearer for the Augustów Chapter of the World Union of Home Army Soldiers.

health no longer allows him to visit other important events commemorating the anniversary of the crime of July 1945. He is pleased with the work of the priest prelate Stanisław Wysocki and local activists. He was happy about the establishment of the Association for the Memory of the

1945 Augustów Roundup Victims in 2009 and the commemoration of victims of this crime by motorcyclists from all over Poland. However, in his opinion, few residents of the Suwałki Region are familiar with the postwar crime committed by the Soviets in July 1945.

His two sons, who are in the medical field—Andrzej, a surgeon in Suwałki, and Robert, a specialist in internal and family medicine, practicing in Augustów—know the truth about the Augustów Roundup and are very much interested in the event. On the other hand, their children, the grandchildren of Tadeusz and Ryta, know nothing about the Roundup. Therefore, the veteran is persistent in emphasizing that it is necessary to never stop reminding people about it and that state celebrations are not enough. What Poland needs today are good teachers in schools and devoted historians in state institutions who will promote the truth.

Does he believe the crime of July 1945 will ever be explained?

"Since Katyń has been explained, I think that our 'Little Katyń' in the Suwałki region will also see the explanation," answers Tadeusz Jagłowski.

After two heart attacks and a bypass surgery, he did not believe he would survive. But he *is* still alive, still waiting for some light to be shed on the matter of the Augustów Roundup. That is why on February 25, 2014, he agreed to supply his DNA material to a public prosecutor at the Institute of National Remembrance. Perhaps future generations will find out what happened in the Augustów forest in July 1945.

Augustów, August 18, 2013–March 11, 2014

Józef Kucharzewski (Giby)
"I heard the moans of my tortured sister"

With regular facial features and dark blond hair, Zyta was a girl of exceptional beauty. She had a joyful, though a bit romantic, personality. She was young (just turned 20) and had a life ahead of her. Her picture shows an elegant young lady, with her hair carefully combed up, her eyes full of radiance, and a smiling, glowing, and somewhat dreamy face. This photo has been hanging at the Kucharzewskis' apartment since the memorable July of 1945 when she was unexpectedly taken away by the Soviets and went missing without a trace.

"She was wearing a green dress, made from a parachute tarp," recalls, in Giby, her only brother, Józef Kucharzewski. Four years younger than she, he is 85 today. He has a furrowed face, gray hair, and problems with hearing but remembers those days well. The recollections are extremely painful. That's why, for decades, he did not want to talk to anyone about them. "Our mother waited for her for all her life—with a rosary in hand," he adds.

Józef Kucharzewski, brother of the murdered Zyta, a sacristan in Giby, in the Sejny area.

They lived in the village of Giby, in Suwałki (now Sejny) County on the shores of Lake Gieret, around which the village spread out in the 16th century. It was surrounded by the Jaćwież Forests—today's Augustów Primeval Forest—on the one side, and on the other, by hills, which often served as a defensive line, including during the memorable Polish-Lithuanian clashes of September 1920. It was then that Giby, Sejny, and the other surrounding regions fought to stay on the Polish side. Blood frequently flowed on this borderland, and even today, the discord between Poles and Lithuanians is noticeable here. It is only a dozen kilometers or so to the current border with Lithuania.

Zyta Kucharzewska at the Giby Elementary School (at the front desk on the left).

Zyta Kucharzewska worked as a typist during the German occupation of Poland from 1939 to 1945.

The only photograph from Zyta's childhood that has survived is the one from her school in Giby; it has faded somewhat since then. It shows an elementary school classroom and the over-ten-year-old girl sitting at the first-row bench with a friend. She has bold, shiny eyes; her hands rest under the chin; she is gently smiling.

"She was a good student," remembers brother Józef. "And she was so clever."

Their father was a blacksmith; the mother ran the house. The younger Józef learned the blacksmith's profession from an early age, under the guidance of his father, and Zyta loved books. The Kucharzewski family lived with two

Józef Kucharzewski (Giby)

children, Zyta and Józef, in the very center of Giby, next to the Szarejko family. During the German occupation, Zyta worked at a sawmill that was owned by a German. Her *Kennkarte*[1] from March 1944 has survived. The girl in the picture has a tanned, serious face and sad, dark eyes. At that time, she had already participated in the underground independence movement as a liaison girl of the Home Army. Her four-year-younger brother did not suspect anything because his sister was always at home. Only years later did he find out that, because of her girlishness and gentle disposition, the insurgents arranged for her to work for the unit to make it possible for her to live with her family in Giby.

In another photo from those war years, Zyta is sitting at a typewriter. She is elegantly dressed and focused.

"They say she was an excellent typist. She worked at a sawmill office and knew the German language well," says Józef's son, Grzegorz Kucharzewski (b. 1969), about his Aunt Zyta. His father would not tell him about the tragedy, but he learned a lot from Zyta's mother and his grandmother, Aleksandra Kucharzewska.

After the liberation from the German occupation, in the summer of 1945, Zyta had little time to enjoy freedom. The family keeps a few of her photos with her peers from the period immediately after the war—mostly

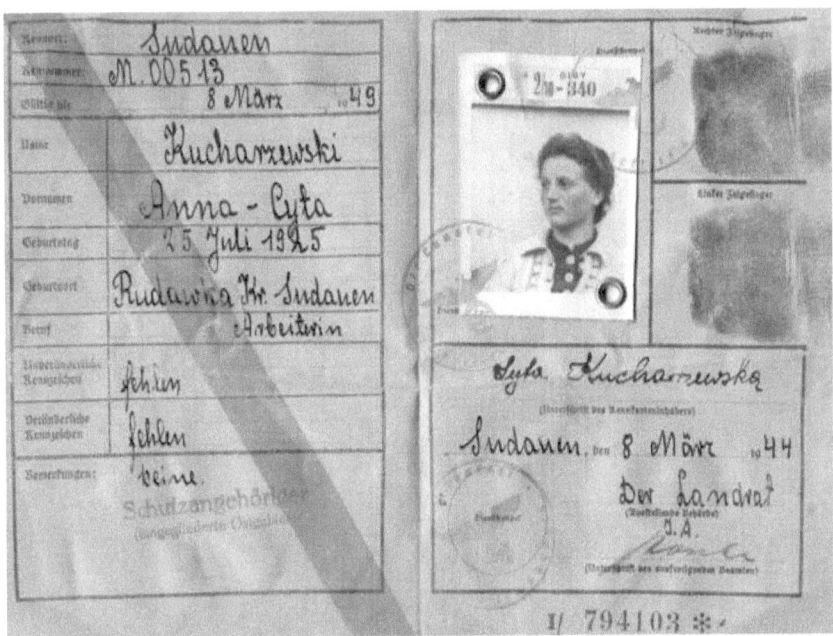

Zyta Kucharzewska's *Kennkarte*, an ID issued by German authorities to a Polish citizen of the General Government.

from walks or social gatherings. They were taken outdoors: among trees, by the lake, or in the forest. Zyta stands out for her beauty, a smile, and some unique charm.

On July 25, 1945, she was to turn 20.

The Soviets, three of them, came for her in the early morning of July 12, 1945. They were looking for a radio station, but they did not find even a transmitter. They tied her hands behind with the wire and led her out. Most probably, a neighbor denounced her. She was placed in a collective "filtration" camp in Giby, located in the neighborhood. The NKVD converted all the farm facilities belonging to their neighbors, the Szarejko family, into a temporary detention center. In two pigsties, a barn, and a cellar, about 150 Poles were imprisoned for almost two weeks, lying on straw, in manure—just like cattle, like pigs. Zyta was the only woman. Probably that's why they kept her apart in a small wooden tool shed. Everyone was starved and deprived even of water.

"It was so tight in the shed that she had to squat all the time. It's hard for me to imagine how Zyta could withstand so many days in this tiny space," says Józef Szarejko from Giby, who was a ten-year-old boy at that time. He knows every farm building well because he was born there, although, in 1940, he and his family had to move out. At the order of the

Zyta Kucharzewska (first from the right), shortly after the war, with her friends in the Augustów Primeval Forest.

German gendarmerie, in April 1940, his parents had to leave their store and family home in Giby. They were displaced to Posejanka, a village near Giby. After the war ended, his father's parents and Józef Szarejko's grandparents temporarily moved into their house in Giby. Their farm and all the buildings, located on the other side of Giby, were destroyed during the war. At the time of the Augustów Roundup, the boy came to his grandparents on vacation, becoming a witness to the tragic events.

The large Szarejko family, including the ten-year-old boy, who unwittingly became an eyewitness to the Roundup, were squeezed by NKVD and UB[2] officers into one small room. They occupied the rest of the house, and, for almost two weeks, they conducted bloody interrogations of Poles captured during the Roundup.

"We could not sleep—there were endless moans, sobs, howls of pain, and cries for help. During the brutal interrogations, the NKVD members horrifically beat and cruelly abused all of the detainees. They tortured them. In one room, on the first floor of our house, the walls and floors were red from the blood of the tortured Polish patriots," says Józef Szarejko.

The Kucharzewskis lived close by, just a few yards from the Szarejkos' farm buildings. Sitting on a ladder hidden in another pigsty, Zyta's brother, 16-year-old Józef, was able to watch what was happening next door. He saw a lot because he spent many days in his hideout. He watched the guards—Soviet soldiers. He saw the officers conducting investigations and prisoners led to interrogations and later—in blood—leaving the house after the NKVD torture. At the bottom stood a large tub of water where battered Poles washed their wounds. The water was red from their blood; it reeked.

Józef Kucharzewski relates:

> There was a table next to the pigpen, and one of the Soviet officers was sitting there. He had to be of Jewish origin, because the Soviet militants who were guarding the detention process were calling him and others "*Еврей*."[3] At the table, the prisoners, who came from the pigsty to the Szarejkos' home for interrogation, answered the investigator's questions and signed some documents. I also saw them many times lead my sister; she often stumbled. Then, I heard her screams and moans from the Szarejkos' house; it was easy to distinguish her from others because she was the only woman. An elderly Pole was beaten to death during interrogation. His body, wrapped in rags, was put on a wagon, and later at night, taken away to the forest.

Zyta never looked into the window of her family home, which was on the opposite side—probably on purpose, so that she would not give away her relatives. Regardless, one day the Soviets wanted to arrest her 16-year-old brother. His mother, however, bribed one of the Soviet guards with one liter of moonshine, and Józek had to disappear from sight for a few days. He went to their relatives in the neighboring village. Through another Soviet soldier, Vania, Kucharzewska gave food and drink for her imprisoned daughter.

After about two weeks, on the night of July 26 or 28, the Soviets loaded and transported the prisoners.

"They loaded them into cars and took them to the forest. Eleven cars were tightly packed. None of them returned. They also led my sister and took her to her own death, right before my eyes."

Józef Szarejko, on the other hand, counted 13 cars. He also claims that they returned every half hour, taking a few rounds. Poles were taken along the Giby-Rygol road towards Grodno. Where? He heard they were killed in Naumowicze, in today's Belarus.

After the detainees had been taken away and NKVD and UB people had left the Szarejkos' farm, Zyta's 16-year-old brother went to see the neighbors. He saw the room in which his sister and other imprisoned men had been tortured and was horrified. The walls were red from blood. So was the plank floor. The perpetrators left a torture device in the room—long, metal needles that the interrogators inserted under the prisoners' nails.

"I kept the device for a long time after the deportation, but then, it got misplaced," says Józef Kucharzewski.

His son, Grzegorz Kucharzewski, has been writing songs from a young age inspired by his Aunt Zyta. He plays the guitar and sings. Once, while sitting in Giby with his family and listening to the memories, he created a song telling the tragic story of Aunt Zyta (available on YouTube).

"The worst thing is when I close my eyes while singing this song. I begin to image this drama and I start shivering," says the bard, taking up his guitar.

> They came in July, warm July, early morning
> Three of them: two privates, one lieutenant
> Sharp, short words, "She's a spy! With us she's coming!"
> Tied her hands on her back with a wire.
>
> Mother quickly threw a coat on daughter's shoulders
> Quietly sobbing, wiping yet another tear
> "Zyta, Zyta," softly chanting name so dear
> Sensing this was the last time she'd ever see her.
>
> The heart of a mother felt in this torment
> That her life would be turned into waiting—
> Life, not long enough to hear—if for a moment—
> Her daughter's voice calling her, calling.
>
> So they took them to a forest, far and dark
> While the witness moon shed silvery tears

Zyta's nephew, Grzegorz Kucharzewski, felt inspired by his Aunt Zyta. For years, he has been writing songs, playing the guitar, and singing. His song, "It Was July," tells the tragic story of his aunt.

> Their lives like candles blown cold and stark,
> Like sickle-slit wheat's golden ears.
>
> Deadly demon led them down a forest path
> Then stacked them over a trench one by one
> A devil with a star and a Pepesha gun
> Aimed at their heads, a quick thunder, and it was done.
>
> No one knows which soil hid their bones
> Which forests muffled hopeless calls
> They're all dead, that's all that is certain
> But where they lie, only You, oh Lord, know.[4]

"My song 'It was July' is an account—kind of a report from those events. Whoever hears it will learn the truth about the Roundup," says Grzegorz Kucharzewski, who has been living Aunt Zyta's fate since he was a child. Her mother, Grzegorz's grandma, waited for her daughter until the end of her life. She never said Zyta was dead, despite fruitless searches all over the world.

Grzegorz Kucharzewski was born in Giby in 1969. He graduated from the local elementary school, whose patron was one of the "Soviet liberators," Captain Ivan Konstantinovic Shandurov. (It was only in the academic year of 1989–1990 that the request to change the patron was sent to the board of education.)

"I remember that as a child, I faced dilemmas. At school, I was taught one story, and after returning home, I heard a different one, from my grandmother," says the singer-songwriter, smiling. Just like his blacksmith ancestors, his father and grandfather, he "knows a little how to strike the iron, too."

Today, he is an educator himself; he teaches at the Stanisław Staszic Vocational High School of Agriculture in Sejny, where he lives, not far from the school from which he graduated. He received a degree in education. While in elementary school, he was already into writing poems and songs. He is a self-taught guitar player and bought the first instrument with his own money. Currently, he is a well-known bard in the area but has also given concerts in the town of Jurata and at the Porczyński Gallery in Warsaw. He usually gets invited by various patriotic circles, such as the Association of the Home Army Soldiers "Łagiernicy," which has printed his poems in its newsletter. Some of them have been turned into songs.

"When I sing some of my songs, I fear their hearts will not withstand the pain," says the artist.

He is interested in the history of his homeland; he likes to read, especially history publications.

"I would like people to learn about our history through my songs. I want them to remember Stalinist crimes, especially the largest one after the end of World War II, the Augustów Roundup. It was supposed to disappear into oblivion, and to this day, the local residents and our countrymen are hardly aware of this crime. Twenty-five years after regaining freedom, there is still lack of information about the Roundup—in textbooks, encyclopedias, even on the internet. However, young people are willing to participate in the preparation of patriotic programs and performances. You just need to encourage them." Grzegorz Kucharzewski dreams of releasing a CD and promoting his work more widely.

He does not approve of the current trend, a specific command to forget about the history of his own nation.

"Other countries care and generously fund historical narration. So why is it different in Poland? Why should we have amnesia about our past?" Grzegorz asks rhetorically. He would like to know the whole truth about the Augustów Roundup and about how and when his Aunt Zyta, died. Therefore, he does not intend to remain silent, which he expressed in this poem:

> You stay silent
> When you should shout
> To raise those who lie in the graves,
> Those with no crosses,
> Those thrown into a ditch,

Józef Kucharzewski (Giby)

And those who were
Denounced by their neighbor,
Whose lives were deemed worthless.

To those who choose to be silent:
I forbid you to be silent
I am a grandson of the mother
Who shed so many tears,
Who exhausted her prayers,
And who departed quietly
without consolation.

Zyta's brother, Józef Kucharzewski, the blacksmith, did not find peace after the loss of his sister. The Polish secret police members often raided his apartment in Giby and took him for interrogation. They locked him in a Suwałki prison four times. Even today, it is very difficult for him to talk about the torture he was subjected to.

"I will remember it until I die, especially the beating on my heels," he waves his hand as if in surrender. "To be left alone, I had to move to Silesia for a few years. I worked in a mine in Katowice."

However, he missed the beautiful places where he had grown up.

A wooden, historic church, dating from 1912, stands opposite Józef Kucharzewski's house.

After returning to Giby, he started a family and bought a nice wooden house with a garden, close to the place of his sister's agony. When, in 1982, a wooden shrine of Old Believers[5] was moved from the nearby Pogorzelec to the area of the former cemetery in Giby, Józef Kucharzewski became its sacristan. He has been continually performing this function to this day.

"I have worked in this church from its beginnings, from the foundations," he says proudly, opening the heavy door of the chapel.

He does not have to walk far to work. The wooden, historic church, dating from 1912, stands opposite his house, on the other side of the road on the Augustów-Sejny route.

The church has retained its original shape but was adapted to Roman Catholic rites. In 1984, it was consecrated as the church of St. Anne and St. Hubert—first as a branch of the church in Sejny, and eight years later, as an independent parish in Giby. From the very beginning, Józef Kucharzewski took care of the grounds of the church—planted bushes and trees around it, built the shrine of the Virgin Mary, and erected commemorative plaques and figurines.

In the well-maintained interior of the church, which exudes the smell of wood, you can see a plaque commemorating the victims of the NKVD-UB crime of July 1945. The church has a unique design. The antlers of the Augustów Primeval Forest animals were used for making a beautiful, yet simple, cross, chandeliers, sconces, and candlesticks.

A plaque commemorating the victims of NKVD and the Polish Secret Service at the church in Giby. Inscription on the plaque: "In honor of the Poles, victims of the Augustów Roundup committed by the NKVD and Polish secret police in July 1945. They died because they were Poles. [From] Mayor of the Village of Giby, The World Association of Home Army Soldiers, Freedom and Independence Association, Association of Siberian Exiles, Association of the Stalinist Political Prisoners, Association of Politically Repressed Soldiers and Miners, and Compatriots. Giby, September 2005."

Józef Kucharzewski (Giby)

In the vicinity of the church in Giby, there stands a monument that commemorates the victims of the Augustów Roundup and was designed by a well-known artist residing in Maćkowa Ruda, Professor Andrzej Strumiłło.[6] Unveiled in 1991, it has been standing there—by the road on the Augustów-Sejny route, on a hill surrounded on two sides by the Augustów Forest—for over 20 years. The monument is in the form of a tall, wooden crucifix surrounded by large, raw boulders climbing up the slope, which can be visible in the sun, especially in the spring. There is a symbolic meaning behind the monument—each boulder stands for one place from which the victims of the crime had been taken. Close to 600 names of the missing were engraved in the granite under the cross.[7] This work of art was created thanks to the cooperation of the following: the local authorities, foresters, craftsmen, clergymen, and people from the whole area who helped with the project with great enthusiasm. At the beginning of August 1991, the first open-air Mass was held there, with a large participation of residents and many notables, including Member of Parliament Bronisław Geremek, the Voivode of Suwałki Andrzej Podchul, and the honor guards of the Polish army. Everyone believed that after the communist authorities were overthrown in Poland, the Augustów Roundup enigma would be quickly resolved.

Since then, every year on the third Sunday of each July, a ceremonial celebration of an anniversary of the Augustów Roundup takes place at the monument in Giby.

And again, the families of the missing people are pleading to God for an explanation of the fate of their relatives who were arrested by the NKVD in 1945. The Kucharzewskis show up every year, and the grandson of missing Zyta's mother, Grzegorz Kucharzewski, sings his songs by the monument and recites poems, including "The Six Hundred":

> We're every clot of blood,
> Stomped into the ground by a murderer's boot
> The breath in us has frozen in the sand
> Tamped down
> Overgrown with grass.
> Nobody knows
> in what sand—
> Polish or Soviet—we lay,
> Nobody has yet moved the soil
> Which, like a dark shroud,
> hides the murder of the innocent.
> We are in every blade of grass,
> Sweaty with dew after a ghastly nightmare,
> Which came true one morning in July.

The house in Giby where, in July 1945, the NKVD arranged a collective filtration camp for detainees during the Augustów Roundup still

A monument commemorating the victims of the Augustów Roundup in the vicinity of the church in Giby. It was designed by a renowned Polish artist, Professor Andrzej Strumiłło, in the early 1990s.

stands there. The property still belongs to the Szarejko family (the next generation). Only the old farm buildings—a pigsty and a barn—have been demolished. The cellar is the only place where the arrested Poles were held to still be there. Currently, everything looks different in this pen—a shop has been set up on the ground floor of the house, and in the place where the former pigsty and barn held the imprisoned Polish patriots, lodgings for tourists have been built. The lake provides pleasant spaces for grilling, swimming, and sunbathing; there are areas for bonfires, boats, and sunbeds. Grzegorz Kucharzewski commemorated this place in his poem, "There is a House":

> There is a house
> Not far from here
> Where walls are screaming
> With hundreds of throats,
> With endless prayers.
> Under the layers of paint,
> That blood
> Still speaks to me
> After all these years.

> There is a house
> Right here, nearby
> Many tears
> And prayers have soaked in,
> And one request—
> To stop the beating.

Today, while living in another beautiful villa located on the other side of Giby, Józef Szarejko, who, as a boy, visited his grandparents and witnessed tragic events, cannot understand why nobody has ever brought the executioners of the crime and the local collaborators to justice. He can name them at any time.

"Some confidants even have the streets named after them today, or public institutions." Szarejko is furious. He believes that many of those who gave away the names of soldiers from the Polish independence underground to the Soviets know where they had been buried. It is certain that some of the Poles murdered during the Augustów Roundup rest in the pits of death in the Augustów Primeval Forest.

According to press releases, the Institute of National Remembrance in Białystok plans to start exploration and geological surveys of several places on the Giby-Rygol route. They were supposed to begin in the spring of 2014, but so far, nothing has happened.

The municipality of Giby was particularly affected by the Augustów Roundup. After the liberation of Poland in May 1945, 109 citizens were arrested and deported, including over 80 people in the July Roundup.[8] Therefore, on November 19, 1945, the authorities of Giby, as the first in the region, fought for their own by sending a delegation to no other than [then President of the State National Council] Bolesław Bierut with a request for a release and to accelerate the inquiry into the cases of the arrested Giby residents. The delegates returned with nothing. The authorities of Giby, therefore, sent further requests for intervention to the following: the Regional National Council in Suwałki, the Provincial National Council in Białystok, the Presidium of the Council of Ministers in Warsaw, the Polish Red Cross, and even the Polish Ambassador in Moscow and the Red Cross in Geneva. The written requests, which included the lists of the missing, emphasized that they were often the only providers, that the families were bereaved of fathers, husbands, sons, wives, daughters and left with no help and that those relatives had been taken away suddenly, without any proof of guilt. No response has been received to this day.

Many families from Giby also kept looking for missing relatives on their own. To no avail, either. The Polish secret police ordered them to stop asking for the missing ones and advised it would be best to conceal the family tragedy and not make life difficult for the next generations (for example, in getting a job or going to college). In this way, the biggest Stalinist crime against Poles after the end of World War II was forgotten.

The Kucharzewskis were also looking for their beloved, lovely Zyta in all possible ways. A great uproar and lively hopes in their family and the entire local population were raised in June 1987 by a resident of Giby, Stefan Myszczyński, who found an unknown grave in the forest near a road on the Rygol-Giby road. Unfortunately, the exhumations proved that it was a grave of Wehrmacht soldiers. However, the emotions suppressed by the authorities for so many years were rekindled. The Citizens Committee for the Search for the Residents of Suwałki Region Who Went Missing in July 1945 was established. Józef Kucharzewski proved to be very helpful.[9] In 1992, the committee provided all the documentation to the public prosecutor's office in Suwałki, which initiated an investigation, but, after a few months, it was closed due to the lack of documents from the archives in Moscow. Currently, the investigation is being conducted by the Institute of National Remembrance branch in Białystok, and the crime is still waiting for clarification.

In this poem, "From the Graves," Grzegorz Kucharzewski appeals to people's conscience and calls for the truth:

> Your conscience lies in the bullets
> That got stuck in pine tree trunks,
> That drilled through our heads
> And painfully pierced to the core.
>
> And we, who are biting the sand in our graves,
> On which no crosses were raised,
> Were the sons of the nation
> Forbidden to dream of Poland.
>
> Instead of pens,
> They put guns in our hands
> To spread death
> Among our enemies, who
> Swarmed our heads like beehives.
>
> The stinger stuck in the larynx of the nation
> So it could not speak, shout did not want,
> To let it die slowly from hunger
> To expel God from its heart.
>
> To make it live on its knees
> And never rise,
> To break its will to fight
> To make it stay in chains forever.
>
> The eye sockets of our skulls
> Look at you today with reproach
> Though they've been long overgrown with forest,

Józef Kucharzewski (Giby)

> Though life was ripped out of them.
> The forest screams for us, the moss whispers,
> Asking for crosses over our heads.
> It's only the truth, the whole truth we want
> Not ribbons cut by scissors.
>
> No more drum roll parades, no grand speeches,
> No military honors and appeals.
> Give us the crosses, give us the coffins
> In places of our last breaths.

The bard's father, the 85-year-old only brother of Zyta Kucharzewska, repeats:

> She had a green dress on, made from the parachute fabric. That's how much I remember. I would still like to light her a candle. I would like to stand over her grave.

Giby, March 2014

Marian Bućko (Augustów)

*"Our family is waiting
for the explanation of this crime"*

It is still difficult for Marian Bućko to talk about the Augustów Roundup, which claimed the life of his beloved father, Konstanty Bućko. He remembers his father well because he was born 12 years before the outbreak of World War II, on August 21, 1927. So when he starts talking about his father, lost during the Augustów Roundup, his voice is still trembling, and he cannot control his emotions or hold back the tears.

They lived in the village of Krasnybór in the Sztabin municipality in the Augustów District. Two Bućko brothers (out of five) and their families lived in one house—the older, Kazimierz Bućko, with his wife and five children, and the younger, Konstanty, Marian's father, with his wife, Magdalena Gos, and the same number of kids. They cultivated the land, but they did not have a lot of it, and the soil was barren. Therefore, the men had to take extra jobs to support their large families. Krasnybór is a large village (one of the largest in the municipality), beautifully located at the junction of the Lebiedzianka River and the Jastrzębianka River,

Marian Bućko.

not far from their mouth to the Biebrza River, stretching on the hills near the Augustów Primeval Forest, 24 kilometers from Augustów. To this day, it has a large school complex and two churches, one of which hosts the famous image of Our Lady of Krasnybór, known for her miracles.[1]

"My father, Konstanty Bućko, was a railroad worker; he worked at a nearby Jastrzębna Druga railway station. But he also had a small, two-hectare[2] farm. He received it from Marshal Józef Piłsudski, as a reward for his services at the war of 1920," says his son Marian, the second of five children and the firstborn son, while sharing his testimony in Augustów. He is 87 years old and has gray hair, but he is very tall, slim, and holds himself straight. His voice is strong and forcible.

"I look like my father—he had the same figure," says Marian Bućko, not without pride. He could talk about his father for hours.

Konstanty Bućko (b. 1900) joined the war of 1920 against the Bolsheviks as a volunteer and was enlisted with the 41st Suwałki Infantry Regiment of Józef Piłsudski. He was only 20 years old. He became a gunlayer and had worked with two helpers. He went through the entire front as a gunlayer, sometimes without leaving the trenches for two weeks. He chased the Bolsheviks all the way to Kiev and then participated in the Battle of Warsaw. For his bravery and courage, the platoon leader Bućko from Krasnyobór was awarded not only with the land in his native village near the Augustów Primeval Forest but also with the highest military decoration, the War Order of Virtuti Militari.[3]

"After he came back from this war, he liked to describe his adventures to his neighbors, who gathered in great numbers at our house. He did it quite colorfully, and, being a boy, I liked to listen," smiles Marian Bućko, explaining why he knows so many details from his father's life.

When World War II broke out in 1939, his father was 39 years old. Still, he went to the army once again, to the same unit of the 41st Suwałki Infantry Regiment of Józef Piłsudski. He was given a machine gun and fought at Brest. In this war, other soldiers called him "grandfather" because of his age. When the Polish troops could no longer cope with the Allied forces of the German and Soviet armies, Konstanty Bućko was saved from deportation, death camps, or Katyń by his ragged hands of a peasant and also by the fact that in Brest, in a tree hollow, he had hidden his military book with all the records of his participation in the Polish-Soviet War of 1920–21 along with his military distinctions.

After the Soviets disarmed Konstanty Bućko's platoon, he returned to his home in Krasnybór, walking from Brest at night with three younger soldiers from Suwałki. They used side roads and forest trails, where they had skirmishes with communists, both Soviet and Polish. It was the end of September 1939.

"I remember when my father came back. It was at night. We were all crying from joy," the firstborn son recalls.

Konstanty Bućko took up a job in the nearby railway station again and farmed with his family on the two hectares given to him by Piłsudski. He also made moonshine as both occupiers of these lands—first Russians, then Germans, then Russians again—enjoyed this type of vodka. During the Soviet occupation, his children, including Marian, attended the school in Krasnybór. Later, the Germans closed it, and education for Polish students was terminated altogether as the Germans claimed they would not need it.

Marian Bućko remembers that during the German occupation, insurgents secretly visited his father. They encouraged him to become a member of the Home Army. Bućko tried to make excuses—he was too old; he had already participated in two wars. When he said that he had had enough of the fighting, they wanted to take his hat, coat, and uniform. He would not allow it and wore his military uniform until it was completely worn out.

"The cap was the only item that served me after the war. I liked to wear it," recalls the platoon leader's firstborn son.

Konstanty Bućko worked on his farm throughout the entire war. And these were busy years—he and his wife had to feed and provide for five children.

His son, Marian, well remembers the end of World War II. German settlers packed in a hurry, leaving the Polish farms that they had taken over a few years earlier. The Red Army, which was pushing from the east, drove people out of their houses, too, while stealing horses and food. The front was approaching. And the NKVD was close behind. They were checking if the locals had any weapons and grenades. They were looking for "bandits." In the autumn of 1944, many residents of Krasnybór and the surrounding areas suffered from Soviet repression, mass arrests, and deportations into remote parts of Russia, including the camps in Ostashkov and Riazan. The Bućko family escaped to the neighboring village.

"At that time, the local farmers helped one another. They shared the last piece of bread, just like brothers. Not like today, when a man is a wolf to a man," Marian Bućko, then 17 years old, shakes his head.

He remembers hunger, poverty, and the insecurity they all experienced. To survive, people had to collect wild wheat in the fields, search the forest for wild mushrooms, herbs, and berries or walk to the nearby areas of East Prussia to loot.

At the end of January 1945, it seemed that peace was at hand. People were returning to their farms after displacement to front zones and from German concentration and forced labor camps. The front units of the Red Army had departed. Also, the soldiers of the Polish independence underground, who, from August 1944, could not conduct operations here due to the saturation of the frontier area by the Russian military, deportations, and horrific Soviet repressions, started to return home.[4] All of them were exhausted, often ill or crippled, but had hope for a new life. They were healing their wounds and patching the roofs of their farm buildings near the forest.

His father, Konstanty Bućko, also returned to work at the Jastrzębna Druga railway station. Until the trains started running again, he worked on fixing the tracks. He had his very own section to care for and supervise.

"I remember that the tracks had to be hand-raked," says the son of a railroader who worked during those difficult years. He adds that he cannot stand the current state of the railway tracks.

However, the war did not end for everyone. The postwar period for Krasnybór, as well as the neighboring villages, turned out to be even harder. And tragic.

Poles in these areas were far from being indifferent to the Lublin government (PKWN)[5] imposed on them by force and to the arrests, deportations, lynching, lootings, and rapes. The independence underground fought as hard as they could not to succumb to the Soviet rule.

In April 1945, a unit of the Citizens' Home Army was established under Władysław Stefanowski, alias "Grom," at the Lebiedzianka River. He became famous for dismantling the Polish secret police (UB) and Citizen's

The Lebiedzianka River in the Augustów Primeval Forest where the resurgence unit under Władysław Stefanowski, alias "Grom," was stationed. Today it serves as a safe haven for beavers.

Militia operational units on April 14, 1945, after these groups had made several arrests in the municipalities of Dębowo and Sztabin. Four militia officers were killed and six wounded. Also, six of the 11 detained Poles were released, including two members of the Citizens' Home Army. Earlier, on April 8 and 12, 1945, the "Grom" unit disarmed militia posts in Sztabin, Jaminice, and Lipsko. Moreover, on April 17, 1945, they totally liquidated the Municipal Office in Lipsko. However, the most famous operation carried out by the insurgents of the "Grom" unit, which is still remembered by the oldest residents of this land, was carried out on May 17, 1945, on the Augustów-Grodno highway. They destroyed a Soviet unit hastily driving 1,500 cattle from East Prussia to the Soviet Union. It counted dozens of people (together with the escort of the "Berling" units[6]). The underground also intercepted one automatic machine, ten guns, and nine German wagons with food and clothing as well as saddles and bicycles.[7]

In the spring of 1945, the Polish independence underground took control of the whole Augustów District, breaking up militia posts and local government offices and liquidating the administration. The Lublin [communist] authorities—unable to keep their control of this area—asked for "brotherly help." In May 1945, large Soviet forces were summoned. In the forest, the insurgency gained strength again.

However, in July 1945, everyone was taken by surprise and terrified by the Augustów Roundup, first of all by its size, then because it targeted the peaceful population. Besides, it was organized two months after the end of World War II in Europe!

Marian Bućko remembers the Roundup as if it were today. He was 18 years old at the time.

"One day in July, I took a scythe and went to the meadows to mow some hay. And suddenly, I saw the whole line of Soviet soldiers, walking tightly, next to one another, and thoroughly combing the forest. They asked me about weapons. Even though I did not have any, they brought me home. And together with my father, they rushed us to a pigsty in the middle of our village that belonged to Bronisława Hornowska. Her husband, Karol Hornowski, was also arrested," he tells me while visiting the crime scene in his home village.

Mrs. Hornowska's pigsty stood almost opposite the church, in the center of Krasnybór. On one side, there stood a cow and some pigs; on the other, the Soviets placed people taken straight from work in the field or on their farms, or their houses—men of different ages, arrested under the pretext of having their documents checked.

Marian Bućko continues his story: "I sat in this pigsty, together with my father, for four days. Then, they drove us, about fifty peasants, to a nearby barn that belonged to Witek. It was a bit better there because

St. Mary's Church in Krasnybór. Opposite the church, the Hornowski family had a farm, which the NKVD turned into its headquarters in this large village. The Soviets interrogated the arrested Poles in the Hornowskis' house, while in their pigsty and cellar, the imprisoned Poles were kept (including Marian Bućko with his father, Konstanty).

there was no dung and that unbearable stench. We spent the next five days there."

In Krasnybór, in the place of Bronisława Hornowska's pigsty, opposite the church with a painting of Our Lady of Krasnybór, some green, juicy grass grows today. In July 1945, NKVD made their headquarters in Krasnybór in the Hornowskis' home, where the interrogations were carried out. Hornowska, who lost her husband in the Augustów Roundup, died in 2014. The house was recently sold, and a new one was built in its place. Witek's barn, which stood nearby, next to the pigsty in the center of Krasnybór, is gone, too.

"After five days of arrest, I was released from Witek's barn. My father also returned home the same day, in the evening," Marian Bućko remembers that the Soviets asked them about whether they belonged to the Home Army or cooperated with "bandits" and demanded they point out Home Army commanders and soldiers as well as the sites where the weapons were stored. Marian did not know anything about it. He had never engaged in underground activities. He did not even know that his father, Konstanty, was in the Home Army and that his alias was "Setny." He did not know that the platoon leader, Konstanty Bućko, a soldier of two wars, was also a soldier of the Home Army in the Sztabin III District.[8]

The following day, after the father and son were released, the NKVD returned to arrest Konstanty Bućko after all. They had a list with them. The Soviets came with Jan Szostak, whom the family knew well. It was him, the "Judas," who identified Konstanty Bućko. However, he was most probably denounced by someone else.

"I have been thinking for a long time if I should speak about it," said Marian Bućko to a reporter while talking to her on the phone in December 2014. "But I cannot sleep at night, and I decided to reveal it. I want this to be included in the book. Well, he was denounced by a not-so-young spinster, a dressmaker from Krasnybór. I had five witnesses, including Szyper and Hornowska; unfortunately, they are all dead. Why did she denounce him? I do not know. She was the sister-in-law of my father's brother Stanisław Bućko, who was her sister's husband. Stanisław Bućko, my father's brother, also fought in the Home Army. Maybe she wanted to save him because he was her sister's husband? He survived, and my father's sister-in-law was sympathetic to the Soviets. She told them that my father fought against the Bolsheviks and took part in the September campaign during World War II.

"When Konstanty Bućko was arrested by the Soviets for the second time, he was taken to Hornowska's house. This time, however, the platoon leader was imprisoned in the basement, together with other men from Krasnybór, ten in all. Most of them were young.

"They say that they were horribly beaten in this basement," wiping his

A miracle-working icon of Our Lady of Krasnobór at St. Mary's Church.

tears secretly, Marian Bućko points to the place where the dreadful basement used to be. It does not exist any longer. An asphalt road was built in its place, and today, cars drive on it.

Then, all the arrested in Hornowska's basement were driven five kilometers away, to the Granackis' basement in Jastrzębna Druga.

"We were told that they were also subjected to cruel beating." Marian Bućko cannot stop the tears anymore. "My father, covered in blood, was taken from the basement; the Soviets poured water on him and dragged him to the basement for more beatings. My mother brought food and clean underwear and took away the blood-stained clothes. The detainees were all interrogated in the same way—by mistreatment and torture until they were unconscious."

These days, Mr. Granacki's son, Zenon Granacki, manages the place.

"My father told me about the secrets of this basement—whispered, I should say, because you could not talk about it loud. I also know that the NKVD occupied our house. We have been living in this house to this day," says Zenon Granacki in Jastrzębna Druga.

The cellar stands in the middle of a spacious courtyard, surrounded by the buildings and an old orchard that belong to the Granacki family. The farm is bigger and modernized now; it is subsidized with European Union funding. However, just as in the past, an idyllic, quiet, and sandy road leads to the farm, which is surrounded by a wooden fence. Just as in the past, storks have built their nests here. Just as in the past, birds in the forest sing most probably the same songs.

A cellar at the Granackis' house in the village of Jastrzębna Druga, which the Soviets turned into a detention center.

The Poles detained in the Granackis' cellar, who were suspected of fighting for the independence underground, were later driven to a barn that belonged to the Szyc family in Sztabin. The prisoners in Jastrzębna Druga went to Sztabin on foot. They were rushed like cattle and treated brutally, like common criminals. They were surrounded by an armed escort. One of the eyewitnesses recalled after many years:

> I saw them being led from Jastrzębna Druga. On the Lebiedzianka bridge, there was a large cloud of dust, and I had no idea what it was. They came closer—it's them! I was terribly scared; they were surrounded by an army. I recognized the young Granacki; he had just returned from forced labor in Germany. I saw Hornowski and Haraburda. I saw Haraburda's wife throw herself on the ground with my godson Marian. He was just a boy, and she began to despair. A major came up to her and started kicking my godson. Oh, my God! The poor men—they were not even allowed to stop; they kept on walking with their heads down, and their hands tied in the back. Soviets drove them towards Sztabin.[9]

After a few days, all the arrested were transferred by cars from the Szyces' barn in Sztabin to the famous "Turk's House," the headquarters of the PUBP[10] in Augustów. It was no longer possible to give them any food or clean underwear or obtain any information about them, even though the PUBP and Citizen's Militia officers took part in the Roundup. From the "Turk's House," they were taken to an unknown location. Nobody ever heard from them anymore.

The families were not informed about the further fate of their relatives—neither right after this operation nor in the 45 years of the Polish People's Republic, which, in the opinion of many, was an independent

Another barn that was turned into a prison during the Augustów Roundup. It belonged to the Szyc family in Sztabin.

country. Nor was it even possible to mention the Augustów Roundup, whether in the media or by telling stories, just like in the case of Katyń. However, the perpetrators of the Augustów Roundup, including many Poles, were known.

The families whose members went missing without a trace were not provided with any help nor support—neither material nor moral—although they needed it very much. Instead of assistance, the authorities gave them a pejorative stigma of "bandit families."

After ten Krasnybór residents disappeared, people mourned for them in despair. Marian Bućko continues: "We missed our father, the head of our family, very much. We missed him; we were worried, and we waited. In order to survive, we, the boys, had to work for other people to make money, mostly by mowing the grass, working at the harvest, digging potatoes. My mother constantly listened for her father's footsteps, waiting. She paid for mass offerings, just like other women did. Still, by the end of her life, none of those men came back. Even Our Lady of Krasnybór did not help." Marian Bućko shows the image of his mother that he always carries in his wallet. He also sobs when the gold-framed image of Our Lady of Krasnybór, in a silver dress and a crown, with the barefoot Baby Jesus, in a golden crown, too, is slowly being unveiled at the church of the Holy Virgin Mary in Krasnybór.

The family looked for the hero of two wars, decorated with the War Order of Virtuti Militari, everywhere. They wrote not only to Warsaw but even to Geneva and Moscow. The Red Cross informed them that they had no knowledge of him, and the Soviet authorities said that none of the missing people were in their territory.

Life, despite the tragedy, went on, like it always does. Five children of the platoon leader, Konstanty Bućko, completed a seven-grade primary school, like many residents of this land. For them, getting a college education was difficult. Four of the orphans of Konstanty Bućko (three daughters and a son) settled in Gdynia. Only Marian Bućko remained on the family land. In 1952, he married Eugenia, née Wojewnik, and moved with her out of Krasnybór to the neighboring Lebiedzin, also in the Augustów District. In addition to helping his wife run the ten-hectare[11] farm, he took up various jobs. He worked at unloading timber at a warehouse in Jastrzębna Druga, then, at the logging of the Augustów Primeval Forest. For ten years he worked as a postman, delivering packages by bicycle, making 40 kilometers a day.

"He can also weave beautiful baskets from the spruce root. At some point in his life, he owned a stonework business and ran a farm with me. My husband was, and still is, a very active and hard-working man." His wife, Eugenia, is full of praises for him.

They are happy to show the photos of their beautiful and well-maintained "ranch" on the Lebiedzianka River, which today is their daughter Alicja's home. She is one of their four children and a teacher in Augustów. In 2000, the Bućkos moved from Lebiedzin to an apartment they had bought in Augustów ten years earlier.

"We can always go to Lebiedzin and stay there as long as we want. It's better there because everything is ours. But at our old age, we need more peace," they say. They are happy to be able to enjoy their four children, ten grandchildren, and two great-grandchildren. They were involved in raising them; they helped their children settle down. Most of them live nearby and respect family traditions.

Alicja, née Bućko, is a teacher in Augustów; she appreciates her parents' achievements and the memory of her grandparents. She also understands the suffering of her father caused by lack of information regarding the resting place of his father and her grandfather, the platoon leader, Konstanty Bućko.

"Every day, I commute from Lebiedzin to Augustów because I love my parents' 'ranch,'" she explains while treating us with a homemade, fresh-from-the-oven cake. We are at the farm in Lebiedzin, which glistens with fall colors reflected from the Augustów Primeval Forest. "The Augustów Roundup is still alive in my father's memory, and so is in us, the next generation. Over the years, my father's suffering grew greater and greater because he does not know where his missing father lies, because he cannot visit his grave, because he cannot pay him homage, and because no longer can he spend time with him in the Augustów Forest. That's why he is fighting for his memory. This crime, however, permeates the hearts of all of us."

When it became possible to speak about the Augustów Roundup out loud a few years ago (although Marian Bućko was never afraid of talking about it, and his whole family knew the truth about this postwar crime), the monuments commemorating the missing began to appear, such as the monument in Giby or a commemorative plaque at the cemetery in Jaminy. An attorney from Łódź, Witold Lewoc, who is a native of the Jastrzębna Druga village and an acquaintance of Marian Bućko, proposed that all the missing in the Augustów Roundup from the parish of Krasnybór should be paid tribute in the form of a monument. Lewoc was also a soldier of the Home Army but managed to escape and survived the Roundup. In a small publication dedicated to his fellow soldiers of the Home Army, the Citizen's Home Army of the III Sztabin Region and the IV Lipsko Region, and all those who helped them and lost their lives in the Augustów Roundup, he wrote that thanks to his mother, "he was only brushed by the shadow of the Angel of Death's wings." The publication is titled *Zaginieni—polegli w Obławie Lipcowej z parafii Krasnybór* ("The Missing: Men Killed in the July Roundup from the Parish of Krasnybór").[12] Only 100 copies were published by photocopying for the families of the victims of the Roundup. The author himself financed the publishing.

"I feel it is my social responsibility to complete the last will of the fallen in the Roundup and preserve the memory of these events among the members of the Polish society and help determine their resting place," wrote Witold Lewoc in one of his letters, also asking the Bishop of the Ełk Curia and the archbishop office in Białystok to have the parish priests initiate events commemorating the victims of the crimes in individual parishes.[13]

Marian Bućko says, not without emotion and tears:

> Our priest announced from the church pulpit the idea of building a monument. We organized a meeting at a school in Krasnybór. The Remembrance Committee of the Victims of the July Roundup in Krasnybór was created, and I became its chairman. It was July 26, 1998.
>
> From the Krasnybór parish, 43 people went missing. Later, two more were added, making it 45 in total. Most of their families agreed to give 400 zlotys each towards the construction of the monument, though many did not keep their word. Engraving one letter cost five zlotys.
>
> The Chairman of the Committee, Marian Bućko, applied for extra funds for the monument in Krasnybór. In 1998, he wrote numerous letters, including two requests to the Council for the Protection of Combat and Martyrdom in Warsaw—to no avail. In 1999, he also sought support from the Voivodship Office in Białystok and the City Hall in Augustów—also without effect. Only the head of the Sztabin municipality donated 700 Polish zlotys. So did the office of the Augustów municipality in the amount of "as much as" 152.50 PLN.
>
> It was not enough because I needed 2,000 zlotys to pay the bills. The cost of engraving the letters was higher than the boulder. I thought that the relatives of the 43 missing would contribute more as not everyone gave the initial 400 zlotys. But no one wanted to help. I spent so many sleepless nights. My way of thought was this: So many people were killed; they have no graves; the need to be honored one way or another. The monument was ready, the letters were engraved, and there was no help! So I pulled 1,300 zlotys out of my pocket—that's how much we were short of—and I paid myself. Somehow, I have managed to live without this money. Somehow, I did not starve to death! I regret that the names of two more missing people—Józef Okuniewski and Adolf Daraszkiewicz—are not engraved on the monument. But I will not pay myself anymore.

In 1999, the monument to commemorate the victims of the crime against the inhabitants of the Krasnybór parish that was carried out by the NKVD and Polish secret police in July 1945 stood at the church cemetery in Krasnybór. The pastor of the Krasnybór parish gave permission to build the monument at a beautiful spot of this necropolis—on a hill among the trees and grass on the left side of the main entrance gate to the cemetery.

A monument in Krasnybór commemorating the victims of the Augustów Roundup from the parish, unveiled in 1999. It was funded by the Remembrance Committee of the Victims of the July Roundup in Krasnybór (with the help of the Sztabin authorities), whose chairman was Marian Bućko. Inscription on the monument: "Dedicated to the victims of the crime committed in July 1945 by NKVD and Polish secret police against the residents of the Krasnybór parish. They gave their lives for the freedom of their Homeland. [Names of the 45 victims of the July 1945 Roundup from Krasnybór.]"

Marian Bućko himself laid the foundations for this monument. He was only helped by Norbert, the then young son of Alicia, who lived in Lebiedzin, now a recently graduated aviator from Dęblin.

"I have good grandchildren; many are taller than me," says Marian Bućko with pride, lighting the candles at the monument in Krasnybór. "Today, I am also proud of this monument, although it cost me a lot of frustration, not to mention the money."

The monument, made from black granite punctuated with colorful mosaics, did not initially gain the approval of the residents. Some even tried to depreciate it with paint. Today, the monument with the engraved names of the victims of the Roundup has become particularly close to the hearts of the parishioners and those who live in the surrounding area. It is a one-of-a-kind memorial, shaping the patriotic consciousness of the local society, reminding them of the greatest crime in Poland after World War II. From the website of the local government in Sztabin, one can find out that in July of 1945, 126 people from this area were arrested and deported.

On the monument, the following names of the 44 victims of the Roundup from 14 villages, including ten residents of the village of Krasnybór, are listed (in this order): Konstanty Bućko, Władysław Błażewicz, Józef Chodakiewicz, Czesław Granacki, Tadeusz Granacki, Józef Haraburda, Karol Hornowski, Stanisław Karp, Ignacy Kopańko, Zygmunt Korniłowicz, Jan Krzywicki, Józef Kulik, Anna Wnukowska, Antoni Gąsiorowski, Edward Gąsiorowski, Józef Kąkiel, Stanisław Franciszek Kukowski, Józef Markowski, Wacław Siedlecki, Władysław Siedlecki, Władysław Zalewski, Stanisław Kuźnicki, Leon Kuźnicki, Piotr Kuźnicki, Stanisław Makarewicz, Czesław Szczytko, Eugeniusz Szczytko, Kazimierz Szczytko, Czesław Szymański, Józef Szyper, Józef Zawistowski, Antoni Zysko, Antoni Siedlecki, Szymon Zalewski, Stanisław Chlebanowski, Jan Krysztofik, Stanisław Malinowski, Józef Okuniewski, Bernard Żywna, Michał Krupinski, Stanisław Gramacki, Helena Wnukowska, Stanisław Tarasewicz, and Edward Tarasewicz.

The whole Bućko family knows the truth about the Roundup. Even the grandchildren are following the latest updates about this crime; they are searching for newer information on the internet and share it with their grandparents. Together with other families of the missing in the crime of July 1945, they also participate in many events related to the Augustów Roundup, such as the unveiling of the epitaph in honor of victims of the Augustów Roundup at Jasna Góra in Częstochowa (May 3, 2014) or the dedication of the cross commemorating insurgents killed in the battle at Lake Brożane (June 14, 2014)—the most significant battle in the Augustów Primeval Forest with the Soviet forces who carried out the Augustów Roundup.

Marian Bućko (Augustów)

Marian Bućko was a flag-bearer during the unveiling of the Cross at Lake Brożane in the Augustów Primeval Forest on June 14, 2014. He is second from right in the leather jacket with a sash on the shoulder.

Marian Bućko was a flag-bearer during the unveiling of the Cross at Lake Brożane in the Augustów Primeval Forest on June 14, 2014. He is in the group to the right of the cross in the leather jacket as a member of the color guard.

Marian Bućko has also agreed to have genetic material for DNA research collected, which is to help the office of the Institute of National Remembrance prosecutor in establishing the identity of the people murdered in the Augustów Roundup.

"Our entire family is waiting for the explanation of this crime," emphasizes Marian Bućko.

He admits that in 1999, they received 200,000 PLN compensation. Each of the five children of the platoon leader, Konstanty Bućko, received 18,000 PLN. However, they still do not know how and when their father, grandfather, and great-grandfather, the recipient of the War Order of Virtuti Militari, was killed or where his body rests. They also do not have a single photo of him. The grandchildren and great-grandchildren of Konstanty Bućko do not know what he looked like because the only photograph of the platoon commander Konstanty Bućko was left, along with his military papers, in a tree hollow somewhere in Brest.

Augustów, March 11–October 12, 2014

Teresa Staśkiewicz (Augustów)
"The Augustów Roundup is still alive"

She holds one of the very few photographs she has of her father as if it were a relic. In it, she is still a tiny, younger than four-year-old girl; she is wearing a white dress and sitting in a bicycle basket, among flowers, after a ride. Her daddy is standing beside her. He is tall and remarkably elegant—he is wearing semi-long white pants, a jacket, a light shirt, and a tie. This photograph, nicely framed, stands on the bookshelf of his firstborn daughter, Tereska,[1] as he used to call her. Thanks to this prominent place, she can look at him every day.

"I remember this occasion well. We had just returned from the forest. In a moment, my father would take me off the bicycle, out of the basket. I was always scared of this. To this day, I have a fear of heights," Teresa Staśkiewicz, née Wołąsewicz, begins her story. We are talking in the living room of her one-bedroom apartment in Augustów that has an intellectual and Catholic vibe. She has served a homemade cake and tea, and I can hear the family clock regularly strike every hour.

She smiles mysteriously: "Twice, my dad has spoken to me from this

Teresa Staśkiewicz, née Wołąsewicz.

photograph. I've heard his voice twice. I even told the parish pastor about it."

Her father, Michał Wołąsewicz, born in 1911, came from a family of landowners from the village of Trycze, near Grodno. In his youth, he liked riding a bicycle. He also used to visit Augustów often; he knew this beautiful area well. When, in February 1936, he married Jadwiga Bołtralik from Sopoćkin, near Augustów, he decided to settle down with his family by the Netta River. They came to Augustów in 1938, at the time, with their one-year-old son, Jurek. At a townhouse on May 3rd St., they established a grocery and a colonial shop. They lived there, too.

But soon, the war broke out. On Friday, September 1, 1939, while the family was having dinner, someone knocked at the door. The father stood up and left. That is what his mobilization to the army looked like. He fought at the Eastern Front, including in Lviv. After the September defense campaign, he managed to get back to Augustów via Vilnius. His colonial shop had been closed down, and he had to find a job in the Soviets' warehouses as a purchaser.

Daughter with her father, right after a bike ride.

"Shortly after that, I came into the world, to be exact, on February 18, 1941, in Augustów, during the Soviet occupation." His daughter, Teresa, shows a different photograph of her father, taken before he joined the army in September 1939. She remembers her father thanks only to these small black-and-white photographs. When she looks at the pictures, some scenes come alive, and old images—even though foggy—pass in front of her eyes.

When she was four weeks old, her father was arrested by the Soviets. They called him a thief, according to his daughter. He was lofty towards the occupiers, so they told him: "Wait and see. You will go to prison because something will be missing

Michał Wołąsewicz in 1939, just before the mobilization to the army in September 1939.

Michał Wołąsewicz in 1941, after returning from a Soviet prison in Białystok.

from the warehouse." That is how Michał Wołąsewicz was arrested and imprisoned in Białystok. His wife, Jadwiga, stayed alone with her two children in Augustów under the Soviet occupation.

Close to June 22, 1941, on the day of another wave of Soviet deportations of Poles to Siberia, Stanisław Zagórski, Tereska's godfather, who worked on a railway, warned her mother that she was on the list of people to be arrested. The Soviets planned to deport her and other Poles together with their children into deep Russia. Jadwiga Wołąsewicz then fled to the Augustów Primeval Forest. She waited the entire day until the train from Augustów, packed with Polish families in cattle cars, left for Siberia. It was the last day before the Germans entered the area previously occupied by Hitler's former ally from the east. While hiding in the forest, she heard the bombings by the German planes that were flying towards the Soviet Union. After returning home, the neighbor told her that the Russians had come for her at night, knocked on the door, and peered through the windows. Also, at the railway station, before the transport with deportees left, her name had been called out. It is a miracle that Jadwiga Wołąsewicz survived together with her children.

"My mother was so brave. After all, I was only four months old, and my brother, Jurek, was four," sighs Teresa Staśkiewicz. She jokes that at that time, she had some "body reserves" as she had been chubby from her infancy. She still is. On the other hand, she is also elegant, probably taking after her father, and, in a green suit, looks stylish today, despite the tough 73 years of her life.

After the German invasion of the Soviet Union, in June 1941, many Soviet prisons were destroyed by the Nazis, freeing prisoners. Michał Wołąsewicz came back from Białystok—battered and emaciated after the tortures, with his nails ripped off. Once again, his daughter, Teresa, shows a few small black-and-white photos, this time from 1941.

"At that time, my father was even slimmer. After all, he had just been released from prison. He always wore a tie, though," she jokes—she is just cheerful and energetic by nature. During the conversation, she likes to interject funny stories from the complicated history of her family.

In 1944, they survived an exile. The front line passed through Augustów, and they had to leave everything behind and flee. They survived the war by fighting mainly in farm buildings in the village of Netta, which had been deserted, because, in February 1940, the Soviet NKVD arrested and deported all residents to Siberia, in one transport. According to the findings of the Association of Siberian Exiles,[2] 203 people from Netta Folwark, 61 from Netta I, and 26 from Netta II were deported to Siberia. Many other villages in this region met a similar fate.

Teresa does not remember much from Netta. After all, she was just a little girl. She vaguely recalls the crowds of different people and the trenches. She can still feel the itching from lice. Her father, like other men, was often taken to dig shelters and trenches, sometimes for several days. His wife and children brought some food. How did they get it?

"When my father was with us, he somehow managed to get some food. On his bike, he brought a piece of mutton or other meat, and my mom cooked," the daughter says.

From the exile, she also remembers some barbed wire. They later sat behind it together with other people in the village of Bogusze, from where they fled to Augustów in February 1945. She knows that her father used to go to Warsaw; he somehow made his way there to get some supplies.

A few years ago she learned from Alicja Maciejowska, who was then writing a book, *Przerwane życiorysy. Obława Augustowska—lipiec 1945* ("Terminated Lives: Augustów Roundup, July 1945"), that her father might have had connections with the "Radosław" Group.[3] Teresa Staśkiewicz was told by the journalist about the so-called "Radosław List" of 45 Polish citizens that Lt. Col. Jan Mazurkiewicz, alias "Radosław," then-chairman of the Liquidation Committee of the former Home Army, had inquired about on March 1, 1946. She saw the name of her father—Michał Wołąsewicz, born in 1911—on that list under no. 38. His occupation was entered as "worker." According to "Radosław," everyone on the list was arrested in Augustów on the same day, July 17, 1945, by troops of the 50th Soviet Army under the command of Col. Polikarpov and deported to Russia.[4]

Did her father indeed fight in the Home Army? The daughter is still surprised and unsure about it. She was too little, just like her siblings, to know about it. She wonders and keeps asking, not only herself. During the entire era of the Polish People's Republic, one would not talk about the Home Army membership, especially to children. It could result in severe repressions.

"Perhaps my father was a Home Army liaison? I know he always owned a radio. He kept it at home, often hidden in the oven.[5] He kept the family in the dark about any matters relating to the underground work," the daughter remembers.

After returning to Augustów, in the winter of 1945, the Wołąsewicz family found a partially abandoned townhouse at Kościelna Street, with broken windows and a heap of debris in every corner. It was cold, dark, and empty. They began their meager existence in these rough conditions.

The father took a job at the Augustów Fermentation Firm as a tobacco cultivation instructor. He was always in the field, riding one of his bicycles. He had two—one pre-war, the other post–German.

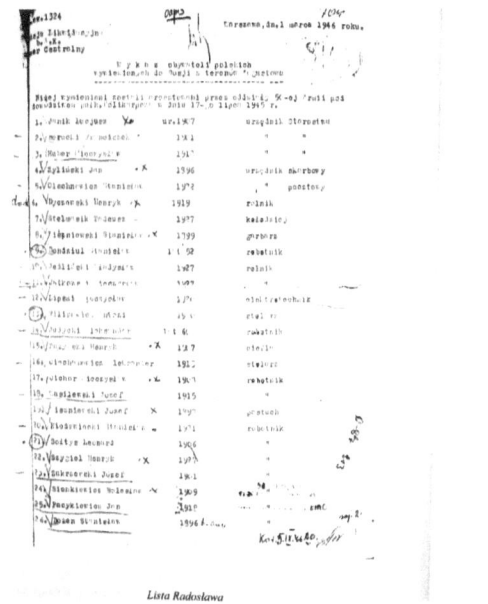

Lista Radosława

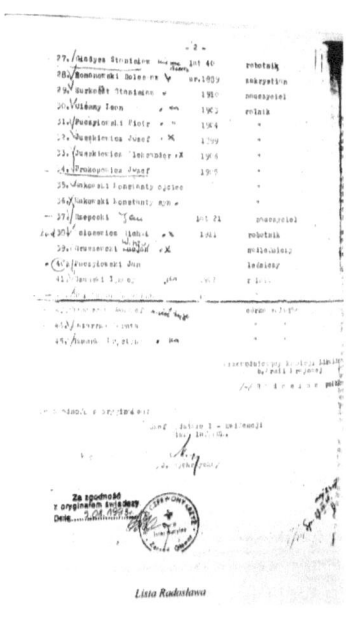

Lista Radosława

"Radosław List."

"That's why it's difficult for me to remember his face. When I got up early in the morning, he had already left; when I went to sleep, he was not there yet," recalls the daughter.

Michał Wołąsewicz, however, was very resourceful and thrifty. During those tough years, he was able to take care of his family; he always brought food and other necessities. When, in the summer of 1945, the news spread about the forthcoming Roundup, he was advised to leave Augustów, hide in a secluded place, and wait. However, his wife, Jadwiga, was pregnant again, and he did not want to endanger the family. Their third child, Basia, was born on July 6, 1945. And 11 days later, on July 17, 1945, Michał Wołąsewicz was arrested by the Soviets.

"I know that he was first placed in the basement of one of the houses in Augustów, at the Dowgierd family. Not far from us. My mother and brother, Jurek, who, by the way, died in 2014, delivered him food. Still, they did not manage to see him." Teresa Staśkiewicz recalls that many Augustów residents heard the moans and cries of tortured prisoners coming from the basement.

The cellars, where the Soviets detained the arrested in July 1945, were under two houses that belong to the Dowgierd family on Partyzantów 9 St. in Augustów. Prisoners were taken for interrogations from the Dowgierds' one-story house basement to the next, two-story building. Across the street, a Soviet officer resided, who was considered a commander-in-chief. It is probably the most critical place in Augustów for the filtration of the detained in the Augustów Roundup.

Second Dowgierds' house.

The father managed to send a secret message to his wife, hidden under the lid of a jar that he gave to his son, the eight-year-old Jurek: "I do not know what will happen to me; you will probably have to manage by yourself." And then, the prisoners were taken away from the town at night. The cars returned many times for the next group of the detained. When, at the end of July, Jurek attempted to give his father a new portion of food, he heard from the guard that Michał Wołąsewicz was no longer in the basement. And the trace of him was lost.

In Augustów, martial law continued for a long time after the Roundup. The destroyed, burned-down city looked like a ghost town. There were stumps and ruins instead of what once used to be a beautiful city on the Netta River at a historic Augustów Canal.[6] Most depressing was the image of the destroyed church towers; the church was also missing the front wall. Darkness was everywhere. Everyone walked barefoot. There was hunger. Also, in the townhouse where the Wołąsewicz family occupied a ground-floor room with a kitchen, the NKVD took over the attic. Some uniformed Soviets left by cars in the morning and returned at night.

"I remember that before they went upstairs, they had to pass our door. I was always scared. All of the summer of 1945 was wasted for me. I was all in fear," says Teresa Staśkiewicz, younger than five years old at that time.

She shares one more trauma from the years just after the war. When Augustów residents were returning from the East and West, Jadwiga Wołąsewicz and her three children were also on the lookout. One day, in July 1945, Tereska, while looking for her father, lost her way in the Augustów ruins. When it got dark, she did not know what direction to go. She cried out loud. She was lucky, though—a good woman suddenly showed up in front of her. She took her hand, helped her find the house where they lived, and took her to her mother.

"To this day, whenever I mention this incident, I tremble. This woman was probably an angel from heaven," smiles Teresa Staśkiewicz.

After the war, extreme poverty prevailed everywhere. It was especially hard for the families without the men who went missing in July 1945 and were often sole providers. Jadwiga Wołąsewicz—with three children and no breadwinner—had no source of income. She did not qualify for a pension or even food stamps after her husband went missing. They did not have an apartment. They survived almost miraculously.

"I remember that food from UNRRA[7] turned out to be of great help at that time. The powder milk was yellow, the aged margarine was hard as a stone, and the corn flour was stale, too, not to mention the horrible fish oil that I had to swallow. Without these provisions, though, in those days of deprivation, we would have starved to death," relates Mrs. Staśkiewicz. She found consolation in books, which provided an escape from the poverty and sadness after the loss of her father. To this day, she is an avid and passionate reader.

To pay rent for a room with a kitchen and to feed three young children, Michał Wołąsewicz's widow—at this point with no profession—learned to sew. The tailoring "business" undoubtedly saved the family. It was still her husband, Michał, who had brought a sewing machine from a post–German loot. He even brought two, so she could sell one. First, she used to make small alterations; later, she sewed underwear, simple blouses, and clothes for her children, including pretty blue dresses for her daughters. She made up for limited tailoring skills and experience with reliability and low prices. Gradually, she gained practice and sewed better and better. The children remember their mother always bending at the machine by an oil lamp or serving customers who came to their one-room apartment. They also had to help her support the family, especially the oldest daughter, Teresa, who learned to sew buttonholes, to do tacking, cross-stitch the bottoms of dresses and skirts, and iron professionally. The younger sister delivered the clothing to the clients, but it was not easy because Basia did not have shoes for a long time. For the tailoring work, they received payment mostly in groceries.

"I never had any vacation. In addition to helping my mother with dressmaking, in summer, we had to pick berries, mushrooms, and fruit to make winter preserves. We also made pickles and sauerkraut. To survive, my brother, Jurek, also raised rabbits. They had to be fed, too." Teresa

Wołąsewicz tells stories about how the siblings used to get greenfeed for the rabbits, even from the cemetery. She also remembers that her mother had moments of despair and breakdowns. After many years, the mother admitted that she even prayed for the death of her little Basia, her youngest beloved daughter. She didn't want her to suffer.

The tragedy was even greater because almost all their relatives died during World War II.

"We grew up not only without a father but without any relatives—grandparents on one side had been deported to Siberia, and the others died early in the war. Other relatives died or scattered around the world in the war turmoil." Teresa Wołąsewicz spins her family story, staring at the painting hanging on the wall of her living room in Augustów.

After this terrible war, the extraordinary, dramatic exodus affected not only people but also all their possessions. Even the monumental image of the Holy Mary, hanging in the center of her living room, at which Teresa often stares, wandered among many homes of her relatives until it came to her. The painting belonged to Anna and Antoni Bołtralik from Sopoćkin, her mother's parents. Teresa's grandfather Antoni Bołtralik acquired it from his parents. Anna and Antoni Bołtralik were deported [by Soviets] to Krasnoyarski Krai[8] just because they were Polish. In addition, her grandfather had fought as a volunteer in the war with the Bolsheviks in 1920. In Krasnoyarski Krai, Antoni Bołtralik soon fell ill and died. His wife, grandmother Anna, who was younger than he, got out of Russia with Anders's Army[9] and ended up in Southern Rhodesia. She never returned to her homeland and died in Africa from stomach cancer.

"Grandfather Antoni helps me in difficult times through this painting. I am being serious." The current owner of this sacred work smiles mysteriously. "For example, recently, my son could not find a job, so I looked at the family painting of the Holy Mary and started talking to my grandfather. I asked him: 'You died of hunger. Do you want your grandson to die, too?' And soon, precisely on the feast of Our Lady of Sorrows, the phone rang. Wojtek found out that he could start his new job the next day."

Czesława Bołtralik, one of the daughters of the exiled grandparents, after her mother's death in Rhodesia, left Africa for the United States. After the war, she found—via correspondence—her sister Jadwiga Wołąsewicz, née Bołtralik, in Augustów. She tried to help them, although she did not have an easy life as an immigrant—she worked hard as a manual worker in America. Teresa remembers that one day another letter from America reached them. It was from Uncle Fabian Bołtralik, the mother's brother, who also survived the Soviet gulags. He also managed to leave Russia with Anders's Army, though in a state of near-death exhaustion. After the war, he also settled in the United States. Teresa's mother's siblings, who found their fate in America, sometimes sent their sister Jadzia[10] and her children in Augustów packages with sweets, so rarely available in the People's Republic Poland.

Her second sister, Władysława Bołtralik, joined the Polish Armed Forces and fought at the Western Front. After demobilization, she married a Polish officer, Mr. Winiecki and settled near London. However, she did not support her sister in Augustów. Sometimes, she only sent English Christmas cards. Still, the kindness and assistance from Jadwiga's sibling was the only aid that the orphaned Wołąsewicz family could count on.

Once, a man who showed a striking resemblance to their father, Michał Wołąsewicz, showed up. He said he was his brother. His name was Bolesław. He only talked with his sister-in-law Jadwiga Wołąsewicz; the children did not hear anything. His mother later told them that he had survived a Soviet gulag. Frightened, exhausted, he did not even want to say where he was or how he was released, nor did he give his address. They never saw him again.

Jadwiga Wołąsewicz waited for her husband for a long time. She never married. She looked for her Michał everywhere; she wrote letters to various institutions. Collective searches, including on her behalf, were also conducted in Augustów by Michał Olechnowicz, a postman from Augustów who spent 28 years of his life searching for his son Stanisław (also on the "Radosław List") and approximately 500 missing (as it was believed) in the Augustów Roundup. Unfortunately, to no avail.

When in 1954, Teresa Wołąsewicz turned 13, she wrote a request letter to find her father, all by herself. And it was addressed directly to President [of the Polish People's Republic Bierut, describing the whole miserable existence of her family. She added that Jan Szostak, who contributed to their misfortune, came for her father at night, on July 17, 1945, along with the NKVD. She also wrote that she could murder him in cold blood. The letter was written in beautiful calligraphy on a formal-size paper. The reaction was immediate—the girl was summoned to the prosecutor's office for interrogation, without her mother. The prosecutor asked her first and foremost who told her to write the letter. She replied without fear: "It shows clearly that it was me who wrote it. Without anybody's coaxing."

Afterward, she kept sending letters to other authorities and institutions. In 1979, for example, she wrote to the Central Committee of Polish United Workers' Party, from whom she received the answer that nothing she wrote was true, that such events did not take place at all. Her letter to a TV program "Witness," with the description of the Augustów Roundup, was left with no reaction. The topic of this crime never appeared on TV.

Almost every time Tereska sent a letter, her mother was summoned to the Polish Secret Police Office in Augustów, to the famous "Turk's House."

During the interrogations, Jadwiga Wąsewicz was also asked about her husband and his past. But she did not know anything. Her husband, Michał, had never informed her about the underground activities. In the end, they left the widow alone. And Tereska regrets that there are no copies of those letters. They all disappeared, because in 1960 she moved out of the house, which underwent cleanups, renovations, and moves.

Under these difficult circumstances, the three Wołąsewicz children attended Augustów schools. They did not receive any pension or benefits or child support. Moreover, the whole family didn't have health insurance. The family was not allowed to use free health care, including any tests. Basia, for example, had a severe illness since her childhood and suffered a lot, but it was only at an adult age that she learned she had been born with three kidneys. The Wołąsewicz children knew from an early age that if their father had died at the hands of the Germans, it would have been a better death, but the death in the hands of Russians and Polish secret police was not officially acceptable. So they told their friends and teachers that their dad had died during the war.

Years passed. All three had to help their mother from early on do various jobs, often overly taxing. With a joint effort, however, they managed to get out of the worst of trouble. All three graduated from high schools, got an education, and became professionals. Jerzy worked as a technician; he lived in Augustów all the time. Basia became a nurse and settled in Ostrów Mazowiecka. Teresa graduated from the five-year Pedagogical Lyceum and for 30 years worked in Augustów County as a village teacher, teaching children, mainly first through third grade. She got married but was widowed early. She has two sons: Wojciech and Grzegorz. She is still waiting for grandchildren. In 1979, she got a one-bedroom apartment in Augustów, where she lived with her mother, who died in 1994 at the age of 86. Yet, Jadwiga Wołąsewicz had managed to help Teresa raise her children. Thanks to her mother, the firstborn daughter could take various courses over a long period of time and even graduated from the Teachers' University of Radio and Television.

In 1991, in a free Poland, when Jadwiga was still alive, the family began to solicit for compensation for the death of her husband and father, Michał Wołąsewicz. It took many years. The widow Jadwiga did not live to see the year 1997 when the three Wołąsewicz children were awarded 13,000 PLN each.

"The court proceedings were humiliating. We were asked, for example, to prove the arrest of my father. It's good that at least there was the 'Radosław List.' If I had today's brains, I would not have taken this money." Teresa Staśkiewicz recalls those years with disgust.

Anatol Batura, Teresa Wołąsewicz's favorite Polish language teacher from the pedagogical high school, instilled in her love for the Polish language and literature, especially poetry. To this day, she owns an extensive library, although lately, she has been giving many books away to others. She loves poems by Fr. Jan Twardowski. Recently, she also bought several audiobooks. She also likes to listen to records—music and poetry. She has a selection for every season and every holiday. Besides, she loves to listen to the radio. Thanks to her sons, she has modern radios in the living room and the kitchen. She rarely watches television. All the time, she follows the development of events pertaining to the Augustów Roundup.

"At the end of the 1980s, some hope was brought to our lives by the Citizens Committee of the Search of the Missing Residents of the Suwałki Region," says Teresa Staśkiewicz. "I am very grateful to Mrs. Alicja Maciejowska and other people from this organization who, while enduring different forms of harassment, traveled around our land and collected the first documentation about the victims of the Roundup."

Recently, there have been more and more searches, events, discoveries, and new publications regarding the crime of July 1945. She is happy about this publicity. She participates in the July memorial services in Giby and other celebrations every year. Only in the last few weeks, she has participated in several extraordinary events: the unveiling of a beautiful plaque dedicated to the victims of the Augustów Roundup at Jasna Góra in Częstochowa (May 3, 2014), the consecration of the cross commemorating the insurgents killed in the most significant battle with the Soviet forces that carried out the Roundup in the Augustów Primeval Forest, on Lake Brożane (June 14, 2014), a particularly solemn Mass in the St. John's Arch Cathedral, and a scholarly conference at the Royal Castle in Warsaw immediately following the Mass, with the participation of Polish historians and Nikita Petrov from the Association "Memorial" in Moscow (July 27, 2014).

"Augustów Roundup is still alive—today, even more than before," assures Teresa Staśkiewicz, née Wołąsewicz. This year, she submitted samples of her DNA to the prosecutor from the Institute of National Remembrance in Białystok. "The Roundup lives, especially for my generation, among families who lost their loved ones in the Roundup. There are many of us, and we will not let it be forgotten."

Augustów, March 12, 2014–August 2014

Afterword—
Why Is This Book Needed?

> For human memory ... fades by degrees
> and barely one life can survive:
> but what is written in the books remains
> forever and is not easily destroyed.[1]
>
> —Jan Długosz

Although the opening passage was written over five centuries ago, the chronicler who wrote these words is bonded with contemporary historians by the desire to preserve the past. Even more so when it comes to events that define an identity; even more so when the individual memory stored in the books is one of the few available resources. Such is the case of the Augustów Roundup of July 1945. Therefore, we are grateful to Teresa Kaczorowska, who undertook an incredible reporting task that resulted in this publication.

This book recreates the memory of the Augustów Roundup, a Soviet crime directed at the Polish independence underground movement in today's northeastern Poland—the crime that is still unexplained and not sufficiently present in the historical consciousness of the Polish nation. In July 1945, the military counterintelligence of a foreign country, the Soviet Union, following not the court of law but Stalin's orders, murdered over 1,000 Polish citizens. This crime cries out for the truth because, after 70 years, we have no answer to the most important question: Where are the death pits and the remains of the murdered? We do not know the full list of the fallen; we cannot fulfill our duty, as [a Polish poet] Zbigniew Herbert put it, "call them by their names" and "provide them for the journey."[2] We still owe the victims a proper burial. The memory and the truth about those murdered and the events need to be restored.

We live in Augustów among people who, during the Augustów Roundup, lost their loved ones. It helps us understand how important it is to give them moral gratification, especially considering that for so many years they have had to deal with the stigma of the so-called "bandit families," given to them by the communist authorities. It's high time they were told, "The death of your loved ones has not been in vain, and free Poland appreciates their sacrifice and your suffering." The time has come to listen to the families of the victims of this communist crime.

Teresa Kaczorowska gives the floor to the closest people to those murdered in the Augustów Roundup—daughters, sons, and brothers, even a survivor, an insurgent who managed to escape the July pacification—while skillfully conveying their emotions. At the same time, she enhances their voices with historical background. The seven heroes from seven chapters are linked by the same traumatic experience. Their message allows us to look at this experience through the eyes of a witness to history, with all the advantages and traps brought by such a narration—the most difficult type of historical source.

The advantage of the testimonies of the book's protagonists lies in their individual perspectives. The emotions of the narrator are passed on to the reader. We look at the crime not through dry facts and figures but through the experiences of the relatives who are still coping with this tragedy. We no longer think impersonally about the murdered as mere victims of a crime. We rather think: Konstanty Bućko, Piotr Jagłowski, Zyta Kucharzewska, Władysław Stefanowski, Klemens Świerzbiński, Michał Wołąsewicz, Aniela, Kazimiera, and Ludwik Wysocki—the beloved and the loving, no longer anonymous.

The book's strength lies in closing the gap between the reader and the past, showing complex human stories that the reader can identify with and thus making them easier to understand. The heroes talk about what they remember, what they experienced, and how they construe the events, which makes the message subjective—and rightly so. The author who describes the past through testimonies can do more than a historian; while a subjective presentation of the past by a witness is naturally accepted, for a historian it is not. A historian must treat the chronicling of individual memory as only one of the historical sources, subject to thorough verification. The participants of an event often do not accept a different perspective on the event they witnessed. On the other hand, a historian must learn and analyze various points of view based on the broadest and most diverse data available. Emotional assessment may distort the interpretation of the past; subjectivism, or sometimes bias if you will, the auto-creation, the selective nature of the memorizing process, and the interference of knowledge from other sources are all the traps of spoken history. For these reasons, testimonies are treated by historians as a supplementary source of knowledge; they are appreciated in research in the field of social history, but in the opinion of many, they are the last to consider as a reliable way to establish "facts."[3]

Afterword—Why Is This Book Needed?

Why, then, do we need a book about the Augustów Roundup based on interviews with witnesses of history if it cannot lead to establishing the craved-for facts behind the crime, which, after 70 years, remain unexplained? Is it worth utilizing the testimonies to enhance our knowledge of history?

Our answer is "yes"—not only because those testimonies are appealing to the reader. We are aware of the shortcomings of spoken history. However, in the case of what we know about the Augustów Roundup, human memory has played and still plays not only a complementary role but has also allowed us to establish irrefutable facts. Without access to the Russian archives, much of the current knowledge about this crime is based on information obtained from witnesses and families and, in some cases, confirmed by documents.

For a long time, testimonies provided the primary source for archival research and establishing facts about the goals, scope, course, victims, and perpetrators of the Augustów Roundup. Thanks to those testimonies, we managed to collect and combine information from written documents stored in Polish archives. With time, the records—incomplete and scattered in various archives—about the activities of the Soviet forces and the participation of the Polish terror apparatus in the pacification, as well as the post–Home Army materials, residents' complaints, local administration documents, and testimonies, helped to build a bigger picture, though incomplete, of events in the area covered by the raid.[4]

The Roundup witnesses identified the places where the officers of the Soviet military counterintelligence SMERSH detained and interrogated the detainees in each region. Particularly significant are the testimonies of the people who were detained at the same time and who, at some stage of the interrogation, were released because the Soviets decided they had nothing to do with the Home Army.[5]

Thanks to these reports, we know how the majority of the soldiers and the command of the Citizens' Home Army (AKO) of the Augustów District, together with a guide of the Augustów and Suwałki regions, were able to leave the threatened area, and, as a result, SMERSH could not carry out the complete pacification. The Polish Underground was decimated but not destroyed.

Let us also remember that up to this day, Russians have not released the list of the fallen and murdered in the Augustów Roundup. The existing lists of names, which are still incomplete and require verification, were created according to the data obtained from families and neighbors. The victims' lists were first documented in the 1940s in the communities whose residents were kidnapped and disappeared in the summer of 1945 and were also created at the time by the Polish Underground.[6] The victims' data includes the following: the inquiries addressed by individual families to the authorities and institutions, the lists made by collective effort with the assistance of the Polish Red Cross and the Catholic Church in 1957, and the information gathered in 1987–1992 by members of the Citizens Committee for the Search for the Residents of Suwałki Region Who Went Missing in July 1945.[7] The priceless material in the form of recorded reports, personal questionnaires of the missing, photos, and documents collected by the still-living mothers, fathers, spouses, siblings, children, relatives, and neighbors of the fallen and murdered in the Roundup became the foundation for the prosecution and, since 2001, for the ongoing investigation by the Institute of National Remembrance (IPN). The depositions of over 700 witnesses questioned by prosecutors[8] demonstrate a unique role of human memory in the process of reconstructing knowledge about the Augustów Roundup of July 1945.

This memory must be taken further (i.e., nationwide). We believe that Teresa Kaczorowska's reports will contribute to this. Her literary talent, willingness to use historians' findings, sense of a keen observer, combined with sensitivity and the feel for psychological subtlety allowed the author to create interesting portraits of the witnesses of history and give the stories she listened to an attractive form.

Although the Augustów Roundup perpetrators' intention was to kill the memory of the event, the book by Teresa Kaczorowska, which honors those who preserved this memory, proves that it is still much alive. It gives us hope the story will be commemorated and disseminated. That is why this book is needed so much.

Just as Jan Długosz wrote in his work, which we quoted at the outset, it is essential that the book about the Augustów Roundup also presents the findings based on documents still available after 70 years to create a picture of the events based on data coming from currently available sources. The author took care of the historical background of the witness testimonies but left us the task of synthesizing information about the crime of July 1945. This is worth doing especially because in 2011, our knowledge was greatly expanded thanks to vital documents. Taking them into account, we will undertake the task of providing answers to basic questions about the communist crime of July 1945 and explore the areas that still have considerable gaps to be filled.

What Do We Know, and What Do We Not Know About the Augustów Roundup?

The essential knowledge about the Augustów Roundup is covered by the following three most important publications. The first one is the result of a conference organized by the Institute of National Remembrance in Białystok on the 60th anniversary of the crime.[9] Papers by the institute's employees and by historians not affiliated with the institute still feed the fundamental research on the origin and various aspects of the Augustów Roundup. In 2010, two publications with primary sources were published: *Obława Augustowska—lipiec 1945. Wybór źródeł* ("Augustów Roundup of July 1945: Selection of Sources") (Białystok, 2010) and *Przerwane życiorysy. Obława Augustowska—lipiec 1945* ("Interrupted Biographies: The Augustów Roundup of July 1945") (Białystok, 2010) by Alicja Maciejowska. Each has its distinctive character and carries significant weight.

However, these publications require supplementation and a new analysis, as they appeared before Nikita Petrov's release—in 2011—of two cryptograms by Viktor Abakumov, chief head of the Counterintelligence Board SMERSH, to Lavrenty Beria, People's Commissar of Internal Affairs of the Soviet Union, dated July 21 and 24, 1945. These secret documents reported on the liquidation of the independence underground in the Augustów Primeval Forest and were created by the perpetrators of the crime during its implementation.[10] Along with the document of the Chief Military Prosecutor's Office of the Russian Federation from January 4, 1995, addressed to the Embassy of the Republic of Poland, they constitute the most critical reference point of research conducted by Poles and remain the only compendium of information from the Russian side so far.[11]

The material contained in these three Russian documents complements one another and supplements the existing determination on critical issues, such as establishing the names of the perpetrators, the crime plan to be carried out against the Poles, and the data on the number of detainees, including those arrested by SMERSH and those already recognized as members of Home Army and intended for annihilation on July 21, 1945.

Who Ordered the Augustów Roundup and Why?

Thanks to the documents created by the crime perpetrators at the level of decision-makers and executors, we can name them. These documents are of great legal consequence.

The Augustów Roundup was carried out at the orders of Stalin. The official position of the Russian Chief Military Prosecutor's Office from 1995 states that the General Staff of the Soviet Union Armed Forces, on the recommendation of the commander-in-chief, prepared a "military operation in the Augustów Forest ... to detect and neutralize all formations of the [Home Army], hostile to the Soviet Union." In both cryptograms from July 1945, the term "Home Army" is not used, but "gangs" and "bandits." On July 21, 1945, General Colonel Viktor Abakumov, head of SMERSH, reported to Beria that, according to his instructions, he sent "the deputy head of the Main Board of SMERSH, General Major Ivan Gorgonov with a group of experienced counterintelligence officers to Olecko in order to 'liquidate the bandits arrested in the Augustów Forest.'" He reported to the superior on the progress and outcomes of the pacification in terms of the number of detainees, the results of their selection, and the seized weapons.

Abakumov consulted on implementing the previously agreed-upon plan of the annihilation of Polish citizens, announced further reports, and asked for instructions. He had to do this through cryptograms (they were marked, "Decipher and deliver immediately," which indicates the high importance of the case) because Beria, the head of the NKVD, was at that time at Stalin's side at the Potsdam Conference.

These sources clearly document the planned—top-down and centrally controlled—nature of this Soviet crime. According to Moscow's military doctrine and imperial policy, the NKVD-NKGB and SMERSH leadership coordinated the activities of the NKVD's internal army units with the Red Army in securing and clearing the backs of the front line, combating all actual and alleged "hostile elements." This was also implemented during the Augustów Roundup.

The Main Board of Counterintelligence SMERSH, while carrying out the orders of the highest authorities of the Soviet Union, supervised the activities of direct executors—officers of SMERSH from the Third Belarusian Front commanded by Lieutenant General Pavel Zelenin.

A large-scale operation required the use of the troops returning from East Prussia. The raid was carried out by units of the Red Army that were part of the Third Belarusian Front. The Russian cryptograms mentioned the 50th Army of this front; other sources go further and indicate the 385th Infantry Regiment of the Internal Forces of the NKVD, which was part of the 62nd Internal Armed Forces Division of the NKVD.[12] The Polish Public Security Office documents estimated the forces used during the Roundup at 45,000 Soviet soldiers.[13] In the Suwałki Region, during the 12 days of the raid, until July 25, 160 soldiers of two units from the First Infantry Regiment of the Polish army also participated in the operation.[14]

Field operations were coordinated by Soviet advisers at the Polish Public Security Offices in Suwałki and Augustów. Polish Public Security officers and members of the Citizens' Militia also assisted. Together with the Soviet units or on their own they prepared lists of Home Army members, acted as field guides, and arrested Poles. Secret police officers and agents were also used during the selection process and often ruled on who among the detained would be arrested. Some people detained during the raid and then dismissed stated that the individual who was doing the selection remained unseen. This took place in several places of detention (e.g., in Płaska, Rygol, and Białowierśnie). The heads of the Polish Public Security Office in Augustów and Suwałki complained in their reports to superiors that the Soviets who carried out the Roundup shared little information from the operation.[15] Even if the Polish helpers are looked upon as a mere tool in the hands of the Soviets, they cannot be absolved from responsibility. Yet, they were never held accountable; they never suffered, except those executed by the Polish Underground for their involvement in the raid.

Where Was the Pacification Carried Out?

The troops of the Third Belarusian Front were combing the Augustów Primeval Forest and the adjacent areas of today's Augustów, Sejny, Suwałki, Sokółka counties and the lands of today's Lithuania and Belarus, which were cut off by the postwar border. This pacification is called the Augustów Roundup precisely because its target was the Augustów Primeval Forest complex, which gave shelter to the insurgents. The cryptograms from July 1945 confirm this unambiguously. The geographical scope of the operation within the present Polish borders was well recognized by historians because of the available sources, including reports and preserved material evidence such as the bloodstained cellars and other places of interrogation and detention. On the other hand, we can only speculate on the pacification implementation in the area appropriated after the war by the Soviet Union.

In this respect, the documents found in the Russian archives by Nikita Petrov are crucial—they state that in the Lithuanian Soviet Republic, "the operation of eliminating bandits was also carried out" at the same time. It had to be a large-scale operation because until July 21, only from the Polish side of the Curzon line, 514 "Lithuanians" were handed over to the NKVD-NKGB authorities of the Lithuanian Soviet Republic; 252 of them were already classified as "connected with bandit formations in Lithuania"; others still required verification.

The term "Lithuanians" may also mean Poles who were classified as such by SMERSH because of their residence and insurgence activities on their family land, which, by the decision of the Powers, would become Soviet Lithuania.[16] During that time, many previous Home Army self-defense units from the Vilnius and Novgorod regions passed through the Augustów-Suwałki land, retreating westward. Probably that's why the number of the detained "Lithuanians" was so high. According to the IPN historians, the Lithuanian archives do not provide any material about the July 1945 raid in the Augustów Forest. However, documents from previous and subsequent operations against the insurgents do exist.[17] It should not come as a surprise that Polish archives pose the same problem. At least in Poland, some sources documenting the search for the kidnapped and missing in July 1945 and complaints about rapes and robberies carried out by the Soviets are available. Comparable sources probably could not have existed in the realm of the territories incorporated into the Soviet Union.

The operation of July 1945 differs from earlier and later methods against the underground on both sides of the Curzon line—Poles arrested in the Augustów Roundup were murdered without a trial, and that's why everything was done to make it a perfect crime. Information about the crime was effectively assessed as classified. Hence, there are no sources.

Cryptograms from Abakumov should inspire an intensification of joint Polish-Lithuanian research of the July pacification. After all, those arrested during the military operation in the Augustów Forest and handed over to the Lithuanian NKVD-NKGB authorities because of their association with the Polish Underground operating in the area are also the victims of the Augustów Roundup. Explaining their fate seems to be the most challenging task. There are no lists with their names, nor do we know anything about their families' search efforts. The IPN prosecutors probably cannot include these victims in their investigations for legal reasons, and the Lithuanian government is not expected to claim them; our only hope remains in historical research.

Why Was Such a Powerful Pacification Carried Out Only Two Months After World War II Ended in Europe?

The Augustów Roundup was organized in response firstly to the patriotic sentiments of the local population, who did not accept communist oppression, and secondly, to the intense activity of the Citizens' Home Army, established in the Białystok region in place of the Home Army dissolved in January 1945. Therefore, the pacification had the following two goals, both equally important from the point of view of the interests of the Soviets and the communist authorities appointed by them in Poland: to destroy the underground and to intimidate Poles. In other words, to create certainty about the irreversibility of the imposed order and the hopelessness of the fight for Poland's independence.

After the troops left the Augustów-Suwałki region together with the January 1945 offensive, maintaining control over the area rested with the militia-military formations of the Polish Committee of National Liberation. With limited forces, the communist authorities were on the defensive from the beginning. In Augustów, as early as in March, they were unable to enforce the regulations; in April, due to the subversive actions of the Citizens' Home Army patrol and self-defense units, they lost control over the county. Suwałki County experienced a similar situation. Intense activities of the Citizens' Home Army led to the disintegration of the county administration and security apparatus.[18] The preserved documents, produced on both sides of the barricade, clearly show that the "homegrown" communist authorities would not have survived in the field without the support of the Soviet forces. Their helplessness and requests for help[19] led to the Soviet takeover of the task to eliminate the independence underground movement in Augustów, Suwałki, and neighboring areas.

This goal was also important from the point of view of the immediate needs of the Soviets, who wanted to secure clear communication routes between the occupied lands and the Soviet Union. These routes were used for transporting war loot collected mainly from East Prussia. The attacks of the Citizens' Home Army patrols on these convoys and the efforts to protect the Polish population against robbery and rape by the demoralized Soviet troops made the occupant's life harder. Impunity would not be tolerated.[20]

An official letter from the Russian Prosecutor General's Office justifies the July pacification by "numerous facts of assaults on soldiers of the Soviet Army." During those operations, Red Army officers and privates were killed. However, the reports sent to the Polish and Soviet authorities overestimated the Citizens' Home Army's size and strength.

That is reflected in the two cryptograms from July 1945 by SMERSH. Its management was clearly disappointed by the number of those arrested and the number of the seized weapons. In the cryptogram of July 24, we find that the "Military Council of the 50th Army had non-validated preliminary data that the bands operating in the Augustów forests possessed artillery. ... Sometime before, the Military Council reported this to the command of the Third Belarusian Front." Meanwhile, a thorough verification carried out personally by Gorgonov and Zelenin established: "During the operation in the Augustów Forest, both branches of the Red Army and the SMERSH authorities did not confiscate any artillery weapons."

It is worth linking this information with Marian Tananis's testimony, published by Teresa Kaczorowska in this book, which provides the only report about the spectacular "show" put on by the Citizens' Home Army Sergeant Władysław Stefanowski, alias "Grom." It has not been verified but is interesting in this context. In 1945, on the anniversary of the Constitution of May 3 [1791], he organized a parade near the village of Płaska of about 300 underground soldiers, combined with a display of weapons, some imitating artillery. Marian Tananis talked about this during the on-site inspection of Lake Brożane in the spring of 2013. By comparing these two sources, we can conclude that in Augustów the Russians used such large forces because of the overestimation of the number and weaponry owned by the Polish insurgents.

What Do We Know About the Time and Course of the Augustów Roundup?

It is hard to determine the chronological order of the Augustów Roundup unequivocally. The reports revealed by Nikita Petrov point to July 12–19, 1945, as a timeframe of the stage of the Soviet operation when SMERSH cooperated with the internal troops of the NKVD and the units of the 50th Army of the Third Belarusian Front returning from the front. This period was indeed the peak of the activity in terms of the number of troops deployed, but it seems to be erroneous to place the Augustów Roundup within this time span. We know that there existed a plan for implementing the operation, although we cannot tell when Stalin gave the orders to execute it and when it was carried out. He certainly took into account the preparation phase, which is difficult to pinpoint, though, because starting in May 1945, there was a gradual increase in the number and activity of Soviet forces in the area covered by the July raid. The underground reports at the beginning of June 1945 establish a high concentration of Soviet troops in Sejny, the presence of cannons on the west side of the city, and news from the Russians about the preparation for the Roundup.[21]

In Augustów County, during the last part of May and in June 1945, the troops of NKVD and the Polish Public Security Office, counting several dozen people, became bolder and bolder in carrying out organized raids on the area of a particular municipality or in one or several villages. They conducted inspections and arrests while committing robberies along the way. Russians strengthened their posts and patrols along the forest sections of the Augustów-Grodno highway, so by the end of June, the possibility of maintaining contact among the Citizens' Home Army soldiers on both sides of the road was cut off.[22] Both the Citizens' Home Army and Polish Public Security Office sources indicate that on July 10, 1945, the rapid increase of the Soviet troops took place in Augustów.[23] The next day, in the city and the whole county, a "state of emergency was ordered by the Soviet Union's military authorities." Checkpoints on the exit roads were created, and freedom of movement was restricted.[24]

On July 12, 1945, a military operation in the Augustów Primeval

Forest and adjacent areas began. Its first day brought success to the Soviets. The Red Army soldiers located and pushed Citizens' Home Army insurgents from the unit under the command of Sgt. Władysław Stefanowski, alias "Grom" (Augustów District), and a much smaller unit of the Second Lieutenant Józef Sulżyński, alias "Brzoza," (Suwałki District) to Lake Brożane. On July 12, 1945, surrounded by the outweighing forces of the Red Army, the Polish insurgents fought over Lake Brożane. As a result, the "Grom" unit was disbanded, and only a few soldiers of both units managed to escape the encirclement. One of them recalled: "[Soviets] were constantly being supplied with ammunition while we were not." The majority of the 200 insurgents fell. Documents confirm that 57 soldiers were captured. Władysław Stefanowski, alias "Grom," may have been among them. They were grouped and murdered with other arrested people, victims of the Roundup, in a still unknown place.[25]

In the whole area of the Augustów Primeval Forest, the Red Army surrounded the villages, detained all men, taking them from their homes, fields, workplace, and other random locations "to have their documents checked." The troops kept combing the woods and meadows in a line formation. Witnesses confirmed that the Soviet soldiers from the skirmish front lines sometimes warned the Poles in the area, but the NKVD units, which followed, ruthlessly detained everyone. In some villages, under Soviet order, men were assembled under the pretense of a meeting and then detained. Arrests also resulted from the lists prepared by the informers. These lists included women.

On July 21, 1945, the head of SMERSH reported: "During the operation, the front troops detained the inhabitants of the towns located in the Augustów Forest, including elderly men and women. In total, the units of the Red Army detained 7,049 people. ... Out of the list of detainees arrested during the movement of military units, after checking, 5,115 residents were released ... as there was no data about their participation in the bands."

The Poles detained by the Soviets were then placed in barns, cellars, and pigsties and were subjected to a selection process. During the interrogations, SMERSH officers checked whether the person was on the list for arrest, asked about insurgents and about who helped them. Edward Piekarski, who was detained for over two weeks in a small barn owned by the Szyper family in Krasnybór, recalled: "They herded us here, around 150 men. Cattle would not survive what we went through." Families and neighbors brought food for the detainees, who were interrogated in the house next door.[26] Such was the scenario in almost 90 locations; in some of them, there was more than one place for the detention and selection process.

After the first stage of the selection process, those suspected of being members of or supporting the Home Army were moved to the next place, where interrogations were exceedingly brutal. On-site inspections of the still-existing places designated at that time for the next selection stage allow us to affirm that they were carefully chosen and, according to the reports, well-guarded. On the outskirts of the Sztabin village, in the sturdy buildings owned by the Szyc family, the tortured Poles were thrown on the dew-covered grass for "sobering"; blood and shreds of flesh were lying next to the manure tanks, where some men had been brutally beaten. Written reports describe the brutality of interrogations in Augustów, Jastrzębna Druga, Paniewo, Giby, Sejny, and Suwałki.[27]

Abakumov reported to Beria that, apart from those transferred to the Lithuanian authorities, "the number of arrested on July 21 ... is only 592 people, and the number of detainees who are being checked is 828 people." According to the document, their selection should have ended within five days, on July 26.

This date does not mark the end of the Augustów Roundup as various sources document that the detentions were carried out by the SMERSH officers until July 28, 1945.[28]

This last stage of the Augustów Roundup (after the preparation phase followed by mass detentions by the Red Army troops) consisted of arrests that were no longer "blind" as in the case of the military operation carried out from July 12–19 which included people who were involved in the Polish Underground, identified by traitors or selected according to forced confessions of the previously detained people.

The roundups of those underground members who managed to survive the July detentions continued in August and subsequent months by the Polish Public Security officers, sometimes also with the participation of Soviet forces stationed there until the end of September.[29] They should be treated as a continuation of the ruthless attack against the independence movement. Still, these were no longer detentions carried out and coordinated by SMERSH in the Augustów Roundup. We define them as a specific Soviet operation carried out under Stalin's orders according to a plan prepared by the General Staff of the Red Army, under the supervision of the head of the NKVD to eliminate the underground independence sheltered by the Augustów Forest and supported by local residents. It was preceded by earlier preparations but carried out in July 1945.

What Was the Fate of the Arrested in the Augustów Roundup?

The only available source to give us an idea about the fate of the arrested in July 1945 is the plan of the crime presented by Viktor

Afterword—Why Is This Book Needed?

Abakumov. In his cryptogram dated July 21, 1945, the head of SMERSH wrote to Beria:

> If you consider it necessary to carry out the operation at this state of affairs, we want to carry out the liquidation of the bandits in the following way:
>
> 1. All identified bandits, numbering 592 people—liquidate. For this purpose, an operational team and a battalion of the SMERSH Board troops of the Third Belarusian Front—already tested out during many counterintelligence activities—will be assigned the task. The operational and battalion personnel will be thoroughly instructed on the liquidation methods against the bandits.
> 2. During the operation, the necessary steps will be taken to prevent any attempts of escape
> 3. by the bandits.... The forest areas where the operation will be carried out will be surrounded by cordons and thoroughly searched before it begins.
> 4. Responsibility for carrying out the liquidation of bandits will be imposed on the deputy head of the General Board of SMERSH, Major General Gorgonov, and the head of the Counterintelligence Board of the Third Belorussian Front, General Lieutenant Zelenin.
>
> Comrades Gorgonov and Zelenin are good and experienced chekists[30] and will carry out this job. The other 828 detained will be checked within five days, and all exposed bandits will be liquidated in the same way. We will report on the number of bandits selected from this group of detainees. Awaiting your orders.

The quoted passage proves that besides the reports to Beria dated July 21 and July 24, there existed another report that clarified the number of the "exposed bandits." Most likely, Abakumov received orders he asked for, but these documents are not available. The cryptogram dated July 21, 1945, contains the crime plan, not a report on its implementation. However, since the detainees meant to be shot were lost without a trace, the rational analysis of the facts 70 years later leads to the conclusion that the plan was indeed carried out. According to the quoted statement from the head of SMERSH, "Comrades Gorgonov and Zelenin are good and experienced chekists and will carry out this job."

Indeed, the effective implementation of the crime plan, which Abakumov presented in the cryptogram dated July 21, 1945, can explain the lack of knowledge regarding the place or places of murder and the location of death pits. The area was carefully selected, checked, combed, and surrounded so that none of the victims could escape and become a source of information. The implementation of the Augustów Roundup was perfect in comparison to the crime committed in Katyń. The discovery of the Katyń death pits by

Germans was a lesson for the Soviets to hide the victims' bodies in the land controlled by the Soviet Union. This leads us to a conclusion that the victims of the Augustów Roundup were taken outside of Poland, beyond the nearby eastern border, perhaps to the territory of present Belarus. Nikita Petrov found the two July reports from Abakumov to Beria regarding the Augustów Roundup in a folder marked "Operation in the Belarusian Soviet Republic."[31]

In the uncovered documents, the place of the murder is not disclosed. An indication that it was to happen in a forest exists only in the crime plan. The fact that a special envoy responsible for implementing the crime landed in Olecko does not in any way help identify the location of the execution. Olecko, in our opinion, could only have been chosen due to security reasons. We have already mentioned the Soviet exaggerated estimation of the number of Polish insurgents and their weaponry. Perhaps during the pacification, the SMERSH Deputy Head, Gorgonov, preferred to land in the territory recently taken away from the Germans, outside the area of intense underground activity, where he did not have to fear the enemy artillery? From Olecko, it was easy to be safely escorted to one or several main operation control points in the Augustów Forest.

Russia never confessed to the murder of the Poles captured during the Augustów Roundup. In a letter from 1995, the General Prosecutor's Office of the Russian Federation confirmed that 592 Polish citizens were arrested during that time but that their further fate was unknown. The Federal Security Service archives hold the files of the 575 persons detained during the pacification, whose purpose, as acknowledged by the Russian prosecutor's office, was to "neutralize" the Home Army. However, they do not include any information about indictment; no criminal cases have been referred to a court.

After 70 years, the conclusion can be only this: the arrested in the Augustów Roundup were probably eliminated following the scenario outlined in the SMERSH boss's cryptogram.

The military counterintelligence of a foreign state—the Soviet Union—murdered a group of Poles without a court order for being members or supporting the Home Army and the Citizens' Home Army. This act qualifies as a crime against humanity, which is not subject to the statute of limitations.

Questions with No Answers—What Don't We Still Know After 70 years?

We do not know the complete list of the Augustów Roundup victims, nor the time, place (or places) where they were executed, nor the location of the death pits.

From Abakumov's words we can conclude that those among the 828 detainees considered by SMERSH (according to their analysis after July 21, 1945) as having links to the Home Army were murdered by the same method as described in the crime plan sent to Beria. However, we do not know whether they were executed together with those uncovered by July 21 or those arrested after this date.

Were the Home Army soldiers arrested in the second and third week of July in the Kamienna Nowa, Sztabin, Augustów, Giby, and Suwałki vicinity murdered at the same time and place? After all, the many recesses of the Augustów Forest made it possible to create a cordon and set up a site for carrying out the crime.

Did the Soviets arrange their death pit at the same place as that intended for the insurgents who fell in the battle at Lake Brożane? Let's remember that the bodies of the fallen were transported from the location of the battle several days before the probable date of the annihilation of the arrested.

According to some reports, people were killed during escape attempts—while detained or escorted—or during brutal interrogations. Where are their bodies? We do not have the answers to these questions.

We must also humbly admit our lack of knowledge about the number of the fallen and murdered in the Augustów Roundup. The reports released in 2011 make it possible to state with certainty that, as a result of the operation carried out in the Augustów Forest, many more people died than the number of 600 that had been assumed so far, but how many more?

On July 21, 1945, alone, 592 Poles and 252 people recognized as Lithuanians were to be killed, and 1,049 detained Poles and "Lithuanians"[32] were still supposed to be checked. Besides, the arrests directed by SMERSH lasted at least until July 28, 1945, and the figures significantly increased by the number of people pronounced by SMERSH to be involved in the insurgency.

Those killed during the Roundup itself must be added to the number of those arrested—the majority of about 200 insurgents from the units under the command of Sgt. Władysław Stefanowski, alias "Grom," and the Second Lieutenant Józef Sulżyński, alias "Birch." We do not know the number of the Citizens' Home Army soldiers killed in other fights and during detention or escorting. We know that Sgt. Wacław Sobolewski, alias "Sęk"—an experienced commander of the Citizens' Home Army branch of the Augustów District—died in Osowa Góra while being escorted.[33]

We would like to point out that in the writings on the subject, the weight of the loss in the struggle with the Soviet forces is underestimated. This is clearly demonstrated by the fact that the name of Władysław Stefanowski, alias "Grom," the commander of the largest active Citizens'

Home Army division in Augustów and Suwałki is not on any list of the victims. However, there is no doubt that he died as a result of the raid.

This must be corrected, and the understanding of the Augustów Roundup, which should be viewed as a communist crime, needs to be re-evaluated. Insurgents—members of the Home Army and Citizens' Home Army—fighting with Germans and Soviets for a free Poland were the main target of the crime. In the narrative about the Soviet pacification, those who died fighting the Soviets in July 1945 cannot be omitted.

After 70 years, we still do not have access to sources that would enable us to determine how many victims the Augustów Roundup consumed—how many fell and how many were murdered. Thanks to cryptograms dated July 1945, we can say with certainty that there were far more than 600 of them.

The Aftermath of the Augustów Roundup of July 1945

The July pacification was undoubtedly a demonstration of strength and lawlessness. However, were the goals set by the Soviets achieved? The answer to this question is not clear-cut.

The severity and unpredictability of what SMERSH carried out well served the implementation of the nonmilitary aim of pacification (i.e., terrorizing the local population). In July 1945, 15-year-old boys, 70-year-old men, and women, including those expecting a child, were arrested. "The Kunda from Jaminy could not be found, so they took Edward Kunda from Jaziew." Then, the 16-year-old Stanisław Cieślukowski was taken instead of his father, Stanisław, who stayed in hiding. Why was Romek Różański, just short of being 15, arrested in Mikaszówka, although the whole village signed a petition that he was not part of the insurgency?

A significant percentage of the murdered were people not linked to the Polish Underground, which strengthened the belief in the new authorities' omnipotence and impunity and the hopelessness of resistance and support for the independence insurgency.

Thanks to the Roundup, the Communist Party as well as administrative and security structures could rebuild, strengthen, and survive.

In the history of the independence insurgency on the Augustów-Suwałki land, the Roundup of July 1945 constitutes a distinctive disruption. The Citizens' Home Army underground structures were smashed; tracking down the surviving members became easier, but the underground was not destroyed. Those who sought shelter in the forest against the terror of the strengthening power, from autumn 1945 to April 1947, got organized within the "Freedom and Independence" Association. The armed resistance against the communists was not broken in July 1945; it remained in the Augustów Forest until the autumn of 1954.

The Roundup created a mental gap between the majority of the population and the imposed power. It was not only the killed and murdered who became its victims. It was also their families. Difficult living conditions deepened the drama of the loss of loved ones. Families remained without fathers and adult men, who were often the only providers for their families.

For many years, the wives did not know whether they were widows or their children orphans. Unresolved legal problems, including property issues, were growing. That led, in the 1950s, to civil court hearings, in which the courts assigned completely different dates of deaths. The real ones remain unknown. The Russian side never confessed to the crime and never revealed its time or place to the families.

The Soviet crime of July 1945 is a particular case in many dimensions; it holds a special place in both the individual and collective memories. This powerful pacification that was carried out when peace had been already declared—two months after the end of World War II in Europe—would have been, for a free society, a turning point for shaping the memory and identity of the inhabitants of the region. For political reasons, this did not happen—in postwar Poland, the Augustów Roundup, like Katyń, was taboo.

There was no natural, intergenerational transfer of memory. Even many families of the Roundup victims did not want to burden the next generations with the past and make their lives more difficult. But what could not be said could not be forgotten, and the memory of the events, though not shared, somehow survived.

This crime is still calling for explanation. It will require action not only by historians and prosecutors. To establish a full list of the victims and find their death pits, the authority of the Polish state must support the efforts of the families, social workers, and the Institute of National Remembrance. Without such pressure, the Russians will not reveal the truth. We must demand it regardless of the status of the Polish-Russian relations. The normalization of these relations can be achieved only by establishing the truth.

Every crime should be accounted for; it cannot go unpunished—this is the foundation of the moral order. An undisclosed crime disturbs the sense of justice; it emboldens the criminals because no punishment means no warning for the future.

We must keep demanding an explanation of the Augustów Roundup of July 1945.

—*Danuta Kaszlej and Zbigniew Kaszlej*

Danuta Kaszlej and **Zbigniew Kaszlej** are Polish historians whose research focuses on the anti-communist resurgence in the Augustów and Suwałki area, especially the Augustów Roundup of July 1945. They have published numerous books and papers on the topic and have presented the results of their research at several conferences. They also organize popular science projects addressed to the youth, educational rallies, and commemorative events. In 2006, they co-founded and now serve as president and vice president of the Home Army Historical Club in Augustów, whose goal is to promote a better understanding of the history of the region. They are both graduates of the History Institute at the University of Warsaw, Poland.

Afterword—
The Augustów Roundup
Crime with No Statute of Limitations

More than 70 years have passed since the sweeping criminal act of the Augustów Roundup was carried out over the territory of two counties: Augustów and Suwałki. The forces of the 50th Army of the Third Belarusian Front were sent to comb the grounds. The responsibility for the selection of those who were later executed without trial lies with the Counterintelligence Board of SMERSH of the Third Belorussian Front. The crime was kept secret for a long time.

The circumstances surrounding this crime began to be clarified quite recently when more and more facts confirmed that the order to conduct the Roundup in the Augustów forests and the decision to secretly murder the detainees came from Stalin himself.[1] In the early 1990s, the Office of the Chief Military Prosecutor of Russia collected materials and conducted its own investigation into this Stalinist crime but, unfortunately, decided not to announce the truth. In the official reply, given to Poland in January 1995, the Office of Chief Military Prosecutor shamefully kept quiet about the murder of the detainees without any trial during the Roundup. However, it did confirm the fact that the SMERSH counterintelligence authorities arrested 592 Polish citizens. To this day, Russian leaders have officially refused to assume responsibility for the murders and have not classified the Augustów Roundup as a crime. There was no dependable investigation with clear and apparent answers where the arrested Poles disappeared. It was decided that silence would cover this crime. The Polish side and families of the Augustów Roundup victims have never received complete lists of those who "disappeared" nor were they given any information about the execution place.

Our current knowledge of what happened to those arrested after the Roundup is random and incomplete. The Poles chosen by the officers of SMERSH for execution were gathered in a temporary camp in Giby at the end of July 1945. Within a few days, they were deported from there to the place of execution. There are reasons to presume that the sites of the execution and the secret burial of the Roundup victims were located in Soviet territory, in the area of Kalety village (in the Grodno region, bordering with Poland)—the shortest route from Giby to Kalety. The fact that the execution took place in Soviet territory is confirmed indirectly by the wording of the heading in the internal description of archival files in which Wiktor Abakumov's two cryptograms to Lavrenty Beria from July 21 and 24, 1945, are stored. The heading reads, "On Operations in the Belarusian Soviet Republic." The files describe the consequences of the Roundup and a plan to secretly murder some of the detainees.[2]

The precise total number of Polish citizens secretly murdered during the August Roundup has not been determined so far. In the archives of the Russian Federal Security Service (FSS) in Moscow, there are only 575 records of Polish citizens who were arrested in July 1945. However, Abakumov's cryptogram from July 21, 1945, lists about 592 arrested. The arrests were also continued later. The names of detainees who were secretly murdered on July 27, 1945, together with victims of an earlier raid, are unknown. One can say this with certainty because their files have been preserved in the archives of the Russian Federal Security Service, and they were the source of information given to the relatives.[3] Each of these 575 files stored in the FSS archives is small and contains only a few documents. All of them, dated July 1945, include decisions (or records) of detention, searches, and inquiries by the SMERSH authorities about the association of the arrested with the Home Army. Some of them also contain transcripts of the interrogations. There are no clues in these files to what happened to the arrested afterwards or to any decisions (whether conviction or release). Each of these preserved 575 files seems to be abruptly broken off, leaving the question of what happened to those arrested unanswered. The fact that these files lack any indication of the fate of the victims confirms the unique nature of these 575 cases. While making preparations for the crime, the officers of SMERSH of the Third Belorussian Front preferred not to leave any traces in the files of the arrested, which is an obvious sign that each arrested person was among the victims executed during the Augustów Roundup.

The discrepancy in the number of victims of the Augustów Roundup in various documents—592 designated to be murdered, according to Abakumov's cryptogram to Beria on July 21, 1945, and only 575 files preserved in the FSS archives—can be explained in two ways. Either not all of the files of the murdered were received or preserved by the FSS archives, or some of the 592 people who were originally supposed to be executed never were. Their cases may have been taken over by the SMERSH war surveillance organs or passed on for consideration and decision to other public security authorities (for example, those of the People's Republic of Poland). In this case, even if we take into account the arrests carried out after July 21, 1945, the total number of secretly murdered actually amounts to 575 people. The exact answer to this question can only be given by examining the files of the victims of the Augustów Roundup kept in the FSS archives.

Currently, Russia's position on the Augustów Roundup is to deny even the facts that had been officially recognized earlier. In 2012, when the Association "Memorial" in Moscow initiated the rehabilitation of part of Polish citizens detained during the Augustów Roundup, the Office of the Chief Military Prosecutor responded with a firm refusal, citing that they did not have their investigation files. Not only that—in the course of the court trial, the Office of the Chief Military Prosecutor began to claim that earlier, in 1995, Poland was "mistakenly informed about the existence of criminal cases of Polish citizens," and these 575 cases, which are kept in the FSS archives, are not criminal or administrative. They are named "archival matters with separate materials on the detention of Polish citizens." This proves that by playing with the terms, the Office of the Chief Military Prosecutor is evading the issue of rehabilitation. In 2012, the Moscow City Court declined to grant the rehabilitation of the victims of the August Roundup to the Association "Memorial" in Moscow.

In June 2013, the Office of the General Prosecutor of Russia officially notified the Office of the General Prosecutor of Poland about its refusal to meet specific requirements and provide legal assistance as part of the Polish investigation into the August Roundup and the murder of Polish citizens.[4]

This was nothing unusual. Now, more and more often, one can hear at the Russian official level about belittling Stalinist crimes or even denying them. In today's Russia, all state propaganda efforts are directed at promoting xenophobia, maintaining imperial sentiments, and aggressively rejecting the idea of freedom and democracy. Much of the archival documentation about the crimes of the communist regime still remains hidden from the eyes of historians and is unavailable to research. Under such circumstances, it is increasingly difficult for Russian historians to talk openly about crimes committed by the Soviet state.

I hope that the Association for the Memory of the 1945 Augustów Roundup Victims, headed by an extraordinary man, a real fighter, Father Stanisław Wysocki, employees of the High School No. 2 in Augustów, Wojciech Walulik, historians Danuta and Zbigniew Kaszlej, the employees of the Institute of National Remembrance in Białystok, a great historian, Jerzy Milewski, and many, many others who have done so much to commemorate the memory of the fallen in July 1945 will continue their enormous work in order to explain all the circumstances of the Augustów Roundup. I hope that by joint forces, they will put this crime at the center of attention of the Polish society. The memory of the victims compels us to do that.

—<i>Nikita Pietrov</i>
The Association "Memorial" in Moscow
Based on the translation from the Russian

Nikita Vasilyevich Petrov, PhD (b. 1957), is a Russian historian, human rights activist, and deputy chairman of the Association "Memorial" in Moscow, which investigates Soviet political repression and crimes. Petrov earned his PhD from the Faculty of Humanities at the University of Amsterdam, the Netherlands, in 2008. His research focuses on the security apparatus of the Soviet Union. Dr. Petrov has written extensively on matters concerning Poland, including the NKVD operations in its territory, the falsification of the referendum and elections in 1946–1947, the perpetrators of the 1940 Katyń massacre, and the Augustów Roundup of 1945. In 2005, Nikita Petrov was awarded the Knight's Cross of the Order of Merit of the Republic of Poland for his efforts into uncovering the truth about repressions against Polish people by the Soviet apparatus.

Notes

From the Author

1. Teresa Kaczorowska, *Zapalę ognie pamięci*, MON, Warsaw, Poland, 2005; *Children of the Katyń Massacre*, McFarland, 2006. Also published as an e-book, McFarland, 2010.
2. As of 2018, he was no longer holding this post.

Marian Tananis (Sejny)

1. Augustów Primeval Forest is a large virgin forest complex known for its rich flora and fauna, stretching over Poland, Lithuania, and Belarus, covering approximately 400,000 acres, 70 percent of which, including the Wigry National Park, lies within the current Polish borders. In the mid-16th century, it became part of the Polish royal estates and hunting grounds for big game: aurochs, bison, elk, deer, wild boars, bears, and wolves. At that time, the exploitation of the forest also started: Trees were cut, and timber was rafted down the local rivers to the Baltic ports; tar, potash, wood tar, and charcoal were made; iron was smelted from bog iron; honey was collected from beehives. The southern edge of the forest became the place of settlement for the guards of the royal forest, the so-called *osocznicy*. They were mostly landless serfs relieved of their obligations towards their master, and their guarding post was passed from father to son. They served until the partitions of Poland (1772–1795). During the January Uprising of 1863, the wilderness created a shelter for the insurgents and was a place of the skirmishes. During World War I, the Augustów Primeval Forest suffered greatly because of the wasteful German logging policy of deforestation (approx. 15 percent of the forest was cut down). During World War II, the Augustów Primeval Forest once again served as a shelter for insurgents. It was also an execution site of the local population.

2. Józef Klemens Piłsudski (1867–1935) was an influential political and military leader of Poland during the inter-war period and a member of the Polish Socialist Party.

3. Danuta Helena Siedzikówna (1928–1946), alias "Inka," was a member of the Home Army, who, at the age of 17, was sentenced to death and executed by the communist authorities.

4. Zygmunt Szendzielarz (1910–1951), alias "Lupaszka," was the Home Army commander executed in the notorious Mokotów prison, along with other anti-communist soldiers, following the Soviet takeover of Poland at the end of World War II.

5. Ignacy Mościcki (1867–1946) was a Polish chemist, scholar, inventor, and politician, author of an innovative method of obtaining nitric acid from the air, founder of the Polish chemical industry, professor at Lviv Polytechnic and Warsaw Polytechnic, President of Poland (1926–1939), first associated with the socialist movement and later with the Sanation camp of Józef Piłsudski. After the outbreak of World War II, he found himself in Romania, where he was interned. On September 30, 1939, he resigned from the presidency. From December 1939 until his death, he resided in Switzerland. Mościcki's remains were brought to Poland in 1993 and buried

in the Cathedral of St. John the Baptist in Warsaw.

6. Hermann Wilhelm Goering (1893–1946) was a German Nazi leader, one of the founders of the Nazi Third Reich, fighter pilot ace of World War I, and during World War II, commander of Luftwaffe (German Air Force). After World War II, he was proclaimed a war criminal, and, during the Nuremberg trials, sentenced to death, but he committed suicide the night before the execution.

7. Witold Pilecki (1901–1948) was an officer of the Polish army and, during World War II, a member of the Home Army and author of the first comprehensive intelligence report on the German concentration camp in Auschwitz. During World War II, he volunteered for the Polish Underground operation that involved being imprisoned in the Auschwitz concentration camp in order to gather intelligence. He escaped in 1943 after nearly three years of imprisonment. He then took part in the Warsaw Uprising of 1944. After the Communist takeover of Poland, he was arrested for espionage in 1947 on charges of working for "foreign imperialism." He was executed after a show trial in 1948.

8. NKVD (People's Commissariat for Internal Affairs) was a central body of the Soviet Union's government which existed under this name between 1917 and 1946. Initially, the NKVD dealt with administrative matters placed on the agenda. After 1934, its role increased, especially during the Great Purge of 1936–1939, when the NKVD took over the entire apparatus of Soviet police repression. It was in charge of criminal investigation as well as intelligence and counter-intelligence, border protection, ad hoc administrative courts, the system of forced labor (the so-called Gulag), and concentration camps. The NKVD also oversaw local governments. In 1946, it was renamed the Ministry of Internal Affairs of the USSR. The name "NKVD" became synonymous with the crimes committed by the Soviets and massive repressions against its own citizens and people outside of the former Soviet Union as well as the mass deportations of various nationalities, including Poles. The NKVD was responsible for the Katyń massacre (the murder of Polish army officers in 1940) as well as the executions of Poles after the war and their imprisonment in the former German concentration camps, such as Majdanek, Auschwitz, Działdowo, Trzebuska and others. Between 1938–1941, the NKVD worked closely with the German Gestapo on liquidating the Polish Underground forces and political opposition in the territories occupied by the Soviet Union and the Third Reich.

9. At that time, the Home Army formally no longer existed. After its dissolution on January 19, 1945 (under the order issued by Gen. Leopold Okulicki), the commander of the Białystok District of the Home Army kept its organizational structure and renamed it Citizens' Home Army (AKO).

10. Sgt. Władyslaw Stefanowski, alias "Grom" ("Thunder") (b. 1914), was a member of the Home Army and AKO, the commander of the insurgent unit of AKO Augustów District. It is assumed he died on July 12, 1945, near Lake Brożane in a battle with Soviet troops during which his unit was destroyed. (According to estimates, approx. 75 insurgents were killed.)

11. Lt. Joseph Sulżyński, alias "Brzoza," was the commander of an insurgent unit in the Suwałki District of AKO. It is not entirely clear whether he fought the Soviets in the decisive battle on Lake Brożane. (According to Marian Tananis, he didn't fight a minute because he collaborated with the NKVD and the UB (Polish secret police)). He survived the Augustów Roundup and came forward in September 1945. The Home Army issued a death sentence against him, but it was never carried out, and, after the war, he lived a comfortable life. UB documents confirm he was under surveillance until 1956. He died in Warsaw in November 1995.

12. The Partitions of Poland were the progressive territorial seizures and annexations of the Polish-Lithuanian Commonwealth that took place at the end of the 18th century. The process ended the existence of the state and resulted in the elimination of sovereign Poland and Lithuania for 123 years. The partitions were conducted by Habsburg Austria, the Kingdom of Prussia, and the Russian Empire, which divided up the Commonwealth lands among themselves.

13. Cursed soldiers (Polish: *żołnierze wyklęci*) is a term applied to members of various Polish anti-Soviet or anti-communist military groups (ranging in size from 150,000 to 200,000) that formed in the later stages of World War II. Their clandestine operations included military attacks against the prisons of the communist regime, state security offices, and detention facilities for political prisoners. Most of these groups ceased to exist in the late 1940s or 1950s, as they were hunted down by agents of the Ministry of Public Security and Soviet NKVD assassination squads.

14. Lavrentiy Pavlovich Beria (1899–1953) was a Soviet politician and administrator and the head of the NKVD, to a large extent responsible for the Great Purge. He was one of the chief perpetrators of Stalinist crimes and considered one of the biggest criminals in the history of Europe. He was directly responsible for the massacre of Polish officers in Katyń. The peak of his influence fell in the period of World War II and immediately after it. Following Stalin's death, he was removed from office and executed by his successors in 1953.

15. UB (Urząd Bezpieczeństwa) were Polish secret police, operating in 1946–1956.

16. The historian Danuta Kaszlej gives a different reason for the death sentence on "Brzoza," quoting an insurgent from his unit, Bolesław Rogalewski, alias "Sosenka," who fought on Lake Brożane. He claims that Sulżyński was not convicted of treason but for turning himself in to the communist regime in September 1945, against the orders of the Home Army commanders.

17. Jan Szostak (1917–1986) was an officer of the security apparatus in the Polish People's Republic, the head of the Security Office in Augustów, chairman of the city council, and a folk sculptor. He participated in the September 1939 defense campaign, but, according to his personnel file, he started collaborating with the NKVD as early as 1940 under the code name of "Wrona" ("Crow"). According to his own account, he handed over more than a dozen people and weapons to the Soviet intelligence. He worked as a liaison, squad leader, and platoon commander for the Home Army, under the alias "Kruk" ("Raven"), until the Soviets came. He became known for his exceptional cruelty and for beating people to death. After leaving the security apparatus, he became a member of the city council in Augustów and its chairman. After he lost the reelection in December 1952, he said: "When it was needed to hang people, shoot them and drown them in pit latrines, nobody was available. And now, nobody takes my merits into account." In the last years of his life, he was known as a folk sculptor. He created religious sculptures, and his house was visited by groups of school students. Szostak rarely left his house, fearing the revenge of his victims or their families. After his death, an obituary with the following wording could be seen around the city: "We are happy to announce that the biggest executioner of Augustów has died." His grave has been repeatedly desecrated.

18. The October Thaw of 1956 (also known as the Polish October or October '56) was a shift in the internal policy in the People's Republic of Poland in the second half of 1956, combined with a change of leadership and the liberalization of the political system. It prompted, among other things, the release of some political prisoners and clergy, including the distinguished Cardinal Stefan Wyszyński, from prison and internments. The October Thaw resulted from several events, including Stalin's death (March 1953) and changes in the Soviet Union which followed, such as the disclosure of a secret speech Khrushchev delivered on February 25, 1956, at the 20th Congress of the Communist Party of the Soviet Union, as well as the mysterious death of the Polish leader Bolesław Bierut in Moscow (March 1956), the political protest in Poznań (June 1956), the split in the ruling party, and coming to power of the new communist government led by Władysław Gomułka.

19. Wojciech Jaruzelski (1923–2014) was a military officer and politician in the People's Republic of Poland who held many top political posts, including prime minister (1981–1985), first secretary of the Polish United Workers' Party (1981–1989), president (1989–1990), and commander-in-chief of the Polish People's Army. He resigned after the Polish Round Table Agreement in 1989, which marks the end of Communism in Poland. Jaruzelski

was a controversial figure, especially for his role in the declaration of martial law on December 13, 1981.

20. The clandestine operation Żelazo ("Iron") was ordered by the Polish Internal Ministry in the 1970s to infiltrate criminal groups by the Polish intelligence. The goal of the operation was to use the illegally acquired valuables (including money, gold, works of fine arts, and cars) for financing Polish secret police. Some of these items ended up in the possession of top leaders of the Communist Party or were being offered for sale at a secret store or given to the Ministry personnel as a bonus. As a result of this operation, two people died.

21. Jerzy Popiełuszko (1947–1984) was a Polish Roman Catholic priest associated with Solidarity, the first trade union independent of the communist rule in Poland. He was a vocal anti-communist and, in his sermons, often preached against the regime. He was murdered in 1984 by three secret police agents, who were soon after tried and convicted of the murder. Recognized as a martyr by the Roman Catholic Church, he was beatified in 2010.

22. Sgt. Wacław Sobolewski, alias "Sęk" ("Gnarl") or "Skała" ("Rock"), was a commander of the Citizens' Home Army unit that operated in Lipsk and Sztabin. During the Roundup, he transferred his men to the command of Sgt. Władysław Stefanowski and went into hiding. He was eventually arrested and shot by the Soviets.

23. First Infantry Regiment of the Praga District in Warsaw was created by a Soviet decree as a unit of the newly forming Polish People's Army, on May 14, 1943.

24. Danuta Kaszlej indicates that after the disclosure of some decoded cryptograms by Nikita Petrov, this number is no longer valid. It is believed that the Roundup wiped out definitely more than 1,000 victims, although exactly how many remains unknown. Prof. Krzysztof Jasiewicz estimates that 2,000 Poles were murdered, and the president of the Association for the Memory of the 1945 Augustów Roundup Victims, Monsignor Stanislaw Wysocki, believes that there were at least 2,000 victims of this operation.

25. SMERSH was a counterintelligence organization created in 1943 with the primary purpose of subverting German infiltration to the Red Army. The name was coined by Josef Stalin from a Russian phrase meaning "Death to Spies." It existed until 1946.

26. Viktor Semyonovich Abakumov (1908–1954) was a general of the Soviet security apparatus of Armenian background (his real name was Aba Kum), an officer of intelligence, counterintelligence, and internal security head of a military counterintelligence organization, SMERSH, and, from 1946–1951, minister of national security of the Soviet Union. He is considered one of the greatest criminals of Stalin's era—he was notorious for brutally torturing the detainees to extort confessions. During the political purge, the so-called Leningrad Affair, he was convicted of mismanagement and executed.

27. Ivan Ivanovich Gorgonov (1903–1994) was an officer of the NKVD and SMERSH and a general of the Red Army. He participated in the Augustów Roundup of 1945. In 1946–1951, he was head of the Directorate of the Ministry of State Security (UMGB) for the Moscow region. In 1952, he graduated from the Pedagogical Institute in Moscow, after taking evening classes. He was stripped of his rank in 1954 for "disgraceful acts unworthy of the high rank of a general while working in the organs of state security," and, in 1955, was removed from the Communist Party of the Soviet Union for "violation of the Soviet rule of law."

28. Pavel Vasilevich Zelenin (1902–1965) was an officer of the NKVD and SMERSH and a general of the Red Army. In 1945, he participated in the Augustów Roundup. In 1947–1948, he worked at the Office of Personnel in the Ministry of State Security (MGB) of the Soviet Union. In 1951, he was arrested for "subversive activity in the MGB" and sentenced to compulsory treatment in solitary confinement. He was released under amnesty in 1954 but was stripped of the rank of general for "disgraceful acts unworthy of the high rank of general while working in the organs of state security."

29. Nikita Vasilyevich Petrov, PhD, is a Russian historian, human rights activist, and deputy chairman of the Association "Memorial" in Moscow, which investigates

Soviet political repression and crimes. His research focuses on the security apparatus of the Soviet Union, which is the subject of his several books and numerous papers he has presented at international conferences. Dr. Petrov has written extensively on matters concerning Poland, including the NKVD operations in its territory, the falsification of the referendum and elections in 1946–1947, and the perpetrators of the Katyń massacre. In 2011, he published a previously unknown Russian document on the Augustów Roundup of 1945 that launched the investigation into the crime by the Polish Institute of National Remembrance.

30. The monument was erected during the writing of this book, at a ceremony that was held on June 14, 2014, with wide participation of local citizens, authorities, and institutions. A nine-meter-high cross, dedicated to the soldiers of Augustów and the Suwałki district of the Home Army and the Citizens' Home Army, was raised on Lake Brożane, where the battle took place.

31. Recovered Territories (Polish: *Ziemie Odzyskane*) was an official term used by the People's Republic of Poland for the former Free City of Danzig and the regions of pre-war Germany that became part of Poland after World War II. The underlying principle was that these territories always belonged to the Polish state but were lost in different periods over the centuries.

32. Based on the information on the website of the Home Army Historical Club in Augustów (www.akklub.pl.).

33. Wronki Prison (Zakład Karny Wronki) is Poland's largest, notoriously overcrowded prison, holding approximately 1400 male prisoners. During the German occupation of Poland in 1939–1945, it served as a prison for Polish political prisoners who were terribly mistreated. 804 of the 20,000 imprisoned at that time died. After the war, the prison was governed by the Ministry for Public Security and again used for political prisoners, mainly former Home Army soldiers. Out of about 15,000 imprisoned during 1945–1955, 250 died due to harsh conditions, mistreatment, and overcrowding.

34. At that time, this equaled approximately $4,000.

35. Cheka is a common name for the All-Russian Extraordinary Commission (established in 1917)—the first of a succession of Soviet secret police organizations. KGB (Committee for State Security) was the Soviet Union's primary security agency in charge of internal security and foreign, military, and industrial intelligence and counter-intelligence. It also served as the secret police overseeing the political invigilation of Soviet citizens, combatting real and potential opposition, and crushing independent press. It grew out of NKVD (see note 8) and existed from 1954 to 1991. After the fall of the Soviet Union, it was officially dissolved and succeeded in Russia by the Foreign Intelligence Service (SVR) and what would later become the Federal Security Service (FSB).

36. The Potsdam Conference, which took place on July 17, 1945–August 2, 1945, in Potsdam, Germany, was a meeting of the leaders of the anti-Hitler coalition, the so-called Big Three: U.S. President Harry Truman, British Prime Minister Winston Churchill (replaced on July 28 by the new Prime Minister Clement Attlee), and Soviet Union's Communist Party General Secretary Joseph Stalin. It followed two other conferences of the Big Three—the Teheran Conference (November 28–December 1, 1943) and the Yalta Conference (February 4–11, 1945). Their objective was to determine the fate of Germany after World War II, the development of peace treaties, and the establishment of the postwar order.

37. Natalia Sergeevna Lebedeva, PhD (b. 1939) is a Russian historian, member of the Polish-Russian Group for Difficult Issues, whose work focuses on the history of international relations and World War II. She graduated from the Moscow Institute of History and Archives and then worked at the Institute of History of the Academy of Sciences of the Soviet Union. Her postdoctoral thesis *Katyń: Crime Against Humanity* (defended at the University of Łódź) was published in Russia (1994) and in Poland (1997). In recognition of her research into the Katyń massacre, she has received numerous distinctions and honors, including the Commander Cross of the Order of Merit of the Republic of Poland.

38. Bolesław Bierut (1892–1956) was a Polish politician, communist activist, and

the first leader of the People's Republic of Poland after World War II, serving as president, then prime minister and general secretary, of the Central Committee of the Polish United Workers' Party. He died in Moscow under mysterious circumstances.

39. Citizens Committee for the Search for the Residents of Suwałki Region Who Went Missing in July 1945 was founded in 1987, after Stefan Moszczyński, whose three brothers and a stepfather had gone missing, discovered unmarked graves on the Rygol-Giby route. The bodies were thought to be victims of the Roundup but it turned out these were Wehrmacht soldiers. The mission of the Committee was to gather and disseminate information and documentation about the Augustów Roundup and its victims. Despite the harassment by the Polish secret police, the Committee visited several dozens of villages, conducted thousands of interviews, drafted hundreds of questionnaires about missing persons, and collected documents and photographs. Thanks to the efforts of the committee, the Augustów Roundup received a lot of media coverage. After the committee was dissolved in 1995, all the materials were transferred to the Institute of National Remembrance in 2001.

40. Andrzej Strumiłło (1927–2020) was a renowned Polish painter, sculptor, graphic designer, photographer, poet, and writer. He was a professor of the Academy of Fine Arts in Kraków and head of the Graphic Design Unit at United Nations Secretariat. He was a recipient of the Medal for Merit to Culture "Gloria Artis" and honorary citizen of the city of Suwałki.

41. The Association "Memorial" is an international organization founded in 1989, engaged in historical research and the promotion of knowledge about the victims of Soviet repression, including during the Stalinist period as well as the protection of human rights in the countries of the former Soviet Union. It has received numerous awards, including the Right Livelihood Award (Sweden, 2004), Medal of the Day of Remembrance of the Victims of the Katyń Massacre (Poland, 2008), Sakharov Prize (European Parliament, 2009), and Curator of National Remembrance Award (Poland, 2012). The Association runs the museum, "Art and Life in Gulags."

42. Bronisław Komorowski served as president of the Republic of Poland from 2010–2015.

43. The book was originally published in 2015 on the 70th anniversary of the Augustów Roundup and was inaugurated in Giby during the anniversary celebrations, which included numerous religious services, concerts, and exhibitions in the Suwałki Region. Afterward, the author, Teresa Kaczorowska went on a book tour around Poland, Belgium, the USA, and Germany. In the same year, the Polish parliament declared July 12 as the National Day of Remembrance of the Victims of the Augustów Roundup, and in 2016, President Andrzej Duda unveiled a plaque commemorating the victims of the crime, at the Tomb of the Unknown Soldier in Warsaw.

Krystyna Świerzbińska

1. During World War II, there were four massive Bolshevik deportations of Polish citizens deep into the Soviet Union, the so-called "anti–Soviet purges." During the first deportation (February 10, 1940), 220,000 Poles were deported; during the second one (April 13–14, 1940) 320,000, and during the third (May–June 1940) approximately 200,000. Further "purges" were interrupted by the German invasion of the Soviet Union on June 21, 1941. It is difficult to determine the exact number of deportees, but the estimate is between 800,000 and 2,000,000 people. All family members, regardless of their age or health condition, were taken at night and loaded into filthy cattle cars. Many did not survive the hardships of traveling. These exiles were part of the planned extermination of the Polish nation in the territories occupied by the Soviets.

2. Short for Krystyna.

3. Some Polish family names are gender-specific. In this case, feminine names end with an "a" and masculine names with an "i."

4. Approximately 50 acres.

5. Krasnoyarsk is the third largest city of Siberia.

6. Over 12 miles.

7. Approximately negative 58 degrees Fahrenheit.
8. Short for Klemens.
9. "Sybirak" is the name for a Polish citizen arrested and deported to Siberia, either by Tzarist Russia or the Soviet Union.
10. This narrative is based on several accounts by Józef Szmygel, the son of Franciszek Szmygel from Jaziewo, who was arrested at the July 14 meeting. This was the second rural meeting convened by the Soviets. The first took place calmly, without arrests, which reassured the men who went to the meeting on July 14, 1945.
11. UB (Urząd Bezpieczeństwa) was Polish secret police, operating in 1946–1956.

Fr. Stanisław Wysocki

1. Approximately 74 acres.
2. Danuta Kaszlej, Zbigniew Kaszlej, "Zbrojne podziemie niepodległościowe na Suwalszczyźnie i Augustowszczyźnie od jesieni 1944 r. do jesieni 1954 r. (zarys dziejów)." *Obława Augustowska (lipiec 1945)*, Prymat Publishers, Białystok, 2005.
3. Leopold Okulicki (1898–1946) was a general of the Polish army brigade and the last chief commander of the Home Army. In the notorious communist phony trial of June 21, 1945, the so-called "trial of the sixteen," he was sentenced to ten years in prison. He was eventually murdered in a Soviet prison in Lubianka on December 24, 1946.
4. In Russian: "soldier."
5. In Russian: "fighter."
6. Danuta Kaszlej, Zbigniew Kaszlej, *op. cit.*, p. 33.
7. The Polish Committee of National Liberation (Polish: Polski Komitet Wyzwolenia Narodowego, PKWN), also known as the Lublin Committee, was a government established in Poland in 1944 by the communists.
8. Ibid.
9. Witold Urbanowicz (1908–1996) was a brigadier general, pilot of the Polish army and lieutenant colonel of the Royal Air Force, After the defeat of September 1939, he fled through Romania to France, then to Great Britain, where he joined RAF. As a pilot of the 145th RAF fighter squadron, he fought in the Battle of England, and on August 21, 1940, he took command of Polish Squadron 303, the most effective unit of the Battle of Britain in its decisive phase. He was the only Polish pilot in the top ten most effective pilots and second on the list of the best Polish fighter aces (after Stanisław Skalski). Witold Urbanowicz also fought in the U.S. Air Force (including the Chinese front) and in the famous "Flying Tigers" squadron. In 1945, he flew from the USA to occupied Germany and from there to Poland, where he was arrested by the communist security services. Following his release, he immediately escaped to the West. He settled with his family in New York, where he worked for American Airlines, Eastern Airlines, and Republic Aviation. After retiring, he was a consultant in the U.S. aviation industry until 1994. In 1995, he was promoted by President Lech Wałęsa to the general of the Polish Aviation Brigade. He published several wartime memoirs. Gen. Urbanowicz was awarded numerous military orders, including the Cross of the Order of Virtuti Militari, the Cross of Valor (four times), the British Distinguished Flying Cross, and the American Air Medal. The School of Aviation in Dęblin and several schools in the Suwałki Region bear his name.
10. A sparsely populated mountain range in far southeast Poland known for its pristine landscape.
11. The John Paul II Higher Theological Seminary in Łomża was established in 1919 by Bishop R. Jałbrzykowski under the authority of the Apostolic Nuncio in Warsaw, Archbishop Achille Ratti, future Pope Pius XI. On June 5, 1991, Pope John Paul II met with the professors and seminarians of the seminary. To commemorate this event, the Pope's monument was erected in the courtyard.
12. Adam Kruczek, "Blisko ludzkich Spraw," *Nasz Dziennik*, No. 250, October 25, 2013.
13. Mikołaj Sasinowski (1909–1982) was the bishop of Łomża from 1970–1982. Born into a noble family, he was ordained as a priest in 1936. During World War II, he was a chaplain of Polish air forces in France, North Africa, and Great Britain. After returning to Poland in 1946, he studied law at the University of Warsaw. In 1967, he became the rector of the

Theological Seminary in Łomża and in 1970 was appointed the bishop of the Łomża diocese. He was also the chaplain of Polish veterans.

14. Juliusz Paetz (1935–2019) was a diocesan bishop of Łomża (1983–1996), Metropolitan archbishop of Poznań (1996–2002) and, after 2002, the archbishop emeritus of the Archdiocese of Poznań.

15. The Appeal of Jasna Góra is an evening prayer to Holy Mary, whose intention is directed towards the homeland and the Church. It can be said in private or with a congregation.

Tadeusz Jagłowski (Augustów)

1. Approximately 50 acres.
2. The Peasants' Party (in Polish: Stronnictwo Ludowe) was established on March 15, 1931, from the unification of three parties: PSL "Piast," PSL "Wyzwolenie," and the Peasants' Party. Prime Minister Maksymilian Malinowski from PSL "Wyzwolenie" became the president of the Congress (the highest authority of the party). Other top officials were elected among members of the other parties and included: Wincenty Witos, Stanisław Wrona-Merski, and Kazimierz Bagiński. Maciej Rataj became editor of the party's weekly, Zielony Sztandar.
3. Witold Siarkowski (b. 1906) was a member of the Home Army and Citizens' Home Army in charge of weapon storage for the insurgents, under the command of Władysław Stefanowski, alias "Grom." He was arrested by the Soviets during the Augustów Roundup on July 12, 1945. Like other victims of the Roundup, he disappeared without a trace.
4. The "Zapała" unit, numbering 40 people, operated in the Augustów district on the Sztabin-Dębowo and Sztabin-Sosnowo routes, under the command of Lieutenant Stanisław Świątkowski, alias "Zapała."
5. District Public Security Office.
6. At that time, there were three categories of war veterans' disabilities, number one being the highest.
7. The People's Referendum of 1946, the so-called Three-Times-Yes Referendum, was carried out in Poland on June 30, 1946, by the communist-controlled State National Council's resolution of April 28, 1946, to test the popularity of the ruling communists, prepare for the forged election in 1947, and consolidate the communist power. In preparation for conducting and protecting the falsified popular referendum, the Political Bureau of PPR set up a State Security Commission in March 1946 to coordinate the activities of LWP, WOP, KBW, UB, MO, and ORMO units. Its task included the liquidation of the independence underground and the assassination of PSL politicians. The referendum included three general questions: 1) Are you in favor of the abolition of the Senate? 2) Do you want to consolidate the economic system introduced by the agricultural reform and the nationalization of the primary branches of the national economy while maintaining the statutory powers of the private initiative? 3) Do you want to consolidate the western borders of the Polish state on the Baltic, Oder, and Nysa Łużycka? The falsification of the referendum was supervised by a team of officers of the Soviet special services, established in Warsaw on June 20, 1946, under the command of Col. Aron Palkin, the head of the department of the Soviet Ministry of State Security. They mainly dealt with the falsification and falsification of referendum documents. At the June 22 meeting, Bolesław Bierut, Władysław Gomułka, and the Soviet adviser at the Ministry of State Security, Col. Siemion Davidov, discussed technical details of falsifying the results of the referendum. Soviet officers falsified 5,994 protocols of the circuit commissions and counterfeited 40,000 signatures of members of the electoral commissions. Packages with real protocols were passed to the Soviet officers for falsification by the Ministry of Public Security officers under the personal supervision of Minister Stanisław Radkiewicz.

8. Stanisław Mikołajczyk (1901–1966) was prime minister of the Polish government-in-exile during World War II, and, after his return to Poland, he was the leader of the Polish Peasants' Party and deputy prime minister in postwar Poland until 1947. Fearing arrest, he escaped to London, but the Polish government-in-exile considered him a traitor and did not welcome him back. He

moved to the United States, where he died in 1966.

9. "Stanisławowicz" is a patronym added according to the Russian custom, after Piotr's father, Stanisław.

Józef Kucharzewski (Giby)

1. Personal ID issued by German authorities to Polish citizens in the occupied territories.
2. UB (Urząd Bezpieczeństwa) was the Polish secret police.
3. In Russian: "Jews."
4. "It was July" by Grzegorz Kucharzewski (music and Polish lyrics).
5. Schism of the Eastern Orthodox Christians.
6. Andrzej Strumiłło (1927–2020) was a Polish painter, graphic designer, sculptor, photographer, poet, writer, stage designer, and professor at the Academy of Fine Arts in Krakow as well as a head of the graphic design department of the UN General Office. He was an honorary ambassador of Podlasie Voivodship and honorary citizen of Suwałki. He was a recipient of the Gloria Artis Medal for Merit to Culture, Poland's highest award in the arts.
7. Although the National Remembrance Institute is still investigating the matter of approximately 600 victims of the Roundup, after the disclosure of Abakumov's cryptograms and the publication of documents by Nikita Petrov, it is estimated that probably there were more than 1,000. According to Prof. K. Jasiewicz and Fr. Stanisław Wysocki, the number of missing people was close to 2,000, but it is impossible to predict the exact number.
8. Jan Jerzy Milewski, "Zaginieni w obławie augustowskiej—poszukiwania i pamięć." *Obława Augustowska (July 1945)*, Prymat Publishers, Bialystok, 2005.
9. Alicja Maciejowska, *Przerwane życiorysy. Obława Augustowska—lipiec 1945*, IPN, Białystok, 2010.

Marian Bućko (Augustów)

1. The beginnings of settlement in the Krasnybór region date back to the beginning of the 16th century when the royal lands were given to Teodor Chreptowicz. The colonization was continued by another member of the Chreptowicz family, Adam Iwanowicz Chreptowicz, who was an enlightened and innovative nobleman. He built a mansion and a Catholic church (in 1598). Through the centuries, it was mostly the priest of the Dominican order who performed the clerical duties there until the 19th century. They also ran a school and took care of the Chreptowicz family church, including the miraculous painting of Our Lady of Krasnybór. Later, a well-known philanthropist, Count Karol Brzostowski bequeathed the Krasnybór property to the local peasants and officials. Both world wars caused enormous, both human and environmental, devastation. On several occasions, once German and once Soviet armies passed through these lands and used ruthless terror against the inhabitants of the conquered territories. The residents were deprived of national and political rights or were deported to perform forced labor. The Polish language and culture were destroyed. The wooded areas of the Augustów region, as well as the virgin and impassable Biebrza marshes, created favorable conditions for the development of guerrilla warfare.

2. About five acres.
3. The War Order of Virtuti Militari is the highest Polish military distinction, awarded for outstanding combat merits. It is the oldest military order in the world, established by King Stanisław August Poniatowski in 1792. Its motto is "Honor and Homeland."
4. Danuta Kaszlej, Zbigniew Kaszlej, "Zbrojne podziemie niepodległościowe na Suwalszczyźnie i Augustowszczyźnie od jesieni 1944 r. do jesieni 1954 r. (zarys dziejów)." *Obława Augustowska (lipiec 1945)*, Prymat Publishers, Białystok, 2005.
5. The Polish Committee of National Liberation (Polish: Polski Komitet Wyzwolenia Narodowego, PKWN), also known as the Lublin Committee, was a government established in Poland in 1944 by the communists.
6. Units that fought during the Warsaw Uprising of 1944.
7. From the biography of Władysław Stefanowski, alias "Grom," by Danuta and Zbigniew Kaszlej (in preparation).
8. Witold Lewoc, *Zaginieni—polegli*

w *Obławie Lipcowej z parafii Krasnybór*, Łódź, 2005.
9. Witold Lewoc, *op. cit.*
10. District Office of Public Security.
11. About 25 acres.
12. Witold Lewoc, *op. cit.*
13. Jan Jerzy Milewski, "Zaginieni w obławie augustowskiej—poszukiwania i pamięć." *Obława Augustowska (July 1945)*, Prymat Publishers, Białystok, 2005.

Teresa Staśkiewicz (Augustów)

1. Short for Teresa.
2. In Polish, "Związek Sybiraków," is an association of Poles arrested and deported to Siberia, both by Tzarist Russia and the Soviet Union. Its purpose is to help honor former deportees and their families, commemorate their sacrifice and suffering, help with getting benefits, and promote patriotism and tolerance.
3. "Radosław" was a code name for a well-armed unit formed before the outbreak of the Warsaw Uprising of 1944. It was the strongest and most elite group of the Home Army fighting in the Uprising. For its name, it adopted the pseudonym of its commander, Lieutenant-Colonel Jan Mazurkiewicz.
4. The "Radosław List" was published in *Przerwane życiorysy—Obława Augustowska—lipiec 1945*, IPN/ Białystok, 2010, by Alicja Maciejowska.
5. Owning a radio by Poles during World War II was forbidden, and the perpetrator could end up with a severe punishment.
6. The Augustów Canal is a waterway connecting the Vistula River with the Baltic Sea via a circular route, which was built in 1824–1839. In 1968, together with a complex of buildings and equipment, it was recognized and later registered as a historical monument. The channel is also included in the European Route of Transport and Communication, which is part of the European Industrial Heritage Route. The length of the Canal is 101 km, including 82 km within Poland (the rest being in Belarus).
7. UNRRA (United Nations Relief and Rehabilitation Administration) was an international organization established in 1943 to help people in the countries destroyed by World War II. The organization was mainly involved in supporting state economies, supplying raw materials, medicine, food, clothing, and even livestock. Poland was among the countries that benefited from this assistance. The organization was dissolved in 1947.
8. Krasnoyarsk Krai, the second-largest (after Yakutia) territorial unit of Russia (2, 339, 700 km², which covers 13 percent of the territory of the country), located in central Siberia. The capital city of Krasnoyarsk has a population of about 1,000,000.
9. Anders' Army is a common name for the Polish Armed Forces in the East (1941–1942), formed in the Soviet Union under the command of General Władysław Anders. Its members were mainly Polish prisoners of war released from the Soviet Union camps under a special amnesty. After the army was evacuated from the Soviet Union through Iran to Palestine, it passed under British command and joined the Polish II Corps (member of the Polish Armed Forces in the West), which fought in the Italian Campaign.
10. Short for Jadwiga.

Why Is This Book Needed?

1. Jan Długosz, *Jana Długosza kanonika krakowskiego dziejów polskich ksiąg dwanaście*, 1867–1870.
2. Zbigniew Herbert, "Pan Cogito o potrzebie ścisłości" in *Raport z oblężonego miasta*, Instytut Literacki, 1983.
3. Piotr Filipkowski, *Historia mówiona i wojna*, in *Wojna: Doświadczenie i zapis*, red. S. Buryła i P. Rodak, Kraków, 2006, pp. 13–35.
4. *Obława Augustowska—lipiec 1945 r. Wybór źródeł*, Białystok, 2010.
5. The testimonies were obtained for the Home Army Historical Club in the Augustów project, "Obława Augustowska z lipca 1945 r. Gdy nie ma grobów—ocalmy pamięć."
6. More information about the relocation of the soldiers of the Citizens' Home Army Augustów District to the Recovered Territories in Ziencina T., "Łącznicy wyprowadzili nas na Prusy Wschodznie" in *Obława Augustowska—lipiec 1945. Wybór źródeł*, Białystok, 2010, pp. 360–368.
7. Alicja Maciejowska, *Przerwane*

Notes—Why Is This Book Needed?   161

życiorysy. *Obława Augustowska—lipiec 1945*, IPN, Białystok, 2010.

8. Based on the investigation of the communist offenses considered crimes against humanity, in this case, of the July 1945 homicide committed in an undetermined place against about 600 people detained in the Suwałki Region during the Augustów Roundup carried out by the NKVD army, with the complicity of Polish secret service, militia, soldiers of the Polish People's Army; Case no. (S 69/01 / Zk).

9. *Obława Augustowska (lipiec 1945 r.)*, Białystok, 2005.

10. Published in Russian in the spring of 2011.

11. Letter from the Head Military Prosecutor's Office of the Prosecutor's Office of the Russian Federation dated January 4, 1995, to the Embassy of the Republic of Poland in Moscow. In *Obława Augustowska—lipiec 1945. Wybór źródeł*, Białystok, 2010.

12. Mariusz Filipowicz, *Obława Augustowska w lipcu 1945 r.* in *Obława Augustowska (lipiec 1945 r.)*, Białystok, 2005, p. 44.

13. Ibid., p. 42.

14. Special report No. 0300 from the head office of the First Infantry Regiment of the Praga District in Warsaw, dated July 15, 1945, in *Obława Augustowska—lipiec 1945 r.*, Białystok, 2010, p. 85.

15. An example would be a report by Lieutenant Aleksander Kuczyński, head of the Polish Public Security Office in Augustów to his superior, Major Piątkowski, about the operations by the Soviet Army in the area, in *Obława Augustowska—lipiec 1945. Wybór źródeł*, Białystok, 2010, p. 94.

16. Officially called the Lithuanian Soviet Socialist Republic.

17. J.J. Milewski, Introduction to *Obława Augustowska—lipiec 1945 r. Wybór źródeł*, Białystok, 2010, pp. 25–26.

18. Danuta Kaszlej and Zbigniew Kaszlej, "Zbrojne podziemie niepodległościowe na Suwalszczyźnie i Augustówszczyźnie od jesieni 1944 r. do jesieni 1954 r. (zarys dziejów)" in *Obława Augustowska (lipiec 1945 r.)*, Białystok, 2005, pp. 31–32.

19. Tadeusz Radziwonowicz, "Władze lokalne a obława," in *Obława Augustowska (lipiec 1945 r.)*, Białystok, 2005, p. 61.

20. The information in this paragraph comes from Władysław Stefanowski's biography at www.akklub.pl/oblawaaugustowska.

21. *Obawa Augustówska—July 1945. Wybór źródeł*, Białystok, 2010, pp. 39–40.

22. Ibid., pp. 77–83.

23. Report by Lieutenant Aleksander Kuczyński, head of the Polish Public Security Office in Augustów to his superior, Major Piątkowski, about the operations by the Soviet Army in the area, in *Obława Augustowska—lipiec 1945. Wybór źródeł*, Białystok, 2010, p. 363.

24. Tadeusz Radziwonowicz, *op. cit.*, p. 64.

25. A paper titled "We fought with the Soviets for five days" ("Pięć dni się bliśmy z Ruskimi") presented by Zbigniew Kaszlej at the unveiling of a cross commemorating the AKO soldiers of the Augustów and Suwałki regions who fought in July 1945 at Lake Brożane, at www.akklub.pl. An account by Bolesław Rogalewski, a soldier who fought in the unit under the command of Władysław Stefanowski, alias "Grom." He was saved from the battle with the Red Army at Lake Brożane in July 1945, in *Obława Augustowska—July 1945. Wybór źródeł*, Białystok, 2010, p. 353.

26. S. Piekarski, Report from June 22, 2013, in Krasnybór during a rally along the route of places related to the Augustów Roundup, at www.akklub.pl.

27. This is confirmed by a fragment of the report by the head of the Public Security Office in Augustów, Lieutenant Aleksander Kuczyński, to the head of the Polish Public Security Office in Białystok, Major Piątkowski, about the start of the operations by Soviet troops in the county. It reads: "The Soviet intelligence apparatus cannot keep up with the interrogations as the detainees testify, also against others." In *Obława Augustowska—lipiec 1945 r. Wybór źródeł*, Białystok, 2010, p. 90.

28. For example, Janina and Edward Miszkiel from Posejnele, in Berzniki County, were detained by the Red Army on July 28, 1945. In *Obawa Augustowska—July 1945. Wybór źródeł*, Białystok, 2010, p. 155.

29. Tadeusz Radziwonowicz, "Władze lokalne a obława," in *Obława Augustowska (lipiec 1945 r.)*, Białystok, 2005, pp. 68–69.

30. Members of Cheka, a Soviet secret-police organization.

31. Discussion of the speech by Nikita Petrov at the conference in Warsaw on July 27, 2014, www.akklub.pl.

32. Cryptogram dated July 21, 1945.

33. Sargent Major Wacław Sobolewski, alias "Sęk" or "Skała" (1916–1945), was a Polish army officer and a member of the Home Army and Citizens' Home Army. Born in a small village in Augustów County, he graduated from a noncommissioned officer academy in 1935, and, in 1939, was promoted to the rank of platoon sergeant and then sergeant. He fought during the defensive war of 1939 in Mława and Warsaw. After the capital city surrendered, he was taken prisoner but fled and returned home. In 1940, he was arrested by NKVD and put in the Grodno prison. He was released after the Germans took control of the city in June 1941. He joined the Polish Underground on August 7, 1941. He was sworn into the Polish Underground on August 7, 1941, by Piotr Milanowski, alias "Ćma," "Łuk," or "Rukść." He was made a commander of an underground platoon in the village of Topiówka and the deputy commander of the II Region of the Augustów Home Army District post in Biernatki-Raczki. At the risk of being arrested, he escaped to the forest in 1942 and organized an insurgency unit. In the spring of 1943, his unit was combined with the group under the command of Walenty Klewiado, alias "Sęp." After the "Burza" ("Storm") operation and the stabilization of the front, he lived in the village of Kamienna-Nowa near Sokółka. By the directive of Captain Bronisław Jasiński, alias "Komar" or "Lom," he was appointed the commander of the Citizens' Home Army corps in Lipsk (to lead the operation "Jodła") and the commander of an insurgency unit. He was appointed the commander of the Citizens' Home Army corps in Lipsk (to lead the operation "Jodła") and an insurgency unit by Captain Bronisław Jasiński, alias "Komar." During the Augustów Roundup, he handed his people over to Sgt. Władysław Stefanowski, alias "Grom," and returned to the Sokólka region. He was detained by the Soviets in the village of Kamienna-Nowa, and, after preliminary interrogations in Kolnica, was shot by the Soviets in the village of Osowy Grąd. He was decorated with the Cross of Valor and the Silver Cross of Merit with Swords and posthumously promoted to the rank of second lieutenant (based on the biography by Zbigniew Kaszlej and Bartek Rychlewski).

The Augustów Roundup

1. Nikita Petrov, *Psy Stalina*, Warsaw, Demart, 2012, pp. 222–230.

2. Cryptograms No. 25212 from July 21, 1945, and No. 25871 from July 24, 1945 (Central Archives of the Russian Federal Security Service, F.4-os. Op.3. D. 24. L. 179–184). Both documents at the request of the Memorial Association were disclosed, and in 2012, their copies were transferred by the "Memorial" to the Institute of National Remembrance in Warsaw.

3. Regarding those arrested on July 27, 1945, in the village of Biała Woda in Suwałki County—Ludwik Wysocki, Kazimiera Wysocka, and Aniela Wysocka—the answers were given by the Russian Federal Security Service, recorded as No. 10/A-B-1573, of June 14, 2013, No. 10/A-B-1575, of June 14, 2013, No. 10/A-B-1602, of June 17, 2013. These records contained information about the date of detention and the fact that in their files "there is nothing on the presentation of guilt, prosecution, vindication, and further fate." This phrase means that their files are among 575 files preserved in the Federal Security Service archives of the victims of the Augustów Roundup, which ended with secret murders.

4. Letter from the General Prosecutor's Office of Russia No. 87–321–2012 of June 19, 2013, addressed to the General Prosecutor's Office of Poland.

Selected Sources

Bosek, Kazimierz, *Tajemnice czarnych baronów. Żołnierze-górnicy 1949–1959*, Bellona, Warsaw, 2013.
Filipowicz, Mariusz, "Obława augustowska z lipca 1945 roku w świetle zachowanych dokumentów." *Rocznik Augustowsko-Suwalski*, Vol. 3, 2003.
Kaszlej Zbigniew, "Walka żołnierzy AK-AKO z Sowietami nad jeziorem Brożane w czasie Obławy Augustowskiej." Speech delivered in Brożane on June 14, 2014.
Kaszlej, Danuta, and Kaszlej, Zbigniew, "Obława Augustowska i pamięć o niej." *Biuletyn Klubu Historycznego im. Armii Krajowej w Augustowie*, No. 6, 2007.
Kaszlej, Danuta, "Obława Augustowska." *Pastores*, No. 63(3), 2014.
Lewoc, Witold, *Zaginieni—polegli w Obławie Lipcowej wojsk sowieckich NKWD w 1945 r. z parafii Krasnybór*, Łódź, 2005.
Maciejowska, Alicja, *Przerwane życiorysy. Obława Augustowska—lipiec 1945*, IPN, Białystok, 2010.
Petrov, Nikita, *Kaci. Oni wykonywali rozkazy Stalina*, Moscow, 2011.
Petrov, Nikita, *Psy Stalina*, Warsaw, 2012.
Radziwonowicz, Tadeusz, "Po obławie. Pierwsze poszukiwania zaginionych (1945–1947)." *Rocznik Augustowsko-Suwalski*, Vol. 10, 2010.
Sewastianowicz, Ireneusz, and Kulikowski, Stanisław, *Nie tylko Katyń*, Białystok, 1990.
Pawluczyk, Józef, *Cierniowa droga do wolności*, Białystok, 2005.
Obława Augustowska (lipiec 1945 r.), ed. Jan Jerzy Milewski and Anna Pyżewska, Białystok, 2005.
Obława Augustowska—lipiec 1945 r., ed. Ewa Rogalewska, Białystok, 2010.

Index

Numbers in **bold italics** indicate pages with illustrations

Abakumov, Wiktor 10, 19–20, 23–25, 29, 133–134, 136, 140–143, 148, 154n26
Anders, Władysław (army) 125, 159(*Teresa Staśkiewicz*)n9
Andracki, Ignacy (alias "Topór" ["Axe"], later "Filtry" ["Filters"]) 71, 73
Andruszkiewicz, Mieczysław 43
AKO (Armia Krajowa Obywatelska) 4–6, 10, 50, 131, 152n9–11, 160n25, 163; *see also* Citizens' Home Army
apparatus: occupying 4; security 8, 38, 50, 57, 137, 150; Stalinist vii, 9; terror 16, 131
Archives: Central Military in Rembertów, Poland 28; of the Federal Security Service in Moscow 28–29, 44, 55, 61–62, 78, 98, 131, 135, 142, 148–149n2, 148–149n3; Lithuanian 136; Office of State Registration and of New Records (at IPN) 78, 131, 136; of the Republic of Belarus 28
Armia Krajowa xii; *see also* Home Army
arrest vii, xiii, 8, 10, 12–13, 24, *41*, 42–43, 49–51, 53–54, 62, 74, 76, 95–97, 102–104, *105*, 1–6-107, 109, 114, 118–122, *122*, 133–134, 136, 138–140, 142–144, 146, 147–149, 152n7, 154n22, 154n28, 156n9, 156n10, 157n9, 157n3, 159(*Teresa Staśkiewicz*)n2, 161n3, 161n33
Association
Association for the Memory of the 1945 Augustów Roundup Victims ix, 23, 29, 59, 61–64
Association for Freedom and Independence 21
Association "Leśni" for Exploring Places of Struggle and Martyrdom and the War Graves 17–*18*
Association "Memorial" in Moscow vii, ix, 19, 55, 63, 67, 128, 149–150, 154n29
Association of Siberian Exiles *94*, 120
Association of the International Katyń Rally 65, *66*
Augustów Canal, 12, 32, 71, 123, 159(*Teresa Staśkiewicz*)n6; Commission 35

Augustów Primeval Forest vii, viii 1, 4, 6–10, 26, 32, 37, 43, 46, 51, 62, 67, 86, *88*, 97, 101, *103*, 110–111, 114, *115*, 119, 128, 135, 139
Augustów-Sejny route 92, 95
Auschwitz (German Nazi concentration camp) 152n7

Baranowsko-Sandomierz front 72
barns (place of detention) vii, 9, 1, 52–53, 74, 88, 96, 139; in Białowiersnie 19, 20; Godlewskis 12–13; Koszyckis *41*, 42; Kozlowskis 42; Olszewskis 38; Szarejkos 88; Szyces 42, 109; Szypers 139; Tomaszewskis 74; Werners 10, 11; Wiśniewskis 10, 12; Witeks 104, 106
barracks 3, 54–55
basement (place of detention/torture) 14, 108, 122; Dowgierds *122*; Granackis 42, 107–108; Hornowskis 106–107
Batura, Anatol 127
Battle of England (Britain) 15n9
Battle of Kuryłówka xiii
Battle of Lake Brożane 14, 17–20, *18*, 114, 128, 143, 152n10, 152n11, 155n30, 160n25
Battle of Stalingrad xii
Battle of Warsaw 101
Belarus 15, 17, 25–26, 28, 67, 90, 135
Beria Lawrentiy 7, 10, 19–20, 23–24, 133–134, 140–143, 148
Biała Woda 30, 48–50, *51*, 52–54, 56, *68*, 68, 161n3
Białobrzegi 10
Białowiersnie 19–20, 135
Białowieża Forest 2, 3; *see also* Augustów Primeval Forest
Białystok 8, 22, 38, 50–51, 78, 112, 119–120, 133, 136, 152n9
Biebrza River 101
Bielawski, Jan 43
Bierut, Bolesław 27, 97, 126
Błażewicz, Władysław 114
Bogusze 120

165

Bolshevik(s) 2, 101, 107, 125
Bołtarik, Anna 125
Bołtarik, Antoni 125
Bołtarik, Czesława 125
Bołtarik, Fabian 125
Bołtarik, Jadwiga 118; *see also* Wołąsewicz, Jadwiga
Bołtarik, Władysława 125
Bondarenko, Yuri 69
Brzostowski, Karol 158*(Marian Bućko)n*1
Brzozówka River 43
Bućko, Alicja 111
Bućko, Eugenia (née Wojewnik) 110
Bućko, Kazimierz 100
Bućko, Konstanty viii, 100-103, *105*, 106, 110-111, 114, 116
Bućko, Stanisław 106

cellar(s) (place/s of detention/torture) 37, 96, 88, *122*, 135, 139; Granackis *108*, 109; Hornowskis *105*
Chlebanowski, Stanisław 114
Chodakiewicz, Józef 114
Chojnowski, Marian 58
Chreptowicz, Adam 158*(Marian Bućko)n*1
Chreptowicz, Teodor 158*(Marian Bućko)n*1
Churchill, Winston xii, 155*n*33
Cichor, Father Dariusz 64-65, *66*
Cichor, Mieczysław 64
Cieślukowski, Stanisław 144
Citizens Committee of the Search of the Missing Residents of the Suwałki Region 27, 29, 98, 128, 132, 155*n*38
Citizens' Home Army (AKO) 4, 15, 18, *18*, 21, 50, *51* 53, 103-104, 131-132, 136-139, 142-144, 152*n*9, 154*n*22, 155*n*30, 157*n*3, 160*n*6, 161*n*33; III Sztabin Region of 111; IV Lipsk Region of 111
Citizens' Militia (MO) vii, 9, 50, 57, 64, 104, 109, 137, 160*n*8
Civic Platform (political party) 61
Communism xiv, 5, 67; administration 58; authorities viii, 24, 28, 49, 51, 56, 58, 79-82, 95, 104, 110, 130, 134-138, 148, 151*n*3; crime 28, 60, 132; forces 50; government xiii; party 144; power 50; prison vii; regime viii, 58; rule viii; secret police 17; security apparatus 38, 44
Communist Committee in Augustów 76
Constitution of May 3, 1791 7, 137
Council for the Protection of Combat and Martyrdom 112
court-martial 21
crime against humanity 28, 142, 155*n*36
cruelty vii, 9
cryptogram(s) vii, 19-20, 133-137, 141-142, 144, 148, 158*(Kucharzewski,Józef)n*7, 160*n*32, 161*n*2
Cwietyński, Włodzimierz (alias "Orłow") 4, 7, 49

Czarna Hańcza River 10, 48-49
Czarny Bród 6

Daraszkiewicz, Adolf, 112
death vii, 5, 7-11, 14, 17, 20, 44, 55-56, 70, 76, 89-90, 98, 111-112, 124-125, 127, 130, 145, 151*n*3, 151*n*5, 152*n*3, 152*n*11, 153*n*14, 154*n*16-18; camps xii, 102; pits 62-63, 97, 129, 141-143, 146; sentence 21, 36, 42, 50
Dęblin 114, 157*n*9
Dębowo 104, 157*n*4
detainees vii, 9, 11, 13, 14, 24, 28, 35, 43, 54, 89-90, 95, 108, 131, 134, 139-143, 147-148, 154*n*26, 160*n*27
detention 35, *41*, 62, 88-89, *108*, 135, 139-140, 143, 148-149, 153*n*13, 160*n*3

District Office of Public Security in Augustów (PUBP), ("Turks House") 8, 14, *15*, 21, 38, 39, 41, 43, 51, 54, 74, *75*, 76, 109
District Office of Public Security in Suwałki 19
Długosz, Jan 129, 160*n*1
DNA (testing, material, samples) ix, 29, 45, 84, 116, 128
Dobrowolska, Kazimiera (Kazia) 11
Dobrowolski, Kazimierz 12
Dobrowolski, Zygmunt 75
Dowgierd family 122, *122-123*
Duchiński, Eugeniusz 74
Duchiński, Jan 75
Dziądziak, Stanisław 43

East Prussia 10, 26, 71-72, 102, 104, 134, 137, 152*n*12
Embassy of the Republic of Poland in Moscow 27, 133, 160*n*11
Embassy of the Russian Federation in Warsaw 78
European Union 108
executions 8, 21, 26, 67, 97, 142, 147-148, 151*(Marian Tananis)n*1

Falkowski, Bishop Czesław 56
Fidrych, Lucyna 65
Fiedorowizna 73
50th Army of the Third Belarusian Front 134, 137-138, 147
filtration vii, 9, 11-12, 88, 95, *122*
First Infantry Regiment of the Praga District in Warsaw, vii, 9, 134, 154*n*23, 160*n*14
Folwark 120

Gąsiorowski, Antoni 114
Gąsiorowski, Edward 114
Germans, xii, 3-4, 35, 49-50, 102, 119, 127, 142, 144, 161*n*33
Germany xii, 2-3, 6-7, 27, 48-49, 54, 72-73, 87, *87*, 101, 104, 121, 151*(Marian Tananis)n*1, 152*n*6, 154*n*25, 155*n*31, 155*n*35, 156*(Marian*

Index

Tananis)n42, 157n9, 158(Marian Bućko) n1; concentration camps 152n7; death camp xii, 101; forced labor xii, 10, 72, 102; gendarmerie 4, 73, 89; invasion xi, 3, 71, 120, 156(Krystyna Świerzbińska)n1; occupiers (occupation) 2, 35, 48-50, 71, **86**, 87, 102; settlers 3, 102
Ghetto Uprising of 1943 xii
Giby 20, 27, 30, 46, 82, 85, **85**, 86-91, 93-94, **94**, 95, **96**, 97-98, 111, 128, 140, 143, 147, 148, 156(Marian Tananis)n42
Giby-Rygol road (route) 46, 90, 97, 98
Giedzie 17
Giżycko 8, 20
Gliniecki, Aleksander 53
Goering, Hermann 2, 26, 152n6
Gołębie 72
Gołębiowski, Eugeniusz 10, 14, 17
Gomułka, Władysław 44, 153n18
Gorgonov, Ivan 10, 23-25, 29, 137, 141-142, 154(Marian Tanans)n17
Gos, Magdalena 100
Grajewo 77
Granacki, Czesław 114
Granacki, Stanisław 114
Granacki, Tadeusz 114
Granacki, Zenon 108
Grand Theatre in Warsaw, Poland 65
Grodno 6, 12, 14, 25-26, 28, 90, 104, 118, 138, 148, 161n33
Gugnowska, Zofia 53-55
Guziejko, Antoni 43

Hańczuk, Eugeniusz 12
Hańczuk, Konstanty (Kostek) 11
Haraburda, Eugeniusz 43
Haraburda, Józef 114
Herbert, Zbigniew 160n2
Hitler, Adolf xi-xii, 2, 3, 31
Home Army xii-xiii, 2, 4-7, 11, 13, 15, **18**, 20-21, 26-27, 29-30, 35, 43, 48-50, **51**, 52-53, **64**, 72-73, 87, 106, 111, 120-121, 135-136, 143-144, 148; II Augustów Region of 161n33; Liquidation Committee of the former 120; World Association of 94; World Union of Soldiers of 78, 81; see also Citizens' Home Army
Hornowska, Bronisława 104, 106
Hornowski, Karol 104
house (of detention): Godlewskis 12, **13**; Hornowskis 106; Jagłowskis 73-74; Kozłowskis 41; Szarejkos 89; Turk 14, **15**, 43, 74, **75**, 77, 109, 126; Werners 12; Wysockis 51; Ziemba 41

imprisonment 21, 36, 152n7
independence underground 102-104, 109, 129, 133
Institute of National Remembrance (IPN) ix, 20, 78, 84, 132, 135-136, 145; Białystok branch vii, 28-29, 45-46, 60, 97-98, 128, 133, 149, 158(Kucharzewski,Józef)n9, 159(Teresa Staśkiewicz)n4, 160n7
insurgents viii, xiii-xiv, 5-7, 10, 14, 17, 19, 26, 48, 50, 52, 72-73, 87, 104, 114, 135-136, 138-139, 143-144, 151(Marian Tananis)n1, 152n10, 157n2
Internal Security Corps (KBW) 51
Internal Troops of the 62nd Division of the NKVD 9, 57, 138
interrogation(s) vii, 11-13, 42, 57, 74-75, 89, 93, 106, **122**, 126-127, 131, 135, 140, 143, 148, 161n27, 161n33
investigation(s) vii, 27-29, 42, 46, 54, 59, 98, 136, 147, 149, 152n8, 155(Marian Tananis) n29, 160n8

Jagłowska, Apolonia 73
Jagłowska, Eugenia 71
Jagłowska, Ryta 70, 84
Jagłowska, Stanisława 74, **75**, 76
Jagłowski, Andrzej 84
Jagłowski, Konstanty 73-74, **75**, 75
Jagłowski, Piotr 71, 73-74, **75**, 77-78, **79-82**
Jagłowski, Robert 84
Jagłowski, Stanisław 74
Jaminy 37, **42**, 43, 111, 144
Jan Paweł II see John Paul II
Janik, Jan 43
January Uprising of 1863 7, 152n1
Jaruzelski, Wojciech 8, 58, 153n19
Jasiński, Bronisław (alias "Komar" or "Łom") 161n33
Jasiewicz, Krzysztof 26, 30, 67, 154n24, 158(Kucharzewski,Józef)n7
Jarząbska, Apolonia (née Kolenkiewicz) 52, 55
Jarząbska, Józefa 48
Jasna Góra viii, 30, 62-63, **64**, 65, 114, 128, 157n15; Monastery viii, 30
Jastrzębianka River 100
Jastrzębna Druga **41**, 42, 101, 103, 107-108, **108**, 109-111, 140
Jaziewo viii, 32, 35, 38-39, 41-44, 156(Krystyna Świerzbińska)n10
John Paul II 59, 63-65, 157n11

Kąkiel, Józef 114
Kalety 17, 67, 148; Sejny Route 3
Kamienna Nowa 143, 161n23
Kamiński, Antoni 75
Kamiński, Franciszek 72; see also Peasants' Battalions
Kamiński, Bishop Romuald 65, **66**
Karp, Leon 43
Karp, Stanisław 114
Kaszlej Danuta ix, 16-17, 29, 65, 145-146, 149, 153n16, 154n24, 156(Fr. Stanisław Wysocki) n2, 159(Teresa Staśkiewicz)n4, 159(Teresa Staśkiewicz)n7, 160n18, 163

Kaszlej, Zbigniew ix, 17–18, 145–146, 149, 156(*Fr. Stanisław Wysocki*)n2, 159(*Teresa Staśkiewicz*)n4, 159(*Teresa Staśkiewicz*)n7, 160n18, 161n33, 163
Katyń vii, 9, 46, 48, 77, 84, 110, 141, 145, 153n14; Massacre *(of 1940)* ix, xii–xiii, 62, 150, 151*(From The Author)*n1, 152n8, 153n14, 155n29, 153n36, 156*(Marian Tananis)*n40; rally 65–*66*
Kępa, Józef 114
Kępa, Father Piotr **66**
Kilnar, Father Nikodem 64
Kłoczko, Jan 27
Komorowski, Bronisław 30, 156*(Marian Tananis)*n41
Kopańko, Ignacy 114
Kopiec 42, 71, 73–75, 78
Korniłowicz, Zygmunt 114
Kozakiewicz, Czesław 43
Krasnoborki 71
Krasnopol 3
Krasnoyarsk 35–36
Krasnoyarski Krai 125, 156*(Krystyna Świerzbińska)*n5
Krasnybór viii, 100–104, *105*, 106, 110–112, *113*, 114, 139, 158*(Marian Bućko)*n1, 159*(Marian Bućko)*n8, 161n26, 163; Church of the Holy Virgin Mary 110; Our Lady of 101
Krasnystaw 72
Kruczek, Adam 56, 157n12
Krysztofik, Jan 114
Krzywicka 53
Krzywicki, Jan 114
Kucharzewska, Aleksandra 87
Kucharzewski, Grzegorz 87, 90, *91*, 91–92, 95–96, 98, 158n4
Kucharzewski, Józef *85*, 86–87, 89–90, *93*, 93–94, 98
Kuczyński, Lieutenant Aleksander 160n15
Kugiel, Adam 43
Kugiel, Honoriusz 38
Kugiel, Romualda 32
Kuklewicz, Barbara 65
Kukowski, Stanisław 114
Kułakowski, Kazimierz 43
Kulik, Józef 114
Kulikowski, Stanisław 163
Kulikowski, Zbigniew 29
Kunda, Edward 43, 144
Kunda, Leon (alias "Nieznany") 73
Kupiński, Michał 114
Kuźnicki, Leon 114
Kuźnicki, Piotr 114
Kuźnicki, Stanisław 114

Lake Brożane ix, 6–7, 10–11, 14–*18*, 19–20, 30, 114, *115*, 128, 138–139, 143, 152n10, 152n11, 153n16, 155n30, 161n25
Lake Gieret 86
Lake Gołdap 26
Lake Płaskie 6
Lake Pomerania 3
Lake Sajno 10
Law and Justice (political party) 60–61
Lebedeva, Natalia 26, 155n36
Lebiedzianka River 5, 103, *103*, 109, 111
Lebiedzin 110–111, 114
Lewoc, Witold 111–112, 159*(Marian Bućko)* n8, 163
Liniarski, Władysław (alias "Mścisław") 50
Lipowiec 14
Lipsk 21, 38, 104, 111, 154n22
list(s) (of detainees/arrested) 8, 10, 13, 20, 32, 67, 97, 119–121, 126–127, 129, 131–132, 134, 136, 139, 142, 144–145, 147–148
Lithuania 17, 21, 24, 26–28, 70, 86, 135–136, 140
Łomża 47, 57–59, *57*, 157n13–14
looting 14, 103
Lublin: Committee 50, 159*(Marian Bućko)* n5; government (PKWN) 103, 157n7
Lubyanka prison 156*(Fr Stanisław Wysocki)* n3
lynch 103

Maciejowska, Alicja 120, 133, 158*(Jozef Kucharzewski)*n9, 159*(Teresa Staśkiewicz)* n4, 160n7, 163
Maćkowa Ruda 95
Makarewicz, Stanisław 114
Malinowski, Maksymilian 157n2
Malinowski, Stanisław 114
Małkowski, Lucjan 75
Mały Borek 4, 10–11
Markowski, Józef 114
martial law 58, 123, 153n19
Matyskieła, Helena 38, 42
Matyskieła, Stanisław 43
Mazur, Bishop Jerzy 76
Mazurkiewicz, Jan (alias "Radosław") 120, 159*(Teresa Staśkiewicz)*n3
Melaniuk, Father Maciej **66**
Michalik, Archbishop Józef 56, 60, 63
Michniewicz, Beata 65
Mikaszówek 3, 10, 144
Mikołajczyk, Stanisław 76, 158*(Tadeusz Jagłowski)*n8
Mikołajewska, Helena 77
Milewski, Jerzy, 149, 158*(Jozef Kucharzewski)* n8, 159n13, 160n17, 163
Milewski, Mirosław 8, 14, 38
Military District Court 21, *22*
Miluc, Franciszek (alias "Karp") 19
Miszkiel, Edward 161n28
Miszkiel, Janina 161n28
Mogilnica 38, 42–43
Molotov-Ribbentrop Pact xi–xii
monument: in Augustów (dedicated to the memory of the Poles deported to Siberia)

Index

60; in Ełk (dedicated to the Martyrdom of the Polish Nation) 59; in Giby 27, 95–**96**; at Jaminy cemetery 42–**43**; in Krasnybór 112–**113**, 114; at Lake Brożane 17, **18**, 155n30
Mościcki, Ignacy 2, 151n5
Mossakowski, Second Lieutenant 19
Myszczyński, Stefan 98

Naumowicze 90
Netta River 14–**15**, 44, 71, 77, 118, 123
Netta village *(Nettal, Netta II)* 120
Niećko, Józef 72
NKVD vii, xii–xiii, 4, 7–14, 16, 21, 23–26, 28–30, 42–43, 50–54, **64**–65, 68, 74, **75**–76, 88–90, 94, **94**, 95, 102, **105**, 106, 112–**113**, 120, 123, 126, 134–136, 138, 140, 150, 152n8, 152n11, 153n13, 154n27, 154n28, 154n29, 160n8

occupier(s): German xi–xii, 3, 102; Soviet 2, 4, 20, 35, 102, 119, 156*(Krystyna Świerzbińska)*n1
Okulicki, Gen. Leopold (alias "Niedźwiadek") 50, 152n9, 156*(Fr Stanisław Wysocki)*n3
Okuniewski, Józef 112, 114
Olechnowicz, Michał 126
Olechnowicz, Stanisław 126
Olecko (Treuburg) 10, 23–25, 134, 142
Operation "Burza" ("Storm") 4, 49, 161n33
Orłowski, Stanisław (alias "Piorun") 7
Ostashkov 102
Ostrowski, Mieczysław (alias "Kropidło") 50, 53

pacification(s) vii, 8–9, 27, 61, 130–131, 134–137, 142, 144–145
Paetz, Bishop Juliusz 58, 157n14
Palczak, Antoni 27
Panasewicz, Benjamin 43
Panasewicz, Stanisław 43
Paniewo 10, 140
Peasants' Battalions 71–73
Peasants' Guards "Chłostra" 71–72; *see also* Żywią i Bronią
People's Republic of Poland 8, 18, 27, **45**, 48; authorities 27, 44, **45**, 51, 61–62, 78, 149
Persecution xii, 9, 48, 50, 56
Petrov, Nikita vii, ix, 10, 19, 23, 25–26, 28, 30; 63, 67
Piątkowski, Major 160n23, 161n27
Piekarski, Edward 139
Piekarski, S. 161n26
pigsty vii, 9, 74, 88–89, 96, 104–**105**–106, 139
Pilecki, Witold (alias "Żwirko") 3, 6, 152n7
Piłsudski, Józef 1, 2 101–102, 151*(Marian Tananis)*n2
Pińczów (Republic of) 72
Płaska (village of) 3, 6–7, 10–13, **12–13**, 43, 135, 137

Polish Academy of Sciences (Warsaw, Poland) 26, 30, 67
Polish Anti-Communist Resistance vii, xi–xii, 3, 48, 71, 145; Resurgence 146
Polish Committee of National Liberation 137
Polish parliament 29, 30, 95, 156*(Marian Tananis)*n42
Polish Peasants' Party 72, 76, 157n1
Polish People's Republic 8, 17, 27, 30, **45**, 48, 77–78, 126, 149, 153n18, 155n31, 155n37
Polish Public Security Office 134–135, 138, 140, 160n15
Polish Second Republic **34**
Polish secret police vii, 16, 20, 23, 54, 57–58, **64**, 69, 93, **94**, 97, 103, 112, **113**, 126–127, 134, 152n11, 153n15, 154n20–21, 155n38, 156*(Krystyna Świerzbińska)*n11, 158n2, 160n8, 161n30
Polish II Corps (in Italy) xiii
Polish Underground xii–xiii, 3–5, 7, 9, 12, 17, 20, 23, 35, 48, 51, 73–74, 131, 135–136, 140, 144, 152n8
Polish United Workers Party (Communist Party) 8, 44, 57, 144, 153n19, 154n20
Polish Uprising Union (Polski Związek Powstańczy) 4
Poniatowski, Stanisław August 159*(Marian Bućko)*n3
Popiełuszko, Jerzy 8, 154n21
Potsdam Conference 25, 134, 155n35
prisoners vii–viii, 4, 11–14, 21, 27, 34, 42–43, 49, 55, 72, 76, 89–90, **94**, 109, 120, 122, **122**, 123, 153n18, 161n33
Putin, Władimir 44
Pycz, Władysław (alias "Twardy" ["Tough"]) 71, 73

Radomsko, 72
Radosław 20, 120, **121**, 126–127, 159*(Teresa Staśkiewicz)*n3, 159*(Teresa Staśkiewicz)*n4
rape(s) 11, 54, 103, 136–137
Red Army vii, xi–xii, 2, 4, 7, 9, 11, 14, 18, 25, 49, 102, 134, 137, 139, 140, 154n25, 154n27–28, 161n25, 161n28
Red Cross 43, 78; in Geneva 27, 56, 97, 110; Polish 78, 132
Referendum 76, 150, 155, 158*(Tadeusz Jagłowski)*n7
Rehabilitation 149
Resistance *see* Polish Anti-Communist Resistance
Rewińska, Jadwiga (née Stefanowska) 16
Riazan 102
Rogalewski, Bolesław (alias "Sosenka") 18, 20, 153n16, 160n25
Romincka Forest 26
Rominty (now Krasnolesie) 26
Roosevelt, Franklin Delano vii–viii, xii
Roszkowski, Izydor 75

Roszkowski, Stanisław 75
Royal Air Force 157*n*9
Royal Castle in Warsaw, Poland 30, 67, *67*, 128
Różański, Romek 144
Russian Academy of Sciences 26, 155*n*36
Russian archives 29, 61, 131, 135
Russian Federal Security Office 148, 161*n*2, 162*n*3
Russian Federation 28–29, 60–62, 69, 78, *79–80*, 81, 133, 142, 149–150, 154*n*29, 155*n*36
Rutkowski, Stanisław 75
Rychlewski, Bartek 161*n*33

sabotage 3–4, 7, 48, 72
Sasinowski, Bishop Mikołaj 56–58, 157*n*13
Secret Police xii, 57, 134, 154*n*21, 155*n*34
Sejny vii–viii, 1, 5, 7, 9, 21, 23, 30, 62–63, *64*, 65–66, 77, *85*, 86, 92, 94–95, 135, 138, 140
selection (process) 134, 135, 139 140, 147
Shandurov, Capt. Ivan Konstantinovic 91
Siarkowski, Witold (alias "Mewa" ["Seagull"]) 73, 75, 157*n*3
Siberia viii, xii–xiii, 31–32, 35–37, 42, 49, 59, *60*, 119–120, 125, 156*(Krystyna Świerzbińska)n*5, 159*(Teresa Staśkiewicz)n*2, 159*(Teresa Staśkiewicz)n*8; Sybiraks 38, 156*(Krystyna Świerzbińska)n*9, 159*(Teresa Staśkiewicz)n*2
Siedlce 72
Siedlecki, Wacław 114
Siedlecki, Waldemar 65
Siedlecki, Władysław 114
Siedzikówna, Danuta (alias "Inka") 2, 151*n*3
Sikorski, Radosław 30
Siwicki, Zygmunt 75
Skalski, Stanisław 157*n*9
SMERSH 10, 19–20, 23–25, 28–30, 131, 133–135, 137–144, 147–148, 154*n*25, 154*n* 26, 154*n* 27, 154*n* 28
Smoleńsk Forest Massacre xii
Sobolewski, Wacław (alias "Sęk") 9, 143, 156*(Marian Tananis)n*22, 161*n*33
Sokółka vii, 9, 30, 62–63, *64*, 135, 161*n*33
Solidarity xiii, 47, 58, 154*n*21
Soviet Bloc xiii
Soviet Embassy in Warsaw 56, 78
Soviet gulags (labor camps) 125, 126, 152*n*8, 156*(Marian Tananis)n*40
Soviet occupation 3, 49, 102, 118–119
Soviet Union 56, 129, 155*n*35
Stalin, Josef xi–xiii, 8, 25, 31, 36, 41, 56, *64*, 133–134, 138, 140, 147, 153*n*18
starvation 74, 88, 112, 114
Staśkiewicz, Grzegorz 127
Staśkiewicz, Wojciech 127
Stefanowski, Fabian 12
Stefanowski, Lucjan 15–16
Stefanowski, Władysław (alias "Grom"

["Thunder"]) *18*, *19*, 103, *103*, 130, 137, 139, 143, 152*n*10, 154*n*22, 157*n*3, 159*(Marian Bućko)n*7, 161*n*33
Strumiłło, Andrzej 27, 85, *96*, 155*n*39, 158*(Józef Kucharzewski)n*6
Strzelcowizna 10, 18
Studzieniczna 51
Sucha Rzeczka 6
Suchwałko, Ludwik 43
Sulżyński, Józef (alias "Birch" ["Brzoza"]) 6–7, 20, 139, 143, 152*n*11, 153*n*16
Suwałki 2–4, 6, 9, 13, 18, *18*, 19, 27–28, 30, 48–51, *51*, 52–54, *55*, 60–63, *64*, 65, 68, 71, 84, 86, 93, 95, 97–98, 131–132, 134, 136, 139–140, 143–144, 146–147, 155*n*30, 155*n*38, 155*n*39, 156*n*42, 157*n*9, 158*(Józef Kucharzewski)n*6, 160*n*8, 161*n*2
Świątkowski, Stanisław (alias "Zapała") 73, 157*n*4
Świerzbińska, Franciszka 32, *32*, 36–38, 44
Świerzbińska, Monika 32, *32*
Świerzbińska, Pelagia 32, *32*
Świerzbiński, Klemens, Sr. *32*
Szabunia, Major Franciszek (alias "Zemsta" ["Revenge"]) 50
Szarejko, Józef 88–90, 97
Szczytko, Czesław 114
Szczytko, Eugeniusz 114
Szczytko, Kazimierz 114
Szendzielarz, Zygmunt (alias "Łupaszka") 151*n*4
Szmygel, Franciszek 43, 156*(Krystyna Świerzbińska)n*10
Szmygel, Józef 156*(Krystyna Świerzbińska)n*10
Szostak, Jan 8, 14, 21, 75, 106, 126, 153*n*17
Sztabin 30, 42–43, 71, 100, 104, 106, 109, *109*, 111–112, *113*, 114, 140, 143, 154*n*22
Sztabin-Dębowo route 157*n*4
Szyc family 42, *109*, 140
Szymański, Czesław 114
Szyper, Józef 114
Szyszkiewicz, Stanisław 75

Tananis, Antoni 1–3
Tananis, Leokadia (née Waluś) 2–3
Tananis, Walentyna 2–3, 23
Tarasewicz, Edward 114
Tarasewicz, Stanisław 114
Teheran Conference 155*n*35
Terror vii, 8–9, 11, 16, 17, 27, 50, 72, 131, 144, 158*(Marian Bućko)n*1
Third Belarusian Front 9, 24–25, 28–29, 134–135, 137–138, 141, 147–148
Third Polish Republic 78, 82
Third Reich 2–3, 152*n*6, 152*n*8
torture vii, xiii, 9–112, 20–21, 49, 55, 69, 74, *75*, 76, 85, 89–90, 93, 108, 120, 122, 140
Truman, Harry 155*n*35
Trycze 118

Index

Tur, Teresa 65
Twardowski, Father Jan 128

Uchan, Father Jacek 69
Union of Armed Struggle (Związek Walki Zbrojnej) 4, 71
UNRRA (United Nations Relief and Rehabilitation Administration) 159*(Teresa Staśkiewicz)n*7
Urban, Jerzy 27
Urbanowicz, Gen. Witold 52, 157*n*9
Usnarski, Jan 43

Vasiliev, A.V. 78
Victory Parade of 1946 (London) xiii
Virtuti Military 101, 110, 157*n*9, 159*(Marian Bućko)n*3
Vistula River xii, 159*(Teresa Staśkiewicz)n*6

Wałęsa, Lech xiii, 157*n*9
Walulik, Wojciech 65, 149
Waluś, Piotr 3, 14
Warsaw Uprising of 1944 xii, 152*n*7, 159*(Marian Bućko)n*6, 159*(Teresa Staśkiewicz)n*3
Węgrzyn, Wiktor 7, 152*n*6
Wehrmacht 2, 98
Wielki Bór 27
Wiśniewski, Józef 10
Wnukowska, Anna 114
Wnukowska, Helena 114
Wojda 72
Wołąsewicz, Basia 122, 124–125, 127
Wołąsewicz, Bolesław 126
Wołąsewicz, Jadwiga 119, 123, 125–127
Wołąsewicz, Jerzy 127
World War I 151*(Marian Tananis)n*1, 152*n*6, 158*(Marian Bućko)n*1
World War II vii–viii, xi–xiii, 2 9, 23, 32, **32**, 48, 62, 71–72, 100–102, 106, 136, 145, 151*(Marian Tananis)n*1, 151*n*4–5, 152*n*6–7, 153*n*13–14, 155*n*31, 155*n*35–37, 156*(Krystyna*

Świerzbińska*)n*1, 157*n*13, 158*(Tadeusz Jagłowski)n*8, 158*(Marian Bućko)n*1, 159*(Teresa Staśkiewicz)n*5, 159*n*7
Wysocka, Aniela 52–53, **54**, 55, **55**, 62–63, **68**, 69, 130, 161*n*3
Wysocka, Józefa (née Jarząbska) 48, 54, **55**, 56, 68
Wysocka, Kazimiera 52–53, *54*, 55, **55**, 62–63, **68**, 69, 130, 161*n*3
Wysocka, Teresa 54, 68
Wysocka, Wanda 68
Wysocki, Alojzy 53, 68
Wysocki, Ludwik 48, 52–53, 55, **55**, 62–63, **68**, 69, 130, 161*n*3
Wysocki, Roman 53
Wyszyński, Cardinal Stefan 153*n*18

Yalta Conference xiii, 155*n*35

Zabielski, Father Piotr 57
Zaboreczno 72
Zagórski, Stanisław 118
Zalewski, Szymon 114
Zalewski, Władysław 114
Zamość (region) 72
Zawistowski, Józef 114
Zelenin, Lt. Gen. Pavel 10, 24–25, 29, 134, 137, 141, 154*n*28
Zięcina, Tadeusz (alias "Sokół" ["Falcon"]) 73
Zieliński, Jarosław 61
Ziemba, Wacław 41
Ziemba, Archbishop Wojciech 63
Żmijewski, Father Edward 65
Żukowski, Konstanty 75
Żwirki (group/unit) 3, 6
Żyliny 6
Zysko, Antoni 114
Żywią i Bronią ("Nourish and Protect") 72; *see also* Peasants' Batallions
Żywna, Bernard 114

www.ingramcontent.com/pod-product-compliance
Lightning Source LLC
Chambersburg PA
CBHW032047300426
44117CB00009B/1223